T0306500

INHABITING HEAVEN NOW

Andrea Mathews writes eloquently in her new book *Inhabiting Heaven NOW* about how we can de-code some of the morals that have been imposed on us throughout history. Spiritual growth is a natural yearning, and this book shows us that we can find our own spiritual strength within, a strength we can call on and rely on no matter what dilemmas come our way. A compelling, and worthwhile read!
Lissa Coffey, author: *What's Your Dharma? Discover the Vedic Way to Your Life's Purpose*

If you are ready to rid yourself of the burdens imposed by the morals and belief structures you inherited from birth, and ditch the fear and hesitation that holds you back, *Inhabiting Heaven NOW* is your book—a wonderful template for greater joy and fulfillment.
Larry Dossey, MD, Author: REINVENTING MEDICINE and THE POWER OF PREMONITIONS

Andrea Mathews hits the crux of where every human being on the planet must go if their world and the world is to change. Its meaning is crucial to the journey of the soul and the catalyst for becoming sacred spiritual human activists for change.
Simran Singh, Publisher of Award Winning *11:11 Magazine* & Syndicated 11:11 Talk Radio Host

Inhabiting Heaven NOW is a thought-provoking book that had me nodding my head and realizing some of my own unconscious habits. Readers will find true freedom in these pages as they uncover and debunk some closely held unconscious beliefs, codes and ways of being. Mathews offers us a new liberating code to live by—one that throws judgment out the window and offers us a vision for embracing our personal power. Her insights into the Bible, "evil," and the nature of power are edifying and offer much to think about—a great book club pick, since it is ripe for discussions.
Lisa Tener, award winning book coach, www.lisatener.com

Andrea Mathews's *Inhabiting Heaven Now* will come to many as a gift. For those who are trapped in feelings of guilt, ought and should—in other words, for most of us—*Inhabiting Heaven Now* shows a way out of the cul de sac that is our unquenchable moral code.

Most of us live our lives circumscribed by rules: we should not be selfish, we should not sleep around, we should not curse or spit or smoke or dance naked in the square. And because we carry these codes, given us by our parents or religions or society, we suffer. We are not worthy, we are not good enough, unless we _____, well, fill in the blank.

And so we live lives of quiet desperation, caught forever between "I am worthy" and "I am not good enough."

What Andrea shows, in very readable prose, is that the problem is not us, it's in our assumption that there is a wrong and a right, that there is a right way to be, if only. The problem is not us, it's in the very split in how we think: good and evil, right and wrong.

What if, just what if, we are worthy because we are here, she asks? "What if our worthiness does not depend on following or not following the rules? What if, like our pet cat or dog, we are loved and considered beautiful and worthy, because we are, we just are."

It is the mystic's journey to which she beckons, the journey within, that is neither good nor evil but beyond that very split. It is to a new kind of life, a new level of living, that she invites and teaches, a level that is large enough to welcome both good and evil, and to be strong enough to naturally tap into that which enhances life, ours and others.

It is to that place inside that, without the cold and lifeless split that is our defined right and wrong, can guide us to do that which is true for us, for others and for the world.

Robert Forman, author of *Enlightenment Ain't What It's Cracked Up To Be*

Inhabiting Heaven Now is a feast for heart, mind, and soul. It shows Andrea Mathews' signature understanding of how our fears limit our vision and our lives. Her arguments for a more compassionate world—a way to inhabit heaven while still on Earth—are stimulating and compelling. This is a book to read, to reread, to savor and to cherish.

Carol Marleigh Kline, author of *Streetwise Spirituality: 28 Days to Inner Fitness and Everyday Enlightenment*

Inhabiting Heaven NOW

The Answer to Every Moral
Dilemma Ever Posed

Inhabiting Heaven NOW

The Answer to Every Moral Dilemma Ever Posed

Andrea Mathews

BOOKS

Winchester, UK
Washington, USA

First published by O-Books, 2013
O-Books is an imprint of John Hunt Publishing Ltd., Laurel House, Station Approach,
Alresford, Hants, SO24 9JH, UK
office1@jhpbooks.net
www.johnhuntpublishing.com

For distributor details and how to order please visit the 'Ordering' section on our website.

ISBN: 978 1 78099 603 5

A CIP catalogue record for this book is available from the British Library.

Design: Stuart Davies

Scripture taken from the NEW AMERICAN STANDARD BIBLE © 1960, 1962, 1963, 1968, 1971, 1972,
1973, 1975, 1977, By The Lockman Foundation. Used by permission.

Unless otherwise stated, all Biblical translations found in this book were taken from the
lexicons of Crosswalk.com. http://www.biblestudytools.com/lexicons
Cover Photo: © Kim D. French

Printed and in the USA by Edwards Brothers Malloy

We operate a distinctive and ethical publishing philosophy in all
areas of our business, from our global network of authors to
production and worldwide distribution.

CONTENTS

Preface   1

Introduction   3

1   Worthy   7
2   Living By The Code   20
    Code: Don't be Selfish   22
    Code: Feel Guilty, It's Good for You   30
    Code: There's Right and There's Wrong   35
    Code: You Ought to Be Ashamed   40
    Code: What Good Does it Do?   42
    Code: Be Loyal First to Duty   44
    Code: Power is Bad   50
    Code: The Culture is Right   55
3   Between the Devil and the Deep Blue Sea   60
4   The Tree   89
5   The Split   107
6   The Judge and the Condemned   124
7   Evil   156
8   Good   179
9   The Well   197
10 The Ocean   209
11 For All We Know   224
12 The Wide Expanse of Love   241
13 Precious Clarity   257

Works Cited   274

To My Grandchildren:
Ian, Olivia and Daniel,
with enormous love
for you, your children,
and your children's children.
And the beat goes on.

Preface

We formulated our morals based on fear. Fear that the gods would not provide the supplies and safety we needed if we didn't conform to what we suspected they demanded of us; fear of punitive responses from both the supernatural and the natural world; fear that we might otherwise be considered to be bad people; fear of mystery; fear of death; fear of some kind of retribution after death; fear of fear. And our larger systems—our churches, corporations and governments—need for us to maintain our individual and collective fears because they fear that otherwise there will be anarchy—in other words *they* (i.e., *we*) will no longer be able suffer the illusion that they control us.

Having said that, we must be clear that this book is not meant to promote anarchy. Neither is it meant to turn loose the wild wolves of passion upon the stanchions of tradition. Nor is it meant to encourage our seemingly ever-increasing devolution into the abyss of immorality. Rather this book is meant to assist us in looking beyond morality for spirituality.

Most of us are ill-informed about the tenets of the dogma, creed or philosophy to which we ascribe. However, we do assert a certain knowledge about what is *good* and what is *bad*. But we didn't get that knowledge from our dogma, creed or philosophy—that came later. We originally got it from our upbringing in our families-of-origin and our particular culture. Though we tend to think of these mores as morals, they are definitely relative to the family and culture from which we hail. They are programmed into our psyches based on the seriousness of the consequences listed or received for not following them. For many of us, attachment to these mores was the same as attachment to our families-of-origin, ergo our very survival seemed to be hanging in the balance. In other words, we were programmed by fear to respond to these mores as if they were morals. This book will call these mores, turned morals, *codes,* and we will spend a bit of time discussing the process of both their development and their impact on us.

The most important part of this book, however, will not be found in the arguments about our morals. Instead it will be found in the explorations of our essence as human beings hungry for a deeper meaning, a more powerful connection, and a wider expression of both. And it is all too often that we are deprived of these because of our attachment to morals. Indeed, our attachment to morality, as a way of explaining our suffering, not only describes how we should live in this life, but it describes the literal *place* of heaven. And as a result not only is our worldview skewed along these lines, but our notion of what is true and false for the soul is likewise skewed along these same lines of a great battle between so-called *good* and *evil. Inhabiting Heaven NOW* offers a new paradigm, one in which we move beyond the constraints of this monumental battle to find ourselves—in fact, to find the divine in ourselves.

Introduction

Not a single day goes by in my practice as a clinician, or in my world as a writer, speaker and radio host, in which I do not encounter someone who is stuck in both the miasma and the quicksand of a moral dilemma. This, however, is not because it is right to be so stuck — though that is what most traditionalists will tell us. This is because we have come to believe more in our morals than we believe in ourselves.

But even making such a bold statement raises the hackles on the necks of traditionalists from all faiths, creeds, dogmas and philosophies, for we fear that if we drop morals, then planet earth will go to hell in one enormous apocalyptic explosion of total immorality. We trust our morals to keep that from happening. And we are certain that without them that is exactly what *will* happen.

Worse than that, however, is the fact that because we trust in morals, we don't trust in our inner and divine essence to lead and guide us. We don't even trust love to guide us, because, you know, love can be tainted with all kinds of loyalties that may or may not be right. No, better stick with the rules.

So, when I encounter these persons who have come to me for help with what they think are their moral dilemmas, I'm continually frustrated by the fact that in order for them to reach into the realms in which they will find their own answers, they will have to find a way to get past the sticky, gummy, hot asphalt of morality paving their own personal narrow road to hell. But you just can't talk about getting past morals, without people thinking that you are coming all too close to the edge of blasphemy — and they don't want to be in the room when the lightning strikes.

Søren Kierkegaard was able to get away with it in his famous book *Either/Or* in which he says:

My either/or does not in the first instance denote the choice between good and evil, it denotes the choice whereby one chooses good *and* evil/or excludes them (Kierkegaard 1992, 486).

But it took him 633 pages to do it. We are not going to go that long. But we are going to be talking not only about excluding them—good *and* evil, that is—but also about what we do with ourselves once they have been excluded. Byron Katie asks the question: Who would you be without your story? I'm going to take that one more step and ask: Who would you be without your morals?

That's a scary question for many to ask, and scarier still to answer, for at base we fear that without our morals we would *all* be sociopathic serial killers. But would we? Or, is it possible that we can find something deeper than morals within us, deeper than the codes to which we conform our behavior or rebel against, deeper than our dependency on the so-called *battle between good and evil* to define us. What if, in fact, that is exactly what Jesus, Buddha, Krishna and some of the other great Master-Teachers were trying to tell us? What if…we have it all wrong?

Truth is, our dependence on morals, on defining ourselves by the supernatural and unnatural battle between good and evil, will keep us from even asking these questions. Why? Because we live our lives and orchestrate our movements based almost entirely on fear. And so it is perilous, indeed, to put such a deep crack in the terra firma on which we walk based on morals, which seem to protect us from our fears. What will we do? Will we just fall for eternity into the airless air between us and the next planet down the Milky Way? Where will we lay our heads at night if we can't look back over our days and determine our worth by our good and bad deeds? These are our fears. And they dictate our willingness to ask these questions.

So, how did I get to be so brave? Well it's not because I'm some

superhero who has come to save you from the traps of unconscious moral meandering. Nor is it because I'm the next Anti-
Christ come to steal your soul and fling it down into hell—
simply so that I won't be alone down there. It's because there is
nothing to fear. It is extremely difficult for most of us, however,
to wrap our minds around that concept and so most of us don't
even try. Rather we imagine that living a moral life will remove
mystery from life and eventually get us to a place in which we
will finally find some peace.

But it is in the midst of the mystic's journey that we come to
realize both mystery and a concomitant experience of peace.
Most of us, however, are frightened of mystery, for our biggest
fear is of the unknown. We go to all kinds of lengths to convince
ourselves that we know things we don't really know at all,
simply because to not know is so uncomfortably frightening.
One of the things we think we know is that there is this
enormous historic and futuristic battle between good and evil.
Even many who are atheist or agnostic believe in some kind of
battle between morality and immorality. But when we look for
true spirituality, we won't find it in morals, and we won't find it
in fear—we will find it in the mystical alliance between mystery
and truth, an alliance which has nothing to do with a historic
and/or futuristic battle between good and evil. What changes in
these mystic encounters isn't a heart and mind that turns from
evil to goodness. These encounters offer to an open heart a depth
awareness of the divine within humanity.

Just so, our journey here will be all about revelation,
realization and mystery. It will provide, for those who wish it, an
open door to walk through, to explore the mysterious realms of
life beyond duality and its subject, morality. You should read this
book with a notebook beside you, so that you can jot down
significant thoughts and ponder them later. Go slow; take your
time to really contemplate what you are reading. You may find
that you need to argue with some of the ideas presented. Do that.

Argue with pen and paper in your hands, so that as you argue, you don't just cave to your resistance to mystery. Rather you argue from both sides, comparing and contrasting. This arguing will be largely intellectual, and so it cannot bring you to the ultimate conclusion, but it is part of the process, so go with it. But as you are so called from deep within you, please also sit quietly and just be. For it is in being still that we come to know.

God speed.

I

Worthy

We live our lives in spaces, circumscribed by rules. Those rules are either passed down to us, or we make them up as we go. Or, we paint our circles with an odd mixture of both. But rules are rules and they are followed. Even if the rule is that we should break all the rules—that's the rule, and it will be followed. And so we build for ourselves a labyrinth within which we walk our lives. Do we pray as we go? Some do, some don't. Do we solemnly seek the center? Some do, some don't. Do we run into others coming back from the center as we go? Sometimes the empty spaces around a corner fogs into the breath of another, sometimes not. Sometimes we walk alone. But we walk, always within the outer circle circumscribed by the rules of our lives.

Why do we do this? Because in this way we divine our worth. Even if our worth is measured by the number of rules we've broken, still it is our worth. Why do we need to divine our worth? Now that, *that* is the question. Why is it that we need to find ourselves worthy? What is it about life on planet earth that makes us believe that we have to feel worthy? And on the flip side of that, why is it that when we don't feel worthy, we feel ashamed.

The interesting thing about this constant measuring of ourselves is that it isn't based in a search for truth so much as it is based in a need for measurement. And even more interesting is the fact that the need for measurement is based in a need for rules, for the rules assure us that we have something against which to measure ourselves. In other words, whether we know it or not, whether we'd like to admit it or not, we measure ourselves because we have rules by which to measure ourselves. And we have rules because we need to measure ourselves.

And as far as I can tell, we are the only creatures on earth who do that. There are many who would say that this means that we are more evolved than the "lower" creatures—the animals and, the lowest of all created life—earth's vegetation and elements. I wonder about that, for as far as I can see into the stillness found in the absolute life energy of earth's vegetation and elements— earth, water, air and fire—there doesn't seem to be any misery. And I often wonder how much better animals would fare if we'd just leave them alone.

Much of our suffering is related to this sense that we are not worthy unless we ____. Fill in the blank. Our worthiness is not, however, just related to our deeds or even our thoughts. It is quite often related to what we have, or even what others think of us. But in all of that, there are rules. Rules that must be followed to gain our worthiness or gain it back.

Later we'll explore how this came to be, but for now, what we need to know is that we have decided to stand in the middle of a chalk circle that we ourselves have drawn. Many will say that we didn't draw the circle, God did. And we'll talk more about that later too, but for now, let's just say that since religion is man-made, it assumes, based upon its beliefs, what God did and didn't do. Spirituality and religion are two different things. Spirituality listens to the divine, while religion defines the divine. So, for now, let's suspend the argument about how it came to be, and let's just talk about worthiness and shame.

How does one know that one is worthy? Well, most of us would say that if a man knows he is worthy, he's probably also narcissistic and arrogant. In this paradigm, one should always strive for worthiness, but never attain it, for the minute he attains it, he is no longer worthy. How does one know that one is unworthy? Now, that's a whole lot easier to answer. One can feel a deep sense of shame about certain areas of life, certain times of life, or certain behaviors or thoughts. And the minute one begins to feel ashamed, one is just that much closer to worthiness, for one who has no sense that he ought to feel ashamed, is truly unworthy.

If you just got through that last paragraph, you already know how convoluted and impossible is our journey to worthiness. In fact, this entire paradigm is one huge double-bind. What is a double-bind? It is a conundrum in which we are damned if we do and damned if we don't. Imagine being told that you must eat your soup or be severely punished, but the minute you pick up your spoon to eat, you are told that if you eat that soup you will get very sick. That's a double bind. The only decision left to you is which is the lesser punishment.

Abusive parents put their children in double-binds frequently. "Tell me the truth, or I'm going to slap your fanny up around your ears!" So, the child figures she'd best tell the truth. But when she does, she is slapped around for the truth she just told. And frequently putting children in double-binds like this can be severely wounding to a child, creating a platform of anxiety from which s/he may live for many years thereafter. In fact, once upon a time, it was thought that such double-binds were the cause of Schizophrenia. That theory has since gone the way of all bad theories, but the fact that double-binds were once connected to the most severe form of mental illness is telling.

And we are in just such a bind with regard to our worthiness. We can't be worthy without being arrogant, and we can't be unworthy without being ashamed. Most of us cope with this double-bind by landing somewhere in the middle. We make rules for ourselves that circumscribe our behavior and thoughts to fit into the middle ground. We don't want to be too *holy*, and we don't want to be too *bad*. Therefore, we get just enough religion to feel okay about ourselves and just enough *badness* to make sure we are not too *holy*. We're now average—even "normal." And because we have found a safe middle ground on which to live, we don't really have to think too much about whether or not any of this makes sense at all.

And thus we live our lives of quiet desperation meandering somewhere between worthiness and unworthiness. But when it comes to both the small and the large choices of our lives, our sense of ourselves as either worthy or unworthy will come up again. And when it does, we will again measure ourselves against our rules.

I see this all of the time in my psychotherapy practice. When a client says, "I mean I guess I'm an okay person and all..." and they look up at me from the usual position of downturned eyes, and add "I mean, I do take care of my kids and my spouse and I pay my bills on time and I work hard." The measurement has been made according to the rules. But there are rules that have also been disobeyed along the way, and it is those that hold the most weight, for if I ask this same person what it is that makes her ponder her worth in this way, she will give me a very definitive answer: "When I was twenty-one I had an abortion." Or, "when I was nineteen my boyfriend broke up with me and I started using cocaine." Or, "I used to sleep around." The list of broken rules lay like dead bodies across a battlefield as she tops the hill and looks back over her life. And the truth is, no amount of measured and so-called *goodness* will ever bring those bodies back to life or compensate for the loss of worth.

Sometimes the so-called *bad* deeds were not really even bad at all, by any standard, except the internalization of someone else's *bad* deeds. Childhood survivors of sexual trauma, for example, often internalize the *badness* of their perpetrator, particularly when he or she is a loved one, because that is the only way they can believe that they will be okay. If they can absorb the guilt and shame and try really, really hard to be *good*, maybe the perpetrator will magically stop—or become the fantasized image the child longs for.

Or, in other cases there is an imagined *should*. Someone dies at the wheel in an auto accident and the passenger assumes the guilt based on the measurable standard "if only I had been driving."

That standard assumes that he *should* have been the one to die. A parent loses a child, and assumes the guilt just by the fact of parenthood. Somehow the child *should* have been protected by the parent even if the child died of leukemia.

There simply is not enough good in the world to compensate for this sense of unworthiness. It wins every time. Trump card played. Game over. Why is this so? Because we believe so much more in our unworthiness than we do our worthiness. And why is that so? Because we have determined that there are no perfect people and anyone who thinks he has arrived at some sense of worthiness must think that he is better than everyone else. Ergo, he is all the more unworthy. There is just no way around it. We are damned if we do, and damned if we don't.

But religion does tell us that there are some ways around it. In some religions we can strive to always live a moral and compassionate life, which in the very striving makes us somehow worthier. In others, our sins can be forgiven by the sacrificial blood of a god-man, who died just for the purpose of washing us clean. But even after the forgiveness of sins there is a perpetual measuring that must be done to be certain that one is living according to the rules one adopted when one was "saved by the blood." In every case, however, we come back down to these rules and this measuring. And worthiness becomes a goal to attain, somewhere further and further off in the distance—a glimmer of a horizon at which we simply shall not ever arrive.

Until we die. We die and arrive in heaven where we are free from our earthly immoral deeds and we can go forward to live forever in the sated bliss of ultimate goodness. That is, unless of course, we go to hell, where we will be eternally punished for our sins by absolute separation from the divine. Just an aside here, but are we saying, through this concept of hell, that while here on earth we are only *partially* separated from the divine? The other punitive option, of course, is that we could go to another life where we will have to live out the karmic punishment for our sins in the previous life. So, I guess, after all is said and done, we don't really even get rid of our dualistic thinking after we die—at least according to most religions—because heaven is ultimate *goodness*, and hell is ultimate punishment for *badness*, and karma, as we have defined it, is punishment or reward for our *bad* or *good* deeds.

But, we say, how else would we live here on a planet on which we bump into each other daily, if we have no rules by which to abide? I would argue that our rules, the ones we actually live by, have nothing to do with the organizational efforts we might have to make to live on the planet without walking over each other. Red lights and stop signs have nothing to do with our worth, unless we make them into moral obligations. We might need to organize our efforts and our pathways in order to live together here, but that is not what happens. We don't just organize, we moralize. We make what we do into *wrongs* and *rights*. We say that when a man runs a red light that he has been *wrong* to do so. Further, the only reason that he should be punished with a fine is to teach him a lesson, so that he won't do that *wrong* deed again. He's not been poorly organized or poorly attached to a system that requires his compliance. No. He's been *wrong*.

What we don't realize in all of our assumptions of *wrong* and *right*, is that these assumptions keep us at the shallow end of the pool when it comes to living a life of meaning and fulfillment. So let's take, for example, the most heinous of all wrongs, the murder of another. We generally say that a person who has murdered another is *bad* or even *evil*. Then we shake our heads in despair, and promptly dust our hands of it. We can clearly see the pain of the family members of the victim and our compassion reaches out to them. But when it comes to thinking about the crime itself, we can stop any further exploration, by simply saying that the perpetrator is evil. We don't have to consider his desperation, his narcissistic wounds that blinded him to the pain of others, his bully or bad-guy identity or anything else. And we, as individuals and as a society, are relieved of the responsibility of solving the problem. Just throw the thug in jail and be done with it. In fact, we are so certain that it is *right* to do this, that those who wish to consider what might be going on in the mind and heart of the murderer are considered to be "bleeding heart liberals" who only wish to let the devil out on the people yet again. In fact, though there are some ultra-sympathizers who think that no one should have to suffer for their crimes, most "bleeding hearts" would simply like the opportunity to understand it all better—without letting anyone out of jail.

Bottom line, wrapping up these things in the old newspapers of morality, does not take care of the stink of these ancient problems. In fact, after a while, that rot just begins to smell worse. Our jails are overflowing, the drug and alcohol problem continues to escalate and we split off more and more from other members of our world, even in terms of the *bad* or *good* sides of town. Now we should be clear here, that I'm not making any suggestions that we should all move in with a gang member, but I do want us to be fair about what is going on at the level of psychology and spirituality, for as we project more and more of our notions about *evil* onto the *bad* sides of town or *those people* we split ourselves off more and more from the Self.

Like any other polarization, the notion of evil lives forever in the polar regions of our minds, because we have sent it there, and there it must stay, for our greatest fear is that we ourselves are *evil*. And so it is that we polarize people who seem to represent that *evil* for us—we throw them in jail. Again, I'm not suggesting that people who have been identified as bullies, even to the extreme of becoming murderers, rapists and serial killers, should be allowed to live within a society filled with potential victims. I'm not advocating that we set all of our prisoners free. I'm simply suggesting that perhaps the polarization of *good* and *evil* is much more of the problem than we think. But most of us, perhaps even many who are reading this right now, would like to stop right here and have an argument about what we should be doing about these horrible people—should we kill them all, should we give all the sexual predators saltpeter for the rest of their lives, should we castrate them, should we send them all to Siberia? Or perhaps all those bleeding heart liberals have some other *better* suggestion—and off we go, forgetting that there is a psychology and a deeper spirituality behind it all.

So, let's pause from the distracting global arguments for just a few minutes. We'll even swallow the keys to our prison systems so that we can give ourselves space to consider how it is that people become so horrible, and in turn begin to consider our own identifications and our own reactions to those of others. Let's explore one example of how a person might become "so horrible."

If, as a young and susceptible child, I am perpetually told, either subtly or overtly, that I am *bad*, because my parent is either unwilling or incapable of spending the time it takes to really teach me to look in the mirror long enough to see self-love, then I might just grow up feeling that if I don't call myself *bad*, I don't exist at all. When I look in the mirror of their emotional neglect I see that I don't really exist. Or, I can look in the one that says I'm bad. So, I'm most likely to choose the bad one, and use it to prove my existence. In fact, I'm going to be inclined to think that I don't exist *unless* I'm *bad*. Ergo, every time I feel that my existence is in question, I'll be triggered to do something *bad* to prove that I do exist. Therefore, as I grow up, being ignored is going to be a trigger for my *bad* behavior. And the more ignored or unnoticed I feel, the worse my behavior is going to have to get. This particular dynamic response to childhood mirroring might even explain why it is that the sociopathic serial killer typically wants enormous attention from the media.

So, the problem here is not that I'm really *bad*, but that being *bad* has become my way of surviving a sense of non-existence. And if being *bad* were not an option presented to me in the mirror of my parents' reactions to me then I wouldn't be able to identify with it. Here we have reached the proverbial chicken and egg question. I say the chicken. The polarization of *good* and *bad*—a paradigm from which we all live—is the penultimate origin of our chosen method of survival. If this concept were not constantly swirling around in the air in our homes and if it were not a primary, even intrinsic part of the relationship children have with their parents, children wouldn't be able to identify with either *good* or *bad*.

Another example can be found in the children, born with a gift/curse for empathy. Many of these children happened to fall down the chimneys of parents who cannot admit to wrong, or feel their own emotions. These parents tend to project all of their own *wrongness* onto their children. Some of the children who come from this household are going to become black sheep—so that they live out all of the *wrongs* their parents would never allow themselves to live out, though they can allow it to be projected onto their children so that their children can live it out vicariously for them. These children, like the *bad* kids from the previous paragraph, will have to do more and more *wrong*, but for a different reason. These children need to stay connected to their parents—and the only way they can do that is to continue to absorb the *bad* stuff their parents don't want to recognize in themselves. Even if the only relationship they can have with their parents is one of constant blame and criticism, and even if they have to eventually stay far away from their parents, the magical thinking that makes them *bad*, still makes them believe that they are somehow doing their parents a big favor.

Some children equally blessed/cursed with the gift of empathy are going to absorb a sense of *badness*, *wrongness*, illegitimacy so that they go around doing *good* deeds in order to prove their worth. These children will learn to be people pleasers, so that they consistently intuit what their parents and others need from them and deliver it before they are even asked. They may even appear to be much more adult then their adult parents. They'll be able to feel emotions the parents are unwilling to feel, because their parents subtly insist that they carry these emotions for them. But they are also often caught in a double bind, because the same parents who insist that they carry the emotions, also mock them for being "too emotional," or "too sensitive." But if you look at these children now grown to adulthood, you would say, "That's a truly good person." They follow all the rules. They know when to appear compassionate, when to be silent, when to say and do all of the correct socially expected behaviors and they are always about the business of taking care of others. Good people. But inside they are anxious, literally driven by guilt and dragging around a ball and chain of resentment. And they typically haven't a clue about who they really are. This *goodness* seems more like an affliction than anything else.

But most of us can also recall having met or heard about at least one person who represents genuine *goodness*. These are truly compassionate and genuinely open, generous and honest people. No one would argue that they are not truly *good*, right? Well, if you wish to give it a polarized label, I guess so. But wouldn't it be closer to the truth to call them *real* people?

Of course, these are just a few of the ways that these masks and costumes are put on for survival, but generally speaking, the way these two different identities, the *bad* kid and the *good* kid, got to be so different is that they identified with one or the other side of the polarization between *good* and *evil*. They didn't come to these identities without looking in the mirrors provided for them by even well-intended parents, who are so wrapped up in this polarization themselves that they passed it on and off to their children. And the hardest part about all of this is that all this passing around of *stuff* is done under the table. It's done unconsciously, so that neither the sender nor the receiver knows that it is being done. Sometimes these families end up in therapy and can begin to come to terms with what's going on in the entire system, rather than just blaming the *bad* kid and praising the *good* kid. But I often wonder about the extensions of family systems. How does the family system fit into the wider system of culture, and that into the still wider system of society, and that into the still wider system of nation and then world? What would it be like, I sometimes wonder, to get the whole world into a therapy session and find out about the roles or masks and costumes used, and the groups of people onto whom we project *good* or *evil*?

This whole battle between *good* and *bad* turns out to be an illusion when we get right down to it. For who defines *good*? And who defines *evil*? If it is religion, we'd have to ask which religion. Osama Bin Laden thought it was a *good* thing to train his allegiants to commit suicide while crashing their planes into the Trade Towers and the Pentagon. And his allegiants believed in their own *good* deed so much that they were actually willing to die for it—while killing many others. His and their interpretation of their religion led them to believe that this was the only *right* thing to do. Many others disagree. Looking at this from an historical perspective, but a few centuries back and largely covered up by Christian historians, blood ran in some of the European city streets as thousands of so-called *heretics* were murdered because they believed in such concepts as divinization and reincarnation. And only three hundred years ago, so-called *witches* were murdered because they used herbs to help their friends and loved ones heal. And these murders were considered to be *good* deeds.

So, what is *good* and what is *bad*? Only your rules know for sure. And yet, we live in a kind of socially acceptable haze of discontent in which we seem to be trying to heave the collective bolder of *goodness* up the hill, only to arrive at the top to see it roll back down picking up steam at every bump in the road. We secret away our *bad* deeds as a general approach to the whole thing. We say, "Everyone has got something hidden in their closets." But the average Joe, trying hard not to be too *holy* or too *bad,* isn't even going to consider cleaning out those closets for fear of what might be found there.

We live out our power trips, our manipulations and our social graces all in the name of being a *good* person without ever wondering why it is that at the upper echelons of the political world, such power trips, manipulations and social graces seem to be so *evil.* And throughout all of this, we've not yet stopped to ask ourselves about anything that looks like truth. In fact, many of us even hesitate to use the word—except when we are defending a lie.

Now, I didn't say all of that to preach about how we are all going to hell in a hand-basket. I said all of that to say this: Until we get past *good* and *evil,* we are not going to be able to find out who we are, and if we can't find out who we are, how the hell do we expect to find out who or what is this sense of reality we call God? How will we ever get genuinely close to the divine, if we can't even get close to ourselves? And we can't know who we are until we can quit asking ourselves if we are worthy. And we won't be able to stop asking ourselves whether or not we are worthy until we can get rid of the measuring stick.

What if, just what if we are worthy because we are here? What if our worthiness does not depend on following or not following the rules? What if, like our pet cat or dog, we are loved and considered beautiful and worthy, because we are, we just are. We are so used to thinking of all of the bits and pieces of the universe as suppliant to humanity. The flower is only worth something if it serves humanity in some way. The tree only has value to the degree that it provides for us. The mountain is there for us to climb, the ocean for us to swim, and the air for us to breathe.

But what if our image of ourselves is skewed along the lines of our own self-importance because to think otherwise opens us to the mysteries of existence? We do fear a mystery don't we? We want to know. We want to be certain. We want answers. And we want the answers to appear in a form we can understand, as in, physical matter, so that if the answer isn't physical, well then, it isn't really an answer at all.

Our scientists look for empirical data. The very definition of empiricism implies physicality. If we can't see it, touch it, taste it, smell it, or hear it, we can't be certain that it is real at all. But this of course leaves out all of the other senses. Intuition is one of those invisible senses that science is only now on the very fringes of accepting, though humanity has known of it for as long as we have existed. But there are other senses that don't even as yet have a name, like that humming sensation that one gets when one has tapped into the deepest roots of oneself. Like that feeling of connection, of inner knowing, that comes about, not as a result of intuition, but as a result of sitting in a room all by oneself and just being.

But we want the kind of knowing we can present to our physical form. Why? Because mystery makes us uncomfortable at best and downright terrified at worst. The very mystery of our own existence is the most uncomfortable of all. So rather than sit with that mystery and just enjoy our own beingness, we try to define it, label it, decide on its value and ultimately find ourselves unworthy.

What if we are wrong? What if for centuries we've perpetuated a myth upon ourselves that can only be demystified by telling ourselves the truth? And what if the truth is that we are already worthy? And what if realizing that is what allows us to stop acting as if it isn't so?

2

Living by the Code

We have game nights at my house. We pick a night, invite a few friends over and play dominoes and laugh, drink, cuss and smoke and generally have a gay old time. It all ends at one or two in the morning and we are all refreshed. On occasion, we've run into a player or two, who is just a little too competitive to really enjoy the game or, for that matter, anything else about the evening. One of these, who no longer attends our little parties, would quite often become agitated and very vocal about it, when the rules of our little game seemed to be making her lose that game. And she would say, "That's not how my family plays it." We would laugh and make a decision that basically said we weren't changing the rules for her, and get on with the game. So, now whenever one of us is losing and finds fault with the way we are playing, we laugh again in sardonic glee as we say, "That's not how my family plays it!"

These are the codes. They basically allow us to fit into a system. They allow us to be a family with other members of humanity. We live by the code because that's the code that our family taught us—whether that family is a literal family or a bunch of gang members, military men or corporate officers. And there's a code for everything.

Several years ago, I worked in an Alcohol and Drug Treatment Center with hard-core addicts and alcoholics who had previously lived largely on the streets. I learned so much from these wonderful people. And one of the things that I learned was that there is a "Code of the Streets." And one of the most basic rules that inhabits this code is the idea that "the snitch is the bitch." This code meant that if someone in the treatment center had found a way to sneak drugs into his room, even if it meant that everyone else in the room had to white-knuckle their way through rehab to avoid using the substance that was being placed right under their noses by their indifferent roommate, they would do it and do it proud—for they were not about to disobey the code. In fact, the more they had to suffer for the code, the better they felt about themselves. Typically, this meant that the addict, who was white-knuckling through, would ultimately relapse, perhaps even relapse in a very dangerous way. But that was okay, because he didn't snitch—and that was really all that mattered. He measured his worth by whether or not he followed the code of the street—even when he was trying to get a life off of the street.

What I found to be even more confounding was the fact that even if he hated his roommate, very often he would still not inform staff that his roommate was using. Occasionally, a code would fall into dust as the snitch finally caved to his hatred. But this was the exception, not the rule. The rule was nobody wanted to be a snitch. That was the Code and they lived by it.

Of course, as they worked the program of recovery, they began to understand that the Code of the Street was going to have to change to the Code of Recovery, if they were going to survive their addiction. And so I learned that this switching of codes was the very essence of survival, for to live without a code would have been tantamount to being utterly lost—which would have meant relapse. Part of the surrender necessary to the Twelve-Step Program of Recovery is a surrender to a new code, a code that says that the recovering person must put recovery before everything else. With this new code he was to work a "selfish-program," in complete opposition to the notion that he should give up recovery for his brother of the street, avoiding snitching at the cost of his own recovery.

And this is how it is for most of us. Whatever code will enable us to survive—in whatever terms we place our survival—that is the code we will use. Whether our survival depends on avoiding abandonment or perceived abandonment by our parents or primary caregivers; whether it depends on using drugs to avoid the painful memories of some trauma or using them to fit in with other adolescents; whether we think our survival depends on harming others before they can harm us, or we think it depends on striving to be *good*; whatever our survival depends upon, from that we will develop a code of behavior—usually assigned to us under the table by family. And incremental to this code of behavior is the idea that this code will somehow make us worthy.

And it is this feeling of worthiness we glimpse that makes us believe that we have a right to stay here on this planet. In fact, very often those who have survived an attempted suicide will tell us that it was shame, or the opposite of worthiness, that drove them to attempt to take their own lives. Shame convinces us that we deserve to be punished, even executed for the crime of feeling ashamed. Whatever accoutrements of *bad* deeds or thoughts to which we attach that feeling of shame, it is the feeling that ultimately makes the decision for us to suicide. We could have gone on for years doing those same exact deeds but until the shame takes over, we don't usually kill ourselves. And the feeling takes charge because the largest code of social order tells us that shame means something. It means that we are *bad* and deserve to be punished.

And this entire circular mind game comes about as a result of our need to obey the code, so if we are going to raise our consciousness about how, when, where and why we are simply following a code rather than being authentic, we need to come to grips with some of these codes.

Code: Don't Be Selfish

From our earliest encounters with other similarly aged toddlers we have been taught to share. And when we didn't share we were told, either subtly or overtly, that we were being selfish. And we intuited, from the expressions of our caregivers or teachers and from the very air around us, that being selfish was a very low form of *bad*. From there we have added a long list of behaviors to which we can ascribe that tell us that we are being selfish. In fact, that list has grown to even include such things as "thinking about yourself." And now, it is not just sharing or not sharing that is at issue, but the notion of selfishness has been equated with a whole identity. A person is either selfish, or he is not. His words, actions and thoughts will define, not just his words, actions and thoughts, but his entire being!

So, if we are to overcome this potentiality, we have to set about the business of obeying the code. We will need to prove in every action, word and deed that we are not being selfish. And if we catch ourselves infringing upon the boundaries of this code even slightly, we will need to compensate for our infringement in some way. Southern women in particular seem to compensate by including a disclaimer on all statements they consider to be selfish. It goes something like this: "That Sally, she can really be a pain! That's an awful thing to say, isn't it?" Or, "This is selfish I know, but I wish she would just do her own job instead of trying always to get me to do it for her." What is meant by the disclaimer is this: "I know I'm really thinking only of myself here, but if I ask for external approval then I won't have to know I'm being selfish." No genuine observation or discernment can be made; no legitimate expression of concern for self can be given without that disclaimer.

Quite often I have clients, male and female, who think that they are honoring this code by inserting disclaimers in front of every self-description: "I know I shouldn't say this, but sometimes I think maybe I've got a talent for that." Or, "It's wrong to think this way, I know, but I just feel like I'm always doing for everyone else and no one is ever even thinking of me." Sometimes, they even whisper!

According to the code, we are simply not allowed to think of ourselves. Any thought, however slight, however genuine, however observatory or discerning, that either honors the self and its needs or honestly discerns the motivation behind another's behavior is considered to be selfish. And because it is selfish, regardless of its merit, that thought is disavowed right after it comes out of the mouth simply because to believe it would mean the believer should outright identify as selfish. This is one of the many reasons we don't trust our own intuition—because to do so might mean we are picking up on information about others that would automatically identify us as selfish people.

When my son had his ninth birthday, his sister was only six. And as he was opening his presents, she sat on the floor beside him and attempted to pick up and play with the toys he'd just opened, which, of course, displeased him—a message he rapidly conveyed. She got up, ran out of the room and dashed down the hallway throwing herself in agony on her bed. Sensing a disturbance greater than the event, I followed her howls and sat down on the bed beside her to ask what was bothering her. She sat up abruptly and said, "Mama, if he doesn't share, he is going to go to *HELL*!" Anger surged through me immediately as I wanted to know who was telling my six-year-old daughter that a child would go to hell for not sharing. So, I asked first who told her that. She answered with the name of her Sunday-school teacher. I calmed myself and my thinking and said, "What was going on in the room just before she told you that?" She answered that the children were fighting and not sharing. I said, "Do you think maybe it's possible that she was just saying that to get you guys to stop fighting and share?" She looked at me, stunned, and said, "Yeah, that's what she was doing!" as if she'd just discovered the light bulb, and ran back out of the room and sat down next to her brother again. I informed her that since this was her brother's birthday, these particular toys were going to feel really special to him for a while but that if she waited a little bit I was sure that he would share with her. And a few moments later he willingly and easily shared one of the toys in which he was less interested.

Going to hell and selfishness seem to go hand-in-hand, simply because once one has done something considered to be selfish, his entire identity is now called into question. Will this child grow up to be selfish? Unless we teach him to share, he just might. I've literally seen parents snatch a toy out of a child's unopened hands and give it to another child in order to "teach her to share." But how does a child learn to share by having her toys snatched from her by an adult? Typically, adults who do this are mostly worried about what others will think of them, as parents, if they raise a selfish child who doesn't share.

Fast-forward to adulthood, and we find these children trying desperately to please others—and calling this *selflessness*. And so it is that we've come to see selflessness as the opposite of selfish. Persons who are selfless are supremely good people. They give of themselves without any thought of their own needs or desires. This makes them exceptional when it comes to obedience to the code.

According to the code, selflessness means that you always put others *first*. When I was a teenager attending church, the code taught me that the way to have joy was to organize my life this way:

J-Jesus
O-others
Y-you

Jesus was to come first, others second and yourself last. But here's the thing. If I'm doing this to get joy, then I must be first— I mean the goal here is joy, right? *My* joy?

This idea that we can put something or someone *first* in our lives is a psychic joke we are playing on ourselves. How does one absent one's self in order to put something or someone else ahead of it? Now you might say that I'm taking the idea of putting others first way too literally. But if you ask people how they put others first, this is actually what they describe. They try to ignore their own desires, needs and impulses and consider only the desires, needs, impulses of others.

So, when people decide to put others first in their lives, they are also deciding to repress their own genuine desires, needs and impulses. What will happen to these repressed energies over time? They will not just go into the unconscious and sit there hidden away forever. No. They are energies and energy is active. Active energy doesn't just sit. It acts. Therefore, just like any other repressed energy, these very powerful and important indicators of our very real and rich authenticity will find a way to make themselves known. But if we are repressing them every time they try to come back up, then they will have to find some other path into conscious awareness. Therefore, repressed desires will often come up in the form of envy or jealousy. Repressed needs will come up in the form of hunger, longing, loneliness or emptiness. Repressed impulses will act, and think later. And if all of these backdoor attempts to be activated fail to garner the attention of the repressor, then eventually bitterness and/or depression sets in.

So, are we selfless or are we bitter, envious, jealous and acting in ways that we ourselves don't even understand? From an external perspective—the image we present to the world—we may be selfless, but what is really going on inside? See, this idea of selflessness goes hand-in-hand with another faulty premise called *sacrifice.* According to the code, people who are selfless sacrifice, and people who don't sacrifice are selfish. But again, with this concept of sacrifice, we are playing a psychic joke on ourselves.

Sacrifice is considered to be the noblest of all possible actions. But in fact, it is an utter impossibility. No one sacrifices. Ever. Either we give a gift out of our passion or compassion to give it— which means it's not a sacrifice at all, but a joyful gift. Or, we trade. Trades work like this: Wife sacrifices her dream of moving to New York and getting a high-powered job in a publishing company, for the husband who wishes to work in Boston at his own high-powered job at a utility company. She loves him, after all, and sacrifice is a part of marriage, right? Fast-forward a few years, and we'll see that she is waiting her turn. She is feeling more and more resentful over time and reminds him occasionally and often in the middle of a fight, that he owes her. Isn't it her turn yet?

Many will say, "Oh, I don't mind," when discussing the sacrifice they've made. "I don't mind helping her, it's just that she's so negative." Or, "He really needs me, so I don't mind helping." When my clients say this, it is often in defense of their own actions. They are doing something that takes a lot of time and energy and if I ask them whether or not this is something they want to continue to do, they often answer with, "Oh, I don't mind." I've asked a few folks what that phrase means, and mostly they answer, that they can tolerate it okay, and on a few occasions they mean that they actually like doing it a little bit. But when I ask "If you had a choice, would you keep doing it?" they often answer again with "Oh, I don't mind." So, generally I have to say, "Let's pretend that you are not allowed to use that phrase for just a few minutes. If you had a choice, would you keep doing it?" They often answer, "If there was something else more fun to do, I'd do it." And then, after a reflective pause, they say, "But I'd probably feel guilty."

Ah! Now we get down to it. The game called *sacrifice* is a way of forestalling the inevitable feeling of guilt. Guilt, the black-mailer. The blackmailer says: "If you do this thing I want you to do, then I won't have to make you feel so awful later." If you keep taking care of Mary, then you won't feel guilty later. So, you keep taking care of Mary and we'll come back to guilt in just a few minutes, for it has its very own code.

The truth is that the only applicable use for the term *selfish* is manipulative. If I want you to do something that you don't want

27

to do, and I accuse you of being selfish if you don't do it, then you are much more likely to do it—especially if you are one who is fiercely loyal to the code. The term, used as a pejorative, informs its victim that he is unworthy or will be if he doesn't do the thing desired by the applier of the term.

Any other use of the term is unfounded—as if manipulation were founded. We cannot put others first or second or third, because there is no first, second or third in the human psyche. It isn't true that when we do something for ourselves we are selfish, any more than it is true that when we do something for others we are unselfish. When we genuinely do something for ourselves, we are showing a kindness to the self. If we do it from obligation or duty, it's just another way of repressing genuineness. If we genuinely do something for others, we are showing a kindness to others—unless we are doing it out of duty or obligation, guilt or fear of being called selfish. In those cases, there is no kindness delivered, regardless of the deed.

Kindness and compassion are motivated from an authentic heart. They are not motivated by guilt, by a fear of having to identify as selfish, or by obligation or duty. Whether that kindness or compassion is delivered to the self or to another, it is no less kindness and compassion. The self and the other are equal in terms of the need and desire to live a fulfilled and happy life. Other is not more important than self and self is not more important than other.

However, it should be noted, that one can do things for the self that one cannot do for others. For example, one cannot motivate others. All motivation is self-motivation. One cannot heal others. All healing is self-healing. One cannot make others feel better. Each individual's feelings are owned and chosen by the individual. However, one can do all of these things for the self. I can motivate myself, heal myself and make myself feel better. I can choose to live my life a certain way, and I can chose to access, accept and receive deeper aspects of myself creating greater meaning in my life. But I cannot make these same choices for others.

So, if you add up the number of things that I can do for myself, and compare them to the number of things I can do for another—I'm thinking that the sum total is going to be quite telling. I am, in fact, able to do far more for myself than I will ever be capable of doing for another. And yet, the code "Don't be Selfish" tells us that we should not be even thinking of doing all of those things, for to do so means we are selfish.

So, how do we self-motivate, self-heal and self-soothe; how do we access, accept and receive deeper aspects of the self, if we are not allowed to consider the self? Well, at this point in the argument, those who advocate for the code will say, that we are taking it to an extreme. And yes, we have. We have, as a global community, taken the notion of self and other to an extreme that is utterly unfounded. And we live our lives out of that extreme by making hundreds of little choices every single day that keep us tied to the masts of our ships instead of being able to steer them. When we honor this code, each one of those choices made during a given day is skewed along the lines of proof. The object of the game is to prove to ourselves and others that we are not selfish.

But then, those who argue for the code will concede that maybe we can do things for the self, because after all, "You can't take care of others, unless you take care of yourself." And they say this, looking you right in the eyes, without even realizing how distorted that statement is. According to this philosophy, you are really here to serve others, and the only reason you would bother to take care of yourself is because it will stoke up that tool that you are and make it a better tool for others to use.

All the while the truth remains that much more than half of the stuff we are trying to do for others cannot even be done! We can't make others happy. We can't make them make the choices we wish with all our might they would make, no matter how much we try to "help" them by teaching them the "right" way. We can't fix them; we can't figure out what they want; we can't make their lives meaningful; we can't love them into self-esteem; we can't love them into recovery; we simply cannot do these things that we are spending a good portion of our time and energy trying desperately to do for them—all the while *not* putting that same energy into doing those very things for ourselves—things we actually can do.

The best, highest, most noble and loving gift we can give to another human being is to be utterly authentic in their presence. And we cannot give that gift without spending considerable time and energy getting to know ourselves and then spending equal time and energy being true to that Self. We cannot give that gift if we are ignoring the self, or repressing its expressions, desires and needs.

In much the same way that an oak tree can only do the job of growing into an oak tree, the only job we are given is to fulfill ourselves. Those who are loyal to the code hear that statement as one of utter selfishness. But the truth is that the more I fulfill my own authenticity, the more likely I am to *genuinely* give to others, for giving is naturally built into the fabric of fulfillment. But this giving will not be done out of obligation, duty, proving selflessness or any other false reason. Rather as authentic beings, we give because giving is in us to do. Such giving is an integral part of the love we feel for self, which is also equally love for others.

This entire code, "Don't Be Selfish," is built on the premise that we are separate from each other and from the divine. But if there is no such separation then everything I do for me is also done for others. So it is that oneness puts an end to the code of selfishness.

Code: Feel Guilty, It's Good for You

The only reason guilt works for us is because we believe it is right to feel guilty. Guilt convinces us that we are doing the *right thing* if we honor it. In fact, millions of people all over the world, from all different cultures and religions are absolutely enslaved to guilt. And guilt is a terrible task-master. Yet because we believe that guilt is a worthy feeling, we allow it to rule our lives.

Guilt—according to the code's definition—tells us that we have done something *wrong*. In fact, for many people the word *conscience* is equated with feelings of guilt. We know that we have a conscience because it can feel guilty. And we *should* feel guilty, when the conscience rings its bell, because if we didn't feel guilty we'd never know when we have done something *wrong*. In this way, guilt is seen as a guide.

In fact, some in certain more fundamentalist religions will inform young people that they can know when they are being "called of God to serve" when they feel "the burden" for a certain group of people. This *burden* is made up of a combination of heart-felt empathy and guilt. So, for example, if a young person learns of the latest genocides in the Democratic Republic of the Congo and she not only feels sorrowful as an empathetic response to the death, starvation and carnage that is going on there, but she also feels a kind of survivor's guilt in which she wonders why this is happening to them instead of her—then she might be told by her Pastor that perhaps she is being called of God to serve in the Congo.

Actually such survivor's guilt is based on the false premise that these terrible things are happening somewhere on the planet because they *should*—that is, the bad thing had to happen somewhere, so why there, and not here? But these things don't happen because some cosmic order has caused such atrocities to occur; they happen because of human blindness. Because we don't know that we are really one with each other. Because we don't know that there is no need to fight over supply, for the divine is always providing, if we could but wipe the scales from our eyes and see the provision right there in front of us. Because some people fear lack so much that they need to take it all. Because some people who survive by greed take power in order to continue to ensure their sense of survival and continue to use greed to maintain their survival at the top of the heap of bodies.

Of course, any young person with any sensibility at all is going to feel some heartfelt empathetic response, and wish that he could do something. On the other hand survivor's guilt often results from an identification with guilt that assumes responsibility for other people's lives. As we've said, some sensitive and naturally empathetic children are given, in their families-of-origin, the responsibility for carrying the emotional content in the family. And so it is quite easy for these children to transfer those same feelings of guilt and responsibility to a monumental global concern. Once, long ago, I knew someone who was living out of this kind of responsibility, in what I refer to as a Scapegoat identity, who said to me, "I feel like I'm responsible for Hiroshima and Nagasaki and I wasn't even born yet!" So if a child, *burdened* with a Scapegoat identity feels responsible for a country where genocide and horror are taking place, this isn't a *calling from God,* it is just more of the same guilt he has always felt, only transferred to the world.

Guilt is the lie. It tells us that we truly *are* responsible for the well-being and happiness of others. It tells the teenage daughter that she *should have* made sure that Dad didn't pick up his keys and walk out of the house, drunk and in a huff that night, because *if only* she'd stopped him, he wouldn't have killed that child on the road. It tells us that we have the power to keep suicidal people alive. It tells us that we can somehow move into another person's heart and mind and make them happy, even when they have a Victim identity and choose misery in order to maintain that identity. It tells us that we *should* always be about the business of making others happy and well, and that if we stop to consider ourselves, well, we are just selfish.

In these cases, if we think about it, we can recognize that guilt is lying. As we said in the previous discussion on the code "Don't Be Selfish," it is not possible for us to make others experience well-being or happiness. Well-being and happiness are inside jobs. The only person who can make me happy or make me experience well-being is me. No one else has any power to do that for me. Perhaps they can do the song and dance with the *intention* to make me happy, but I still get to choose whether or not I will receive that gift. We can't make other people's choices for them. We can't keep someone else alive—unless they are already unconscious and they need and we know CPR. We can't *make* anyone feel anything—not happy, not sad, not angry, not afraid, not guilty, not anything. Feelings arise from within the complex interaction of belief, emotion and thought that occurs *within* a given individual. Feelings *cannot* be created from the external. Period.

This belief that we can make others feel is one of the most damaging of interpersonal beliefs on the planet. How many mistakes, small and large, have we made in the attempt to make someone else feel, think or choose something different! If we could ever stop and consider the reality that no matter what one person does, the other still has a choice about what they are going to do in response, we could change the world. Response comes from within a person. It is not orchestrated from outside of the person. But the idea that we are somehow in charge of others' emotions, reactions, choices, thoughts, and behavior is taught to us on every level—from individual all the way up the food chain to corporate. How many middle managers, for example, have been fired because they couldn't make an employee behave correctly, or make the market behave correctly, or make the customer behave correctly? How many customer service seminars are being held right at this very moment, in which the participants are being taught that they must please the customer! But what do you do then if the customer refuses to be pleased? We are taught that we must *influence* others—a euphemism for control—and *make* them like the product, the service, the whatever. And in the same way we are taught that we can make others mad, or unhappy, or the biggest lie of all—we can hurt their feelings.

The notion that we can hurt another person's feelings is one of the primary myths of guilt. I can't even say how many people I've worked with over the years, who stayed in very dysfunctional relationships because they were afraid that creating boundaries would hurt the other's feelings—even though they no longer really wanted to participate in this relationship at all. And if I were to venture to ask, "What about your feelings?" they would often answer that they didn't want to be selfish—and they *really* didn't want to feel guilty. So, they spent years in a highly dysfunctional relationship in order to forestall having to feel guilty. Now *that's* some pretty powerful stuff!

Guilt lies. Always. Even if we've done something that most consider to be *wrong,* feeling guilty only exacerbates the problem. The argument that guilt is our conscience talking to us, denies the reality that feeling guilty only depletes energy. It forces us to have to wade through that *bad* feeling and the shame to which it leads, and this means we have even less energy to correct the problem. Once guilt has led all the way to shame—which not only tells us that we've done *wrong,* but that we *are wrong*—we can get lost there. A more effective response would be empathy, in which we recognize both the responsibility for our own behaviors but also clearly see and feel how another feels in response to those behaviors. Empathy urges us to make amends. Guilt is a product of dualistic thinking—about which we will learn much more as we go. And actually, that is all that guilt is. It serves no other purpose—that is, unless you are one of those people who knows how to use it to manipulate others.

From the perspective that guilt is conscience, guilt becomes necessary for us to live our lives within certain constraints. But that idea is based on the one that says that if we didn't have guilt or conscience, we would all just run amuck. Chaos would rule the world. Insanity and anarchy would ensue. Guilt is our savior. Guilt keeps the earth spinning on its axis. But if guilt is our savior, then why do so many think that we needed another savior to come and save us from our guilt?

The feeling of guilt is not necessary to inform us of our so-called *wrong doing*. Empathy is enough, by itself, to inform the mind of the heart's wish to make amends for a certain behavior. But guilt doesn't just tell us that we'd like to make amends, it tells us that we can add this *bad* behavior to a long and ever-growing list of *bad* behaviors that will eventually add up to an identity— one that has to do with our worth as a person, one that is based in shame.

So, guilt does not align us with our deeper truth. In fact, it separates us further from it, for guilt is part of the paradigm of duality that keeps us believing that at our core, we are separate from the divine, due to our intrinsically evil nature. We will say much more about that as we go, but for now, we need to know that the code of guilt is false guidance and it comes from another likewise false code.

Code: There's Right and There's Wrong

Not only does this code spin us off into the polarities of who we are as a species, but it assumes that what is *right* for one is *right* for all, and what is *wrong* for one is *wrong* for all. It is out of this belief that we create our judgments of ourselves and others. Through TV, film, radio and history books, as well as novels, poetry, art and other media, we know that the definitions of *right* and *wrong* have changed over the centuries. Once it was thought *wrong* that an African American should be set free from slavery. Once it was thought *wrong* that a woman should wear pants. Once it was thought that a child born "out of wedlock" was a bastard who should forever after that birth be put into a rigid caste system in which only poverty and shame were possible.

Once it was thought that a woman was to blame for her rape. Once on a global basis it was thought that gays and lesbians were, at best, mentally ill, and at worst, perverted and evil. All of these ideas have changed a great deal, though we still have a long way to go.

In these and many other ways we have changed our definitions of *right* and *wrong* to a more inclusive and less rigidly judgmental stance. That said, we also look back on our history and judge ourselves, saying that we were *wrong* to have done the things we did back then. In fact, I would say that rather than being *wrong,* we were blind to our own humanity. We were blind to the impact of our judgments, assuming that our fears *should* dictate our morality. But it was no more than fear.

In fact, in most cases it is our fear that assumes *wrongness*. It was fear that said that an African American slave should not be set free. That fear objectified African Americans in the same way that a serial killer objectifies his victims. They were not people. They were things. As things we could make whatever use of them we desired. The fear said that a previously unknown darker race, which in the deepest jungles of the uncivilized world was black-skinned, must have something to do with evil. That fear said that the economy of a plantation depended on maintaining an objective, if not abusive relationship with the slave. That fear said, "I need, and I must protect myself."

That same kind of fear is what said that women were to blame for their rapes. Men were just physically incapable of controlling their libido, so that women had to dress down, so as not to provoke the male's primal urges. Men were, after all, the rulers of society, and their needs must be met. So, if a ruler, supposedly a fatherly ruler, raped a woman, then it must have been her fault. This is the same kind of fear that a child holds against an abusive parent. Rather than acknowledging that the parent is abusive, the child takes responsibility for the abuse by assuming the *wrongness*. She caused the parent to abuse by being *bad.*

That same kind of fear dictated how we have viewed the gay, lesbian, bisexual and transgendered populations for centuries. They were different, and difference is frightening. We looked at that difference as if it were some kind of mirror, so that if *they* could be *like that,* then so could I—but no way am I like that—so *they* are sick, perverted and evil. Keep them away from me. So it is again that our fears have dictated our morality.

And so it is that all *wrongs* and *rights* are made up of fear. They depend on fear for their power to persuade. Osama Bin Laden was a terrorist because he elicited the same amount of fear from the public that he himself, and his followers, held within. They feared the infidels and the power of heretic Western politics and so they had to sneak, hide and sabotage in order to bring down that power. And yet this fundamentalist sect believed that what it was doing was *right* and that the Western politic was *wrong.* And now, there are many fundamentalist Americans, successfully creating false propaganda, which says that *all* Muslims believe as this fundamentalist sect believed. All of this fundamentalism happens under the guise of righteousness, when actually it is totally fear-based bias.

In our Western politics today much of the rhetoric we still hear, even though Obama has been re-elected, has to do with fear, though it seems to come from a moral base. We must not have a national health care plan because that would make us socialist—and we fear that socialism will rob us of the freedom we've fought so hard to attain. We must not allow gays and lesbians to marry because we fear the differentness that is being presented by the LGBT population in general. We must keep the budget down because we fear that not doing so will disrupt the economic strata we've set up—a strata that errs in favor of the wealthy, who are worshipped and idolized by the poor plebs who give up their own economic well-being by continuing to vote their fear of disrupting the status-quo. Though each of these issues comes from a base of fear, each one is presented under the guise of morality. Socialism is evil, gays and lesbians are bad, sick and perverted, and the good people are rewarded with wealth — an archetypal syllogism of monumental power.

We fear the murderer, the robber, the persuasions of the prostitute, the pedophile and so we call each of them *wrong,* or *evil.* To be clear here though, we must add that this fear is one that should have us problem-solving and finding a permanent solution to the issues that create such identifications. Instead we just label and swallow the key. And worst of all, we make the assumption that people who don't do any of these things must be *good.* We trust these people because we are not afraid of them. We trust them, so they must be good, right? And when one of these seemingly *good* people does something that we fear, we feel betrayed and we say now that we were *wrong* — these were not *good* people, they were really *bad* people who had us fooled.

Actually, people don't kill because they are *wrong* or *evil.* They kill because they think that they have to. They are blind to their own inner protector, the divine Self, and so they believe that in order to survive — in whatever way they see survival — they must kill. The gang member sees his survival based on the rules and codes of the gang. He must kill in order to not be killed — even his initiation is a joining that allows him to survive a little longer, or so he thinks. The robber believes he must kill in order to keep himself out of jail or make sure he gets the money first. He believes that his survival depends not only on the money, but on the role he plays in life as the *bad* guy. Even the serial killer, who has so totally identified with *evil* that he plays it out daily as a way of being visible first to himself and then to others, believes that the next kill will somehow make him real and that if he cannot be real he doesn't exist at all — ergo he survives based on the next kill.

In the same way, every *wrong* is but a blindness to the truth that we are not separate from the divine and never have been. The prostitute very often lives out an identification with her guilt and shame reenacting her own childhood sexual traumas again and again in an effort to make it okay. The pedophile has in some way attached the power of the bully with his or her sexuality and feels addicted, compelled to act that out again and again. Of course, we don't want the pedophile or the serial killer loose on society to harm our children or our loved ones, but this doesn't make them *wrong* or *evil*.

Similarly, the concept of *goodness* is but a blindness to the truth that we are not separate from the divine and never have been, for the idea of *goodness* is exclusively based on its polar opposite, *badness*. We are *good* when we are not *bad,* and vice versa. And *good* is defined by the culture we live in. As we said, Osama Bin Laden thought it was a *good* thing to fly airplanes into the trade towers. *Good* is defined by those things that make us unafraid. A person is *good* to the degree that we are not afraid of him. Many a kind and generous person has been persecuted for his or her *evil*, simply because people were afraid of his unique form of living. And many a harsh, cruel and manipulative person has been promoted and given adoration and praise because he was able to feign trustworthiness, so that people were not afraid of him.

In fact, these two polar opposites, *good* and *evil*, were created as very early coping skills in our ancient archetypal collective history. Just as a child believes that having a *good* or *bad* day is his parents' fault, so the ancients of our early collective history thought that when fate was *good* to them, it was because the gods were pleased, and when it was not, they were displeased and punitive. If the ancients could just figure out how to please the gods, then they would have good crops and their children would survive the winters. This collective archetypal thinking is the basis of the battle between *good* and *evil*. Therefore, we have included this code, from which we have created our sense of morality, into every aspect of our lives, because deep down we believe that our fates depend upon it. This is fear-based thinking at its best. And we have bargained for centuries with this thinking that says, IF I do this morally correct thing, THEN *good* things will happen to me, and IF I do morally incorrect things, THEN well, what goes around comes around, right? Wrong. What goes around quite often flies off the other side like a whirlpool spits out its holdings. What goes around sometimes just keeps going around. What goes around does not really hold itself responsible for teaching us the lessons we are supposed to be learning.

The whole basis for the paradigm of *good* and *evil* is intellectual abstraction. We have given the name *evil* to those things that frighten us, and to those things that do not frighten us, we have given the name *good*. In this way we can intellectually categorize all of life, so that we do not have to question life any further or feel our fears. We do not have to come to terms with the mystery of love that loves beyond *good* or *evil*. We do not have to try to understand our seemingly *evil* neighbors or even our own shadows—all we need do is categorize. The end.

But we are not *good* or *evil*—we are either blind or we see. And we can see by degree. Some of us see completely that we are one with the divine and that because we are we cannot want for anything. Some of us only see that partially, and some of us haven't a clue. But whatever the vision—that is the reality we live from. We will have much more to say about this vision as we go, so for now, we'll move on to the next code.

Code: You Ought to Be Ashamed

We've briefly mentioned this notion before, but let's clarify. Shame is an identity. Unlike its brother, guilt, shame does not define what we've done so much as it defines who we are—or at least who we think we are. Shame says: I AM *wrongness*, *badness* or *evil*. But guilt as habit leads eventually to shame in that the sum total of all of our *bad* deeds makes us *bad* people.

And in the same way that we think that guilt makes us better people by keeping us in line, the idea that we ought to be ashamed of ourselves likewise is thought to keep us in line. If we can feel ashamed, perhaps we won't repeat our crimes. Most baby-boomers are very familiar with this statement literally said by our parents: "You ought to be ashamed of yourself." Some who come even from generations X and Y still have parents who make that statement. It is meant to make a child feel so bad that s/he will be motivated to self-correct. But shame is not a motivator. It is a deflator, a downer, a de-motivator. If shame creates anything at all, it is depression, for shame says that we are not even worthy to feel our feelings—for to do so implies that we are deserving of some form of pity. But shame tells us that we deserve nothing, so we cannot feel our feelings and it is the denial of these feelings that creates depression. Not one child has ever become a better person because he was shamed. That child may have put on a mask and costume to please the shaming parent, or put on the shame itself as a bad-guy identity, but he did not become a better person.

Some would say that it is good enough that the child puts on a mask and costume—I mean, don't we all have to do that in order to be *good* people? In fact, shouldn't we all be willing to try to wear a *nice* or *good* mask? The problem with this reasoning is that it assumes that without the mask to cover up our intrinsic *badness* we are left to its powerful persuasions. Civility, indeed, society itself requires that we don the mask and costume to keep society safe from our innate evil urges. And if we cannot keep that mask on good enough, well then we ought to be ashamed of ourselves.

But what if we are not intrinsically *bad*? Or, even intrinsically *good*? What if we are just intrinsically real? What if the mask and costume only keep us from being true to who we really are? Well, then when we are told that we ought to be ashamed, what we are being ashamed of is our own truest Self. Is this really what we are looking for?

Shame says I AM *bad*, worthless, not enough, not good, cheap, damaged goods. But, as we said when we were talking about the code of worthiness, the double-bind here is that when we feel ashamed of ourselves it is evidence that maybe we have a little hope—for to feel shame means that we are really not all that bad. The bottom line of the code of shame is this belief that we are put here on this planet to work our way out of our intrinsically *evil* natures. In fact, it is our *evil* nature, that caused God or nature to turn against us in the beginning of time when we were kicked out of the Garden of Eden. We are all victims of original sin, which has been passed down to us generation to generation since that first bite of the apple. We will be discussing this mythology in later chapters, so for now all we need to know is that this mythology has been implanted like a computer chip in our unconscious archetypal understanding of ourselves. And because it has, we all carry within us at least a seed of this idea that we are intrinsically bad, and ought to feel ashamed.

The code of shame is meant to help us correct that *badness*, and turn it into at least a fake *goodness*. And you know what they say: Fake it till you make it. But, I'm afraid that this time faking it doesn't really make it—it just fakes it. We pretend, because we don't know what else to do, especially when we are getting pressure from parents, whom we desperately need and willingly adore, to perform in some way that meets their needs. We can put on a *bad* mask and costume that meets their needs for someone to carry and act out their feelings of worthlessness. We can put on a *good* mask and costume that meets their needs to be seen as worthy by society. Most of us straddle this fence most of our lives, moving at times from one mask to another, never arriving at our own authenticity. And *that* is a shame.

Code: What Good Does it Do?

When I have worked with groups in treatment centers in the past I've very often encountered this code. We'll be doing a group on anger and its ability to help us build appropriate boundaries and rescue us from toxic situations, but someone in the group will inevitably say, "What good does it do me to be angry, it won't change anything!" In other words, unless anger can change the person they are mad at, it has no value. And so they just don't allow themselves to feel the grinding frustration of their own anger, because feeling it only means that they feel bad. This is just one example of how we turn off the inner world in favor of compliance with the external world because what good does it do to go there?!

We have been subtly and overtly taught by the whole of society that externals matter and internals matter very little if at all. In fact, anyone who focuses on the internal is suspected of being selfish, if not a little weird. Preachers and teachers down through the ages have taught us that our feelings change, so they cannot be trusted. Thoughts, however, especially those thoughts that match what the rest of society thinks, can be trusted, because they don't change. I remember once hearing a pastor say that love could not be defined as a feeling but only as a behavior. It set me to thinking about all those people who live entire lifetimes doing things for other people because they should, rather than because they felt a true passion for doing it. I wasn't buying it.

In fact, part of the reason that we do not trust ourselves to delve into the inner world, is because if we do, we might be putting ourselves within the realm of influence of that *evil* nature within. If we go far enough down into ourselves, surely we are going to run into that nasty beast we are. And since we don't want to do that, better to stay in the externals and fake it till we make it. The code tells us that going in there would do us no good, so why bother.

The code tells us that we can be defined as the sum total of our interactions with the external world. Of course, this doesn't account for the pure poetry of essence that rambles and rumbles around inside of us with or without our conscious acquiescence.

It doesn't account for our dreams and it offers us nothing whatsoever for our desires—unless our desires fit into the current external idea of appropriateness of expression. Very often we tell ourselves that our desires are silly, that our intuitions are judgmental and that our needs are just plain selfish. And so it is that we are never privy to the rich treasures of our own souls.

What good does it do to feel our desires, when to do so is thought to be silly if not selfish? What good does it do to recognize our intuitions, for to honor them would be thought unfounded in our world in which empirical data is still seen as far superior to intuition? This is one of the reasons why so many of us stay in marriages in which we are being betrayed again and again, for though our intuitions are telling us something is terribly wrong, unless we can prove it, what good does it do? That is why private detective agencies are making a killing right now, for they can offer us the proof that our intuitions already offered years ago—only we weren't listening.

What good does it do to recognize our fears—we can't change them! What good does it do to feel angry at someone who is not going to change? What good does it do to recognize an authenticity that no one else respects or, for that matter, even sees? What good does it do to go internal and get grounded when the whole world seems to be against me being grounded?

Here's the good it does: It gives us power over our lives. When we go internal long enough we eventually find ourselves and it is upon this Self that we can then base the rest of our lives. When we go internal we get true direction from our own souls, and we can live out that direction and feel the blessings of living fully alive. When we go internal we are no longer blind. We see from the soul the truth of our selves, of our lives and of our world. Really now, what else is there?

Code: Be Loyal First to Duty
A person who consistently does her duty is considered to be a

good person. A person who does not is considered to be a *bad* person. Simple. No gray. Very Western. And another lie. Duty, a somewhat more euphemistic term than its synonym, *obligation*, tells us what we *should* do. Of course, what the specific *should* is varies from culture to culture, family to family, dynamic to dynamic, but if you are loyal to that system you *will* do your duty. And you will do it based solely on your loyalty, for to do it for any other reason calls the power of your loyalty into question.

Loyalty is also based in a *should*, which basically says one is *good* if one complies with the constraints of loyalty and *bad* if one does not. Lack of loyalty is traitorous in the more formal systems of society, such as the military. And somewhere along the lines of our history of relational interaction, we filtered the beliefs found in the military down to the common interactions between human beings, so that now lack of loyalty to some family systems is considered to be a betrayal of traitorous proportions. Why did we do this? Because going to war for one's country was considered to be the ultimate sacrifice—meaning it was the ultimate in *goodness*. So, every other system should be organized similarly if that system wanted to consider itself to be *good*.

Now, let me be clear. I am certain that in times of war, lack of loyalty to the command could mean danger and even death for self and others. And since war does seem to still be something in which we are always invested somewhere on the globe, then during war soldiers are still probably going to need to be loyal to the command. But our decision to pass those beliefs around to every other interactive system was a mistake.

And the biggest problem of all with that mistake is found in the concept that we must be loyal to our duties. Here's how that works. There are certain duties that are incumbent upon a daughter as she matures if she wishes to see herself and be seen as a *good* daughter. There are certain duties incumbent upon a son as he becomes an adult, if he is to be a *good* son. There are certain duties incumbent upon all children—even when they are children—which will win their parents' approval. And lack of loyalty to duty loses that approval. There are certain duties a husband or wife *should* do in order to evidence loyalty to the spouse. I could go on and on, but you get the idea.

But some of you are asking—what's wrong with that? Surely a husband should be faithful to his wife and she to him. Surely children need certain guidelines and disciplines in order to grow up well. Surely adult children need to return the favor to their parents who raised them by attending to those parents when they grow old. This is how we take care of each other, right?

Well, it is definitely true that children need loving guidance, discipline and enough light to see who they are. They need to be kept from danger and they need to understand the basics of healthy interaction so that they can play well with others. But guiding them is not the same as teaching them to be loyal to the system which holds them to a structure of duty. Children will associate parental insistence on loyalty to duty, whether communicated overtly or covertly, with parental approval. And they will associate parental approval with parental love. In fact, parental insistence on loyalty is often communicated as a demand to win parental approval and even parents often associate approval with love. So, bottom line, there is no unconditionality in this demand. This is not healthy parenting.

And yes, we would love to have our spouses provide us with the security that comes from faithfulness. But frankly, if a spouse is being faithful only because he or she *should*, then I'm not interested in their faithfulness. In a love relationship, I don't want duty and loyalty. I want love. I want faithfulness that comes from loving me so much that the heart wants only to be with me and doesn't even consider being with someone else an option. I want the real deal. And I want to build so much intimacy into that relationship that we will always look to each other to meet our needs for a primary relationship. The truth is that *all of that loyalty and duty just amounts to lack of faith in love.*

Well, we might say, that's pretty unrealistic. People do have fantasies sometimes about other lovers. They do have temptations. To that I respond with this: The greater the reliance on loyalty and duty, the greater the number of fantasies about other lovers, and the greater the number and depth of the temptations. Love, not duty and loyalty, needs to be the primary motivator of everything else that happens in a primary relationship. Though it also takes compatibility and some strong relationship skills to make a relationship grow in strength and intimacy, we simply won't stay attached to someone anymore based solely on the power of duty and loyalty. We thought we would—which is why we created the institution of marriage in the first place. We thought that if couples were legally bound to each other, loyalty and duty to that bond would be enough to keep them together. And for centuries it did—or at least it seemed to—while people married for security, dowry, good hips or child-bearing capacity, and stayed in those marriages even as they were holding bile behind their teeth and commonly seeking their intimacy needs elsewhere. The rare exception was the marriage made of two people who really loved each other, wanted to be together and built into the dynamic the intimacy essential to grow the bond between them. It was much more common for people to marry for security and grow apart.

Today, it's different. Today love and passion matter in a marriage—sometimes even more than loyalty and duty. But there are still many who decide to stay married for the children—who would in many cases be much better off if the parents would just go ahead and get that divorce. There are still many who believe that they made a promise and you just don't break your promises no matter what. And there are many who still believe that the marriage vow makes magical things happen so that people will never be unfaithful once they have said "I do." These hold-outs to a history of ineffective relating, however, are not telling us the truth about relationships. *Love, compatibility and effective relationships skills* are the three key ingredients in a healthy growing relationship. All the rest—even the rest about loyalty and duty—is pure fantasy.

And whoever said that children owe their parents anything at all was simply bargaining with the reality of human interaction. Particularly when it comes to aging and death this bargain is: IF I can make my children believe that they should take care of me when I'm old, THEN they will and I'll have nothing to worry about. But, of course, making someone believe something is not the same as making the premise of the forced agreement true. Explain to me, please, how it is that a child who did not ask to be born or parented owes anything to the parent who simply did his or her job. Parenting is a choice—particularly in this age of birth control—but actually anytime. The first choice is to get pregnant. Whether we get pregnant by planning or by just not using birth control, or not using it appropriately, we are still making a choice or several choices that result in pregnancy. The second choice is whether or not we will parent the child once s/he is conceived. This simply means we may choose to run away, give up the child for adoption, have an abortion or abandon the child at any point in his or her upbringing. Or, we may choose to stay and parent. And the third choice has to do with how well we will parent. All of these choices belong to the parent—not the child. So, how do we conclude from these facts that the child now has to pay the parent back—what, for loving the child?

Seriously? Love needs a payback? I don't think so. Healthy parenting is all about unconditional love. There are no debts to pay. The child is simply loved because the child is. The child's existence is enough to elicit love. And what the parent does out of that love will be a gift for the child to receive. But even in this day, when "the child comes first" is the mantra, which in fact is teaching many a child that he or she *should* be entitled to all things, there are still many who believe that the duty and loyalty of being a parent is what makes them a good parent. You sacrifice, you give, you do your duty and you are loyal to that duty, come what may. *Therefore,* your child owes you the same kind of duty and loyalty.

We've discussed sacrifice earlier in this chapter, so I won't go any further here than to say, if we are giving loving gifts to our children, there is no sacrifice. And if we are trading our sacrifice for the one that we hope our children will later make for us when we are old, there is no sacrifice there either. So, how again is it that our children owe us? No, these are games we play with our fears. We are afraid of aging and death, so we fool and betray our own and our children's authenticity by bargaining with their lives for ours.

So here's the real deal about duty and loyalty: They are concepts developed to help us to deal with huge collective fear. The fear is that the majority will not follow the leader. So the leader's job is to convince the followers that IF they can prove their loyalty to the system by doing whatever duty is prescribed, THEN they are good people and will get their just rewards. As a collective we have accepted this bargain as truth and have followed this propaganda—many times straight to hell on earth. And even when we weren't following so well, we still passed on the propaganda to our smaller cultures and even on down to our family systems.

Duty and loyalty are but bargains we make with the reality that we have absolutely no control over other humans and what they are going to do, say, think or feel. Duty and loyalty delude us into thinking that others *should* be able to control us, especially when they are trying to lead us in the *right* way— whatever that is. Duty and loyalty delude those who wish to have control over us into believing that it is *right* that they *should* be allowed to control us with these loosely structured concepts.

The thing is that regardless of how loosely these concepts are structured, every single one of us knows when there is a duty to be done and when we should be loyal. How do we know this? These concepts have become so ingrained in us over the centuries that they have become archetypal. This means that they have their own psychic pull—as strong as gravity—and the pull informs us of what we *should* be doing. How do we know, for instance, when someone tells us that something is our duty, that they are telling the truth? Because we already have an archetypal pull toward duty.

Some would argue that this archetypal pull is the same as conscience and that it is telling us that we really *should* do our duty and be loyal to some system. But how do we know? The fact is that we don't know, but these concepts are so ingrained that we *think* we know. If conscience is a valid concept at all—its points of reference are more appropriately based in love, not duty or obligation. Duty and loyalty to systems build resentment, not love. They make us feel trapped, inhibited and guilty. They accomplish much less than love would accomplish if it were set free to do its truest bidding. And further, they are generally based in what someone else says—i.e., they do not come from authentic self-examination and self-love.

Code: Power is Bad

The code tells us that having power is equivalent to having wealth and both are basically evil. Everybody knows that wealthy people are greedy and intent on having their way and that they will get their wealth no matter how many dead bodies they have to step over to get it. Or, at least that's our bias—particularly if we have no wealth. And the truth is that there are enough wealthy people who actually do operate this way, to convince us that the bias is true. And since money is often seen as power, the same bias holds sway over the notion of power.

Interestingly enough, we also believe that if we were just good enough, we would be successful at attaining the money, power and prestige we are seeking. Thus, we worship those who have what we want, idolizing them so that a good percentage of the income made in the West is made by publicizing the antics of the rich and famous. So, while on the one hand we think of those who have power as evil monsters, on the other we assume that they must have done something right in order to have attained such amazing fame, power and money. This is a double bind for it assumes that those of us who do not have such power, are both wrong for not having it, and right for not having it. This conflict creates a great deal of anxt within the everyday Joe, so that it's just easier to assume the old Machiavellian theory that power corrupts and perfect power corrupts perfectly. That anxt is usually made up of the irrational idea that those powerful people have taken something from us that we want (i.e., our own collection of power and wealth), and they must be bad for having done so. After all there is a limit to how much is out there, so, how am I going to get mine if they already have so much of it!

We have old archetypal images of power that include the one of Nero playing the fiddle while the Christians burned. This is because we perceive power as a tool to be used to control others. But more and more these days people are talking about *personal power*. Yet when asked, many will define this phrase as the ability to influence and even control the behavior of others. People who have personal power are those who have charisma and a powerful persona, they say, as well as the confidence to win friends and influence people. And then they talk about self-control as personal power as well. Self-control, they say, has to do with being able to control one's emotions and behaviors. So, according to this definition, personal power is about controlling self and others.

But actually, a person who has personal power, has a keen awareness of what is going on within, and knows how to mine the psyche for its jewels, then gather them up and bring them out into the external world in a healthy and effective way. Rather than controlling his emotions, this person knows how to use the messages he finds within his emotions as guidance. He is not guided by the emotions themselves, but by the messages within the emotions, messages that inform him of what he needs to do to honor his own authenticity. He knows what belongs to him, and he is also very clear on what does not belong to him. This means he knows, from the soles of his feet to the top of his head, that there is absolutely nothing he can do to get someone else to do, say, think or feel anything. And it also means that he does not control himself or his emotions, but lives from the initiation of the authentic Self.

We are not personally empowered by gaining control over self or others. We are empowered when we learn to receive and make use of our own authentic power. People who are personally empowered do have a persona of confidence, but they are not confident that they can control others, nor are they confident that they can control their own emotions. Rather they are confident because they are sure that no matter what happens in life, they know where to go to get their peace. They can always go within to find peace waiting for them there. How do they know it's there? Because once they found it, they returned to that place within them again and again until they came to call it home.

Quite often when a person who is so empowered walks into a room, others intuitively sense that power. For some this feels like charisma, and for others it feels intimidating. But these responses belong to the receiver, not to the sender. In other words, the personally empowered person is not controlling the responses he receives. Rather, he is just being true to himself. People who are truly personally empowered don't need to take their power from the hearts and minds of others. And people who are intimidated by the personally empowered are so because their intuition is telling them that this is a person who operates beyond *their* control. Further, those who are moved by what appears to be the charisma of the personally empowered person are actually moved by his authenticity and by the connection they feel to it.

There are many, far too many, who know how to use charisma and intimidation in an interesting mix in order to have their way with others. Many sociopaths are quite charming in an attempt to woo their potential victims. Some of these sociopaths become politicians and CEOs. Some become petty con-men and the spouse abusers. But the fact is that for the most part, these people know more about selecting their victims and choosing the grooming techniques that fit the victim's needs, than they do about actually controlling others. In fact, they cannot control others. What really happens in these dynamics is that the so-called *controller,* usually highly intuitive, is a student of human behavior and has learned a great deal about where people are most vulnerable. He or she then plays on these vulnerabilities with charm and pretense, and the so-called *controlled* **give over their own personal power** to the controller.

All so-called control over other human beings is an illusion. No one can reach inside of another person and push all the right buttons and flip all the right switches to force that person to do something. The victim of control is always choosing. Sometimes, such as in the case of violence, the victim may choose to give over control in order to survive—often a very smart choice. But always, choice is operative. There is no such thing as being out of control. We may die choosing, but we are still choosing something. So regardless of how charming or how violent the person who is perceived to have the most power is, everyone in the room still has several options from which to choose.

Therefore, power cannot possibly mean control over others. In fact the only real power is authentic power—that power that comes from our most true, most essential natures to care for and about the self. But most of us think that in order to live a safe and happy life, we have to fight off our enemies and keep the wolves from our door, by effectively guarding ourselves and threatening perceived enemies. Most of us think that we have to fight our way through school, job and career and finally fight our way to the top. Most of us think that if we don't fight, we'll get walked on. Some of us even prefer being walked on to fighting—as we think that fighting is the only other option. Because of this fight or flight thinking, we've come to believe that those who have reached the top must have had to step over some bodies to get there. And because of this fight or flight thinking, indeed, sometimes those who reach the top have actually left some bodies back there on the path to arrival.

But the personally empowered person doesn't believe that she has to fight to get there. Rather, she believes that whatever truly belongs to her is already hers, and all she needs to do is receive it. So, while she may speak from her authenticity when it comes to board-room agreements and relational interactions, she won't be doing this because she needs to win the argument or fight the battle. Rather she will do it because it is authentic to do. And while others may perceive her as confident and assertive, she's really just being real.

So, this confusion over the definition of power keeps us in a state of suspended personal power. In other words, we refuse to receive our own empowerment, because to do so would mean that we'd be like Nero, fiddling into the wee hours of the morning while others are burned at the stake. To receive empowerment might mean that others would think we are greedy, arrogant and indifferent to the needs of others. To receive empowerment might mean that we were actually *bad* people after all. Further, to receive empowerment might mean threatening the interactional dynamics we've already got set up—a set up based most commonly on manipulative interactions rather than authentic ones.

So, we walk around in our everyday worlds either refusing to acknowledge our power and simultaneously wondering why we don't have any, or using manipulation to get our way and calling it power. Either way we are not receiving our own authentic power. We blame others for our misery while we refuse to take responsibility for making ourselves happy. We spend hours figuring out our next strategy for controlling someone else to get our own happiness. And worse than that, we believe that we are right to do it this way, for to receive authentic personal power is simply way too frightening. This deep-seated fear is somehow associated with that sense of ourselves as evil, discussed earlier. All the while our personal power is waiting in the wings for us to both receive it and take responsibility for it.

Code: The Culture is Right

There's a culture for every group in which we are involved – and a code for every culture. There's the church we attend, that requires, with both subtle and overt language, that we dress a certain way, only speak of certain things, and never do this, that or the other. There's the clique of friends that requires that we dress a certain way, weigh a certain amount, work out a certain number of times per week, eat only certain foods and speak only of certain things. There's the workplace, where we are required to compete in certain ways, discuss only certain things, have a certain kind of work ethic, make our requests in only certain ways, and work only for the ceiling of a certain height. And then, there are our families.

Usually the cultures of our families, typically designed by the parents, are so ingrained in us that we hardly notice their influence at all. Often included into the making of the family culture are the values and requirements passed down to them by their parents and the parents' parents. Other times, it is just the parents who develop the code. But if we pay attention, we can come to recognize the codes of the family. Here are some with which we've become more familiar over the years of studying families:

- don't express your feelings around here;
- don't have a different opinion than ours;

- don't speak of "family business" outside the family;
- keep the family secrets, even from yourself;
- put family first;
- honor your parents;
- don't talk back;
- don't embarrass us;
- we don't show affection around here;
- don't ever disappoint us;
- we are all smart people here, no dummies allowed;
- our children are the fairest in the land.

We could go on and on, but the bottom line is that many of these messages and others like them are not spoken, yet they are known by everyone in the family. And everyone in the family follows these codes to the letter. Sometimes the code comes down to something like how far the weekly fight between father and son will go before they can allow themselves to make eye-contact. These are the codes we obey, even to our own detriment. They tell us to stay in the role that has been designated for us and not ever get out of it. They tell us who we are and how much self-esteem we are allotted. When we want to grow, we have to consider these internalized messages to which we've been paying obeisance since we were too small to remember, for to disobey them is to be disloyal to the system—a fact for which we will surely pay with a vague sense of betrayal and guilt.

But while the family serves as a focal point of cultural background for each of us individually, there's really a different culture everywhere we go, and there's usually another culture behind that culture. For example, there's a larger not-for-profit cultural persuasion that governs the smaller individual not-for-profit organization. There's the larger hospital culture that governs the individual hospital, which in turn develops its own culture within that larger structure. There's a for-profit culture that serves as backdrop for the individual corporation's culture.

There's the ethnic culture that serves as a guide for the development of any subcultures within that ethnic group. There's the American culture, that serves as the foundation upon which are based all of the societal cultures. If you really want to sort out the codes, you can.

But the bottom line of these cultures is this: If you want to belong here, you have to do what we want you to do, because we think we've figured out how it should be done. Otherwise, find yourself a different culture. When we were in high school, we all saw this fairly clearly. There were the cheerleaders and the football players who had their own culture and codes. There were the geeks or nerds who had their own culture. There were the shy, quiet types who if they found a group at all, found their home in groups of one or two other shy, quiet types. There were the super-religious, the thugs, and the gang members each of which had their own culture and codes. And then you had cultures like the choir and the band.

When we graduated from high school, we thought all of that was over. But some, who went to college found similar cultures there. And then when we graduated from college, we thought that all of that was over, but when we went to work, we found similar cultures there, within the cultural milieu of that company. And when we had children, we found that they played in cultural groups very similar to those in which we still play. So, we figured that this must just be the way it is. Besides, we were obeying the codes without ever noticing that we were so obligated and without knowing how much energy such obeisance cost us.

Since belonging is such a huge part of how we see ourselves and even of how we survive, we continue to obey the cultural demands, even when they no longer make any sense to us whatsoever. That's the code. You have to do what they want, or you won't belong anymore, and then what?! And *they* order our lives along the lines of the culture's subtle demands before we ever even consider what is true or false within ourselves.

The truth is that if we ever do break free of our assigned roles within a given culture, we will experience the consequences. Some people will get mad at us. Others will stop speaking to us. But if we keep hanging out with these people, yet remain true to ourselves, we often find that eventually at least some of them adjust and come to accept our change. This takes some bravery on our parts, but the alternative is to keep on doing the same old thing, looking for different results.

It is also true that we have just as much power to be the rejecters as do *they*. But our thinking is skewed in this regard. We've lived for so long with the cultural sword of Damocles hanging over our heads that we fear *their* rejection first, react to that fear and ask questions later—if at all. So we rarely-to-never ask ourselves if *we* want to hang out with *them*. Why? Because that would be against the code.

But the worst thing about these cultural codes is that every one of them takes on some moral tenor. For example, if we don't wear what is expected in church, we are quite often shamed as a result. This often works to get us to conform because there is an assumed *rightness* to the expectation. If we act in socially odd ways, we are often shamed, even ridiculed for doing so. And if after receiving our just punishment we still do not conform, we are often completely ostracized. The shame, as it is given, carries with it an assumption of *rightness*, and as received, an assumption of *wrongness*. Even when the ostracized person becomes angry about it, he is still carrying shame—and shame means you are *wrong*.

Basically our cultures tell us that these are the rules, and rules, by the very fact that they are rules, assume the disposition of morality. These are the *right* things to do and these are the *wrong* things to do. Do the *right* things and you'll be seen as a *good* person. Do the *wrong* things and you'll be seen as a *bad* person. If we were to ask how a person's dress or odd behavior were actually immoral, those who insist on these rules would deny that there was any moral code behind the cultural mores. But the *feel* of these codes carries tremendous clout. And so it is that we sacrifice an identification with the authentic Self in favor of belonging to a group.

All of the codes discussed above seem to be running through our blood stream—even our DNA. They dictate the way we walk and talk and think. They even dictate our feelings when our self-talk honors the code first and self later, if at all. In fact, the codes most often tell us to repress our feelings so that we won't know that we are betraying ourselves in order to obey the codes. But authentic feelings don't really go away, nor are they dissolved by the codes—they just go underground to arise again later. This is why the door to any real psychic change opens as a result of feeling our feelings, *good* or *bad*, *positive* or *negative* and listening to their underlying messages—because when we do so we come to know ourselves beyond the codes. We come to see ourselves as individuals first, who belong to ourselves and after that decide where we belong in the world. In fact, we come to see that many of our needs for belonging are but desperate attempts to regain a connection to the Self.

3

Between the devil and the Deep Blue Sea

Most of our thinking regarding morality has come from our religions—not our spirituality. Religion is defined, herein, as a group of codes followed by a group of people who all agree to, more or less, follow the same codes. Religion has a culture of its own too, within which the codes of the dogma are transcribed onto the dress, habits, words and deeds of the individual within the culture. And again as with other codes, our religious cultures ascribe morality to these codes.

Spirituality, on the other hand, is a deep inner connection with a certain philosophy, or with the divine—and the divine can be viewed from several different perspectives, each of which resonate from within the individual. Now it is true that many people can come to see the divine in the same way and may, as a collective, behave, think and feel very similarly. And some of these people may begin to affiliate with each other. But as long as they do not develop codes to which all members of the group *should* ascribe, this group cannot be called a religion. Religions define a code. Spirituality does not define a code. Of course, it does seem to be very difficult for us to join into groups without dictating the behavior of the group's members, but that is largely because of morality.

Morality is a code organized around concepts of so-called *right* and *wrong*. And most of us think of religion, any religion, as being highly organized around morality. Each religion has its own *prima facie* evidence which serves as foundational premise— and much of that is all about morality. In most Western religions, this means that God is good, man is evil and man must learn to be good or he can have no real affiliation with God. And, the evidence of his affiliation with God will be found in his words, behavior and demeanor, i.e., his compliance with the requisite moral code. Eastern religions still have moral codes, even some very strict moral codes, but many of them, particularly the mystic elements of Eastern religion, are not so determined to believe that there is such a wide chasm between the divine and humanity. In fact the premise of much of Eastern mysticism is that the divine is the essential core element of the nature of man. Rather than actually being separate from the divine, as is true in Western religion, Eastern mysticism typically believes that we are blinded to our truest essential nature. That said, however, the evidence of both Western and Eastern affiliates to a specific religion, will be found in their compliance with the moral code of the culture. And the moral code usually includes some kind of agreement that bridges the gap between the divine and humanity.

Historically speaking, and from the Western religious perspective, the Israelites of the Old Testament, or the Tanakh—the canon of the Hebrew Bible—believed that covenant was the mediator between God and man. The basic idea was that if the Israelites honored the covenant, God would protect, supply and support them. The covenant was made up of several moral codes. When Jesus came into the picture, he seemed to inform us that he was "the way, the truth and the life; no man comes to the father but through me" (John 14:6). Of course, we can look at various other interpretations for that message and we will, but in the largest part most Christians believe that Jesus made himself the mediator between God and humanity by coming, living, dying and resurrecting from the dead. So, in that sense, he took the place of the covenant. And most Christians believe that this role is exclusive to Jesus. But shortly before his death, he seems to be offering another mediator in the Holy Spirit—for he said, "But the Helper, the Holy Spirit, whom the Father will send in My name, He will teach you all things, and bring to your remembrance all that I said to you" (John 14:26).

Of course, we know that the holy spirit impacted others well before Jesus ever came to be, from stories in the Old Testament or Tanakh. In fact it was seen at the very beginning of human history, when God was said to have created heaven and earth: "and the Spirit of God was moving over the surface of the waters" (Genesis 1:2). In Numbers 11:25-26, we see that God took some of the spirit he'd placed on Moses and put it upon the seventy elders, so that they began to prophesy. Each of the Judges, who ruled Israel for a time, was anointed with the holy spirit and when Saul was chosen to be king, the spirit of the Lord came upon him and he prophesied (1 Samuel 10:10). Later the holy spirit was removed from him (1 Samuel 16:14), David was anointed as King and "the Spirit of the Lord came mightily upon David from that day forward" (1 Samuel 16:13). So, when we realize this, we have to wonder if Jesus as mediator is the correct format, and if the holy spirit really came in the name of Jesus or in the name of the I AM. Nevertheless, most Christians believe that Jesus appointed the holy spirit to take his place as mediator. Now, Christians could get to God directly through the holy spirit.

But then that was why the church later had problems with this mediator. So much so, indeed, that they began to assert authority over it by giving the power of the holy spirit only to the church. People were no longer permitted to commune directly with God in this way, and so, without a mediator, the people began to look for other mediators. Mary became one of these because she was both human and the mother of Christ. And as Jesus was given more and more divine power and less humanity by the church he resumed his status as mediator.

All of this, however, came about as a result of the belief that humanity was sinful, or immoral, and needed a mediator to bridge the chasm between itself and the divine. So, actually, morality is the original and final mediator. Morality has the power to judge humanity. Morality determines whether or not we are worthy and, therefore, in need of a mediator. And while the love of the divine has, according to Christian tradition, provided for forgiveness of our sins—it is still sin from which we must be forgiven—giving the code that created sin, morality, the ultimate power. Were there no sin, there would be no need for forgiveness—or a mediator. Therefore, whether forgiven or not, we still appeal to morality as the measurement we use to determine what else we need to do to gain some modicum of association with the divine. And when we have complied with its orders, we feel a sense of accomplishment, whereby we can call ourselves *good* people. The church has never stopped promulgating the power of this mediator, for the power of morality is also the power of fear. Fear tells us that if we are not moral people then we are *evil* people in alliance with yet another mediator, Satan.

This super-villain, known variously as Satan, the devil, Beelzebub, Iblis, Satanael, Mara, Set, and other names throughout the world, is not known to all religions. Hinduism, the Bahá'í Faith, and a few other religions and persuasions have no supernatural evil force. But in those religions where Satan exists, he is supposedly in some kind of battle-of-the-universe for a seat at the table of the divine—and he would prefer to take over the very throne of the divine. From this perspective, the divine is seen as the ultimate goodness—referred to as holiness—and Satan as the ultimate evil. These two forces are at war for control over the mind of collective humanity. And it is this theory that is the basis for much of our morality, a morality based, as we've previously pointed out, in fear.

So, who is this character called Satan, the devil? The word *devil* derives from the same root word as *divinity*. Indeed, legend tells us that the gods did evil because they were mad, and the devils did good when they'd been pleased. The word carries the connotation of supernatural—a force seemingly beyond the capacity of human management. Satan has a long and ornate history in which his character and power change from one country to the next, from one polarity to the next, even at times being a personality whose name was interchangeable with God's. You can learn these things and more about the history of Satan and the devil in Barbara Walker's beautiful book entitled *The Women's Encyclopedia of Myths and Secrets,* one of the best and most thorough of books on its topics I've ever seen.

The Greek word, *diabolos (διαβολοσ)* is often translated as Satan in the New Testament, and it means *slanderous* or *prone to accuse falsely* — which meaning alone tells us enough — that we, in fact, are not being tempted to do wrong, but rather falsely accused. But the word is actually a combination of two words, *dia (δια)* and *bolos (βαϖλλω)*. The word *dia* is a primary preposition denoting the channel of an act, as *in, through, the reason for* or *on account of.* The word *bolos* means *to throw* or *let go of a thing without caring where it falls*; or, with regard to fluids, *to pour out.* So, actually the word means *the channel through which we throw something out, without regard to where it falls.* And because we have thrown something out without regard to where it falls, we are slandered or falsely accused. Taken then from a more metaphorical perspective the devil would be the channel through which we throw out awareness of soul without regard to where it falls. The channel is the method we use to frivolously toss away our awareness of soul. And we do not regard where it falls because this channel is the unconscious. And because we have become unconscious of who we are as soul, we falsely accuse ourselves of being less than soul.

But the metaphorical rendition of this potential is rarely considered when people are using the words *Satan,* or *devil.* Typically, these words have a literal translation, so that you hear very avid Christians of various denominations, talking about a devil, *who* comes to them personally and tempts them or causes them to do bad things. And they quite often attribute to the Bible their understanding of this literal character in the drama of their lives.

But actually, the Bible describes the God it espouses in multiple ways, yet describes the devil, if at all, in infrequent and vague terms. For example, there are only four references in the Old Testament to the word *devil*. Lev. 17:7 and 2 Chron. 11:15 talk about sacrifices to *sair*, meaning *hairy one; kid, goat*, which has been translated to mean sacrifices to the devil. Deut. 32:17 and Psalms 106:37, talk about sacrificing to *shed*, which means *spoiler* or *destroyer*. This word *shed* also has been translated into English as *devil*. It was only when these words were translated into English that they took on their demonic power.

It should also be noted that though from this English translation we can and often do assume that destruction comes from the devil, the Bible often attributes supernatural destruction to God by his own admission: Lev. 26:30, Deut. 2:21, Deut 4:3, Deut. 9:19, Isa. 13:9, Lam. 3:66, Amos 9:8, Num. 21:2, etc. Often in Christian churches today, we spin this admission back on itself by arguing, "Well, that was just Old Testament thought. It was attributed to God, but it was really the Devil."

The New Testament's 110 references to the word *devil* are, in the majority, references to possession by a devil and/or casting out of devils. The Greek term, *devil*, in these references, is *daimonion*, (δαιμονιον) which means *demon*, but also *shade*. The next highest number of references in the New Testament is to *diabolos*, which we've already discussed. But this devil is also translated as one who takes on several other attributes in the New Testament. He is an oppressor, (Acts 10:38), one who puts thoughts into the hearts of men (John 13:2), one because of whom we can fall into condemnation (I Ti. 3:6), one whom we can resist (James 4:7), one to whom we belong if we sin (1 John 3:8), a deceiver (Rev. 20:10), and one who casts into prison (Rev. 2:10). Jesus even goes so far as to say that Judas *is* a devil (John 6:70). But we rarely hear of god entering into and controlling the minds and hearts of humans, without their prior consent or even special anointing, as does this devil. Why is that? Could it be then that the devil is mere metaphor for the power of the human psyche to trip itself up, sabotage itself?

The few other references to a devil in the New Testament are defined as a deified spirit: Matt. 8:34, Mark 5:12, Luke 8:29 and Rev. 16:14 and 18:2. In Matthew, Mark and Luke, these are the demons who recognized Jesus, as the Son of God. The Greek word for these deified spirits, however, is *daimovnion* (δαιμοσνιον), which means *a divine power, deity, divinity, a spirit,* or *a being inferior to God.* And that word is rooted in *diavmwn* (δαισμων), or *deity* and in *daio* (δαιο), which means *to distribute fortunes.* If we realize the root meaning as a powerful connotation for the words used in the Bible, we might have to conclude that the author of these words was referring to the distribution of fortunes, rather than to literal demons—particularly when a person was said to be possessed of a demon.

The word *Satan* (Σατανας or Σαταξ in Greek, and שׂטן in Hebrew) is used over all in the Bible 51 times, all translated as *the hater, the accuser.* Sixteen of these are in the Old Testament and 12 are in one book, the book of *Job.* The rest of these references are in the New Testament, beginning with very personal references to a very personal power that is apparently very close to Jesus. The phrase, "Get thee behind me, Satan!" (Mat. 4:10, 16:23; Mark 8:33, Luke 4:8) was used by Jesus to forestall a personal hater, or some personal accuser. The rest of the New Testament references seem to indicate that this theory is plausible, as Satan is considered to be a very personal, internal, or, at least internalized force, who buffets (2 Co. 12:7), tempts (Mark 1:13, 1 Co. 7:5), takes advantage of (2 Co. 2:11) and fills one's heart (John 13:27, Luke 22:3, Acts 5:3). If we take all of this literally, we must assume that there is a real supernatural character who can be found "roaming about on the earth and walking around on it" as he describes himself in Job 1:7, and "seeking someone to devour" as he is described in 1 Peter 5:8.

Furthermore, in Zech. 3:1 of the Old Testament, Satan is said to be standing at the right hand of God to resist Him. And back in the New Testament, there are two references to "delivering" someone "unto Satan" (1 Co. 5:5, and 1 Ti. 1:20). Now, if Satan is so personal to Jesus that Jesus can tell him to "get thee behind me," even in the desert where Jesus is alone; if Satan sits at the right hand of God to resist Him; if he can be useful to Christians in that we can "deliver" sinners over to him; and if he can buffet, tempt, take advantage of us, and fill our hearts; and can cause us to fall into condemnation, set up a resistance against us, deceive us and even own us, casting us into a metaphorical prison, even a literal prison; isn't it possible that this Satan, this devil, is indeed, at least a part of the shade, or shadow of our own psyches? And if we have projected onto our God the attributes of humans, could it not also be true that we have projected onto this idea of Satan or devil, all of the unacceptable parts of ourselves thought to be found in the unconscious shadow material? And could it not also be true that we perceive the grand supernatural powers of the universe to be split, even as we are split, between good and evil?

If this is true then, just as we have named and described the nameless and indescribable divine, we have likewise given ourselves the power to name and describe a polar opposite to the divine we ourselves designed. Just as we ourselves are split between conscious and unconscious—with the unconscious being the reservoir of every idea of ourselves that we cannot accept—we see the divine split between a divine good and a divine evil. I find it very interesting that nowhere in the Bible do we find God having the power to walk about on the earth, seeking someone to devour. In fact, we see Psalm after Psalm in which the author is virtually begging God to intervene. Many a struggling ascetic has begged to be devoured of the divine—to become holy even as "He" was attributed holiness—and yet was left praying to a seemingly empty sky in the dark night of the soul. Why is Satan given all the power?

Could it possibly be that we believe more in Satan than we do in the divine? And if that were true, why would we want to do that? One theory is that we formulated our ideas of the divine and Satan based upon our fortunes. A good crop, a good wind for the sail, a good market all meant that the gods were smiling favorably—which was assumed to mean that the receiver of such fortune must have done something *right*. A bad crop, or a bad wind, or a bad market meant that the gods were not smiling, that in fact some other dark side of the gods, or an enemy to the gods had taken over. And since there is so much suffering on the planet, well, it follows then that Satan—the collective motif of all bad fortune—is mightier than the divine. Some Christians even call him the ruler of this world. And so it is that when we continue to live split off from awareness of what we have hidden in the unconscious, the unconscious is mightier than the conscious mind.

It is also compelling to examine the fact that of the 591 references to the word *evil* noted the Bible, by far the majority are references to evil in and of people, not the devil. In fact, in some (for example, Isaiah 4:5-7, Jeremiah 36:31) the evil is attributed to God and not Satan. Only five of the references to *evil*, found in the New Testament, are attributable to the devil or a demon and these are references to casting out of evil spirits. Only four of the references to *evil* in the Old Testament are related to the devil and only sixteen to Satan.

And what are we to do with scriptures like:

I am Yahweh, and there is none else. I form the light,
and create darkness: I make peace and create evil.
I Yahweh do all these things. (Isaiah 45:7)

Isaiah, most often thought to be the author of the above confession of God, uses the term YHWH more often than not for his references to God. YHWH, the phrase *I AM that I AM*, given originally to Moses, later became the name Jehovah. Charles Fillmore, author of the 1931 *Metaphysical Bible Dictionary*, tells us that Jehovah means, "He-who-is—who-was—who-will-be manifest; the self-existent One; Ipseity; He who is eternal." He explains that in the original YHWH, I AM that I AM, "the absolute verb remains the same, but the prefix changes from manifestation to power, 'he' to 'I.'" And he tells us that the word-for-word translation of YHWH is, "I-am—I-was—I-will-be because I-am—I-was—I-will-be the power to be eternally I." Fillmore adds that Hebrew students use the original word JHVH, which means "the ever living male-and-female principle." And he further explains that the word "Lord" as it is often used in the Bible, and which carries the connotation of an external ruler, is a misnomer. He recommends that "instead of reading 'Lord' we should read 'I AM'" (332).

If it is true that we generally see the divine as an external ruler, though it is actually the very I AM nature within us, then we can clearly understand why it is that this I AM would have to take responsibility for both the light and the darkness, for to do otherwise would be to deny the complete fulfillment of the universality of oneness, which is the I AM within all beings and all things. Therefore, if this passage from Isaiah is spoken by the I AM, then it can be counted on to be less contaminated by the needs and fears projected onto the "Lord," as our external ruler. This I AM reports to Isaiah, that it is the source of all things, including the apparently polarized concepts of good and evil or the one concept of duality. But it is so very hard for us to wrap our heads around the idea that the I AM, who eternally manifests I AM and can only be I AM, manifests the polarized realities of *goodness* and *evil*. And so we find within this riddle given to Isaiah, the truth that *goodness* and *evil* are but words used by humanity to describe divine events. Because of the duality trance state—about which much more will later be said—in which we all live and which was a part of the creative endeavor manifested by the divine, we see good or evil when in fact, all things are one thing. All things are I AM.

Yet we find ourselves, our lives, our finances, our governments, our religions and our very identities categorized between these two concepts. Even for those of us who espouse no religious affiliation at all, everything we can name is, by our judgment, either *good* or *bad*. Our circumstances, our finances, the food we eat, the lovers we've had, our own thoughts, words and deeds— everything fits into one or the other of these two categories. But how can this be if all things exist as one source, the I AM in all things?

As we look at the story of creation, as it is found in the Old Testament, (in the first few chapters of the book of Genesis) or the Hebrew Torah, some very interesting facts emerge. First, the word used for "God" or "Lord God" is *'elohiym* (אלהים), which means *gods* or *divine ones*. And it is the plural form of *elowahh*, (אלוהה) which means *God* or *false God*. *Elowahh* is rooted in *'el* (אל), which has several definitions, including *God, god-like one, mighty one, mighty men, false god, strength* and others. *'El* is further rooted in *'ayil* (איל), or *ram, as food or sacrifice, door, door posts, mighty tree* or *mighty man*. And *'ayil* is finally rooted in the primitive word, *uwl* (אול), which means *prominence, body, belly, wealthy men,* and *nobles*. Not only does this understanding of the root words help us to begin to see the divine as one with humanity, but it also appears to be telling us that the use of these early words, which we have translated to mean God, are not trying to define a specific God. Rather they are attributing power to much more general *gods*. If this is so, then the writer of this book is not intent on starting a religion, but rather in giving a metaphor for understanding the origins of human thought.

In this ancient text, written by an unknown author, we find that God is not given a name or described in any way, but rather the definition leans toward the mysterious. As we look at the root words above, we find that our definition of God, includes both the divine ones and human ones; both the divine and the sacrifice to the divine; both the belly of man and the food; both mighty man and a door by which he enters. These beings in whom we originated are never weak, but neither is goodness attributed to them. And, it should be noted, that this definition also includes the potential for falseness, the false god—or a god of uncertain power and realness. The writer of this part of the sacred text seems to be telling us that this god represents the mystery of creativity itself.

Creation by its very essential meaning is indefinite. It roams the wide expanse of infinite possibility. Every form it creates can reform. Every possibility is always extant. There is no definition for creation that operates in the past tense—though we often use it that way when we are talking about the Christian Bible. Creativity is an ever evolving process of unfoldment—so that if, for example, I paint a picture, those who see the picture are recreating it in their own interpretive way. Thereby, the creative process is never complete. This fact will be an extremely important premise to whatever else we discover as we study our origins here on planet earth.

It is also significant that these beings, the 'elohiym, were intent on being the primary active force. They planted, they formed, they created, they put the man in the garden, and they made many helpers for him, including the woman. Humanity, on the other hand, was only given two powers: 1) to name all things and 2) to keep and cultivate that which had already been created and named. This concept of an appointment to name is quite compelling, for it informs us that, in much the same way that someone might observe my picture, as above, and interpret it differently than what I had in mind when I painted it, humanity has that same power over creation—and *only* that power. When we name a thing, we interpret its meaning. We are deciding on its essence, how it should be forever after that interpreted. And we cultivate that meaning. We don't just cultivate the created; we

71

cultivate our interpretation of what was created. And so it was that at the point of our creation, this mysterious force: The many-one, *'elohiym* created all as oneness. One power. One creation. No duality. All that has happened since that time has been based in the naming and the cultivation of what was named.

And so it is that when Moses was spoken to by the mysterious power in the burning bush, in another metaphor of beginnings, he was instructed to go to the Israelites and tell them that I AM had sent him to them (Exodus 3). "I AM sent me to you." It's pretty apparent that this means something like "The deepest essence of who I AM, my divine essence, has sent me to you." But what began at that moment was not an understanding of I AM, as the very basic nature of Moses and all of humanity, even though this is clearly what the divine said to Moses. Instead, from that moment forward we began to define "God" as a personality—not as the mysterious essence of who we are, but rather as a separate entity with human-like emotions such as jealousy and rage. That entity was then given a gender and was storied as a frustrated super-power who, in spite of omniscience, omnipresence and omnipotence, just couldn't seem to win humanity back from the wiles of that evil force, Satan.

One of the most mysterious and yet empowering books of the Bible, which seems to clarify this intense struggle between God and Satan, is the book of Job. In this book Satan comes into the royal palace of God to taunt and tease God for his powerlessness, telling him that the only reason that Job follows God's tenets was because God rewarded him for doing so. And because of this taunting God allows Satan to cause great suffering for Job. Previously very wealthy, Job is, in a single day, stripped of all of his riches, loses all of his children, and as if that is not enough, he is given a horrible physical illness, which leaves him crouched in front of a fire scraping boils from his naked skin. And the cherry on the cake is the fact that he gets absolutely no support from either his wife or his friends.

The interesting thing about this poetic and metaphorical story is that it not only tells us about the fabled battle between *good* and *evil*, but it also tells us about the psyche of humanity. Most interpretations of this book leave us wondering what the hell is going on as it seems to end on a note that explains absolutely nothing. But when we look at the book as poetic and powerful metaphor, we see much that cannot be explained by most of its traditional interpretations.

It starts with a name. The name Job means *hated,* and though we are told very little about his parents, we do know that if we put this story into its appropriate cultural context, we are reminded that parents named their children for how they felt about their own lives. That in and of itself provides an interesting view of the power of projection in the human psyche, for whether we admit it or not, we frequently tend to do that very same thing to our children. They represent aspects of ourselves that we've either denied, glorified or longed for. And Job was hated. We cannot look at his wealthy and seemingly fulfilled life and glean any notion that he was hated by life, or its circumstances. We must assume that in his early childhood, he represented some hated aspect of his parents' lives.

Essentially this means that Job lived as a scapegoat, the blamed one, the one who carried the responsibility for the dark underbelly of his family. Whatever it was that his parents hated, he was given the power to either be that hatred for them, or overcome it. It looks like he chose the latter, for he'd lived a very upright life, had developed great wealth, had many children and was called on by his village to give wise counsel as he sat at the gate to hear the problems and issues of his fellow villagers. He was a good-guy. In becoming the good-guy, he'd completely compensated for the hatred his parents had put upon him.

Enter Satan who challenges that goodness by trying to convince both Job and God that it isn't real goodness. It is, after all is said and done, merely a result of positive reinforcement.

Job has been rewarded for his goodness with wealth, power, prestige and many children. Let's take all that away and see if there is any goodness left. Though Job is unduly lauded for his patience during his suffering—an interpretation that does not at all match the story—of course he laments his suffering in all the ways that we lament ours. "Why did I not die at birth?" he says (3:11). "Why is light given to him who suffers, and life to the bitter of soul?" (3:20).

And then, out of the dark recesses of his negative anima—his own unconscious or shadowed feminine energy—his wife appears to tell him to just curse God and die. "What's to live for?" she seems to say. "God's done nothing for you, why do you continue to honor him?" Job has lived solely from the masculine archetype of push, penetrate, go out. He's built his wealth and family from the external, and had accepted his image of the divine from that same external source. His life was lived according to the codes passed down to him. His God was the God of his fathers. This was not an internal God, a place inside of humanity, but rather an external ruler—not really I AM—but rather the character invented through humanity's definition and design. And his wife is a metaphor for the ignored internality of his psyche. This energy is dark, not because it is evil but because it has been repressed for so long that its messages seem foreign or alien to him—thus his wife carries that projection for him.

Left in the unconscious any energy must find a back door for expression. Passive-aggressiveness is the result of the strict retention of very active psychic material held in the prison cells of the unconscious. And all manner of difficult human interactions are created out of passive-aggressive behavior that can be quickly denied by its owner. Active energy must find expression. But highly moral people, such as Job, tend to use repression as the primary method of attaining their highly moral character.

This means that the unconscious becomes the home of all of the so-called *negative* traits, thoughts, deeds, and wishes. These very active energies are, therefore, left to the wild untamed forces of the shadow where they become rather feral and will express at will. But the conscious identity does not wish to know about these active and feral energies, and so will not allow them to express in ways that the identity can recognize. So these energies will only express in ways that the conscious identity does not have to notice or can quickly withdraw back into the unconscious. There is no room in this psychic inter-dynamic for the healthy feminine approach.

The healthy feminine approach would be one that receives life from an internal perspective. This approach allows the individual to explore his own psyche and receive what is found there, rather than just accept what has been handed to him by those who have already named and defined life. Indeed, as we put feminine and masculine together through the integration process, we can see that the healthy feminine requires that we go within to receive information, responses, creative impulses, emotions, original thought and many other internal treasures, and then the healthy masculine carries outward to the external, through the power of manifestation, what was found in the internal.

But in Job's world there was no room for the healthy feminine; the only feminine archetype we see in the early part of his story is this negative, hostile force whose only impulse is suicide found in the metaphor of his wife. Indeed, he tells us that "the arrows of the Almighty are within me; their poison my spirit drinks" (6:4). This is all that Job can find within—arrows that come from the external to the internal. The internal can only drink in what the external delivers. There is no power, no force from within that can present itself before the external as real and valid—at least not in the beginning of the story.

Next come Job's so-called friends, each of whom has a long lecture to give him on his morals. They tell him that he has committed some sin, which he denies. Then they tell him that he's committed some secret sin that God means to bring out into public awareness—which is why this suffering is so obvious and intense. But again Job denies it. The final friend, and the youngest, comes around to tell Job that even though he claims no sin, he really has no right to complain for to complain against one's life is to complain against its creator for "God is greater than man" (33:12), and when God brings suffering to man it is only to keep "back his soul from the pit, and his life from passing over into Sheol" (33:18).

And so we see that all of the things that humanity typically thinks about suffering are brought to the floor of the great hall where God and Satan met. Our suffering comes to us from the external and it comes as punishment or consequence for our misdeeds and if not that, well then it comes as a lesson to us, even as protection from ourselves—for God is not man, and man should just shut-up and deal.

But Job says, "No." This is not good enough. He wants to meet with God face-to-face and hear some kind of explanation from the external God he's always worshipped. And so this externalized projection of God appears in a whirlwind. The whirlwind represents confusion, a conflict whirling about in Job's own mind between that projection he's worshipped and an emergent internal divine. Now, he sees his own image of God so clearly that that very image is called into question. Job's confusion, in the form of this projected image of God, asks these questions and more:

> Have you seen the gates of deep darkness? Have you understood the expanse of the earth? Tell me, if you know all this. Where is the way to the dwelling of light? And darkness, where is its place, that you may take it to its territory, and that you may discern the paths to its home? You know, for you were born then, and the number of your days is great! (38:17-21).

The traditional interpretation of these verses is that God is mocking Job for his smallness and ignorance, that God is insisting that Job really has no right to question God, for after all, God is God and Job is just a puny little man. But if we look at these poetic verses metaphorically—in the way that most poetry should be seen—we see something else entirely.

Has Job looked within himself at the gates of deep darkness? Has he understood his own limitlessness? Has he been able to go into his own dark unconscious and find its place, to find within that very unconsciousness, his own home—to find beneath the darkness the dwelling of light? Has he not known that he himself is eternal?

You see, not only are all of our unacceptable impulses found in the shadow, but also hidden there, in that same receptacle, is the divine Self. Because we find it so very hard, due to our heritage of duality, to imagine that we, like Jesus, as well as some of the other great masters, are one with the divine; we have sent that awareness far away into the unconscious. It is deeper even than all of the attributes that we think of as *bad*, for we can easier accept our *badness*, than our wholeness. And again, we see the so-called *bad* and the so-called *good*, living together in the same house. And indeed, our home is found there, within. Under all of that so-called *bad*, we find the truest Self, the eternal and limitless divine nature.

The imagery used in this dialogue, by Job's projected God, (which is slowly morphing into I AM), goes on to explain to Job that his image of the divine has been skewed. He tells Job that "the first of the ways of God" (40:19), can be likened to an ox, or Behemoth, who eats wherever he wants, because he can. The first image we created of God, made of our dualistic thinking and naming, was that the divine was simply bigger than us, could do whatever it wanted and there was nothing we could do about it. This is the same image that most children have of their parents when they are small—parents are just bigger, which pretty much means that they have the total say.

And so the real message here is that Job's image of the divine is skewed along the lines of this infantile reasoning. But then the projection says something quite compelling:

> Can anyone capture him when he is on the watch, with barbs can anyone pierce his nose? Can you draw out Leviathan with a fishhook? ... Will the traders bargain over him? Will they divide him among the merchants? Who can open the doors of his face? Around his teeth there is terror. His strong scales are his pride, shut up as with a tight seal. One is so near to another that no air can come between them. They are joined one to another; they clasp to each other and cannot be separated.... His heart is as hard as a stone; even as hard as a lower millstone. When he raises himself up, the mighty fear; because of the crashing they are bewildered (41:1-25).

There is a distinct shift in metaphor here. First, his projection is telling Job that his image of the divine is skewed to look like that bold beast, the ox. But just as the projection is asking Job if anyone can capture the ox by piercing his nose, the metaphor suddenly shifts to Leviathan (וְתָיְיל). That Hebrew name is rooted in *Levah* (לוה), which means *to join, to be joined, to be joined unto, to borrow* or *to lend*. This root connotation makes the poetry regarding the joining of the scales of Leviathan all the more interesting.

Leviathan is traditionally seen as another name for Satan, as is that other name given to the ox in the book of Job, Behemoth. But the poetic text does not tell us this. In other places in the Bible, Psalms 104:26, 74:14 and Isaiah 27:1, Leviathan is a sea creature with more than one head who can be both made and crushed by the power of the divine. But there are only five mentions of this so-called creature in the Bible and so we are left to wonder.

But Leviathan has also been equated with Lilith—an ancient and mythological female who has served many purposes over the centuries of mythology. Mostly she has been seen as Adam's first wife, created like unto Adam from the dust, who refused to comply with his wishes that she allow him the superior position during sex. She is said to have left him to make her home by the Red Sea, which meant that God had to create another female to be Adam's bride—this one taken from his rib—the much more compliant Eve—who turns out to not be so compliant after all.

But there are older myths that speak of Lilith. The mystical *Treatise of the Left Emanation*, written by Rabbi Isaac ben Jacob Ha-Kohen sometime in the 1200's, is elucidated in *The Early Kabbalah*, edited by Joseph Dan and translated by Ronald C. Kiener. There we learn that Lilith is the consort of Samael, who is referred to as "the first prince and accuser, the commander of jealousy...called evil" (172) and "the great prince and great king over all the demons" (175). Samael and Lileth "were both born in a spiritual birth as one, as a parallel to the forms of Adam and Eve above and below: two twinlike forms" and "emanated from beneath the throne of Glory" (173). The Treatise goes on explain that the Leviathan referred to in Isaiah 27:1 as "'Leviathan the twisted serpent and Leviathan the tortuous serpent'—this is Lilith" (180).

If we look at the Leviathan/Lilith connection from a metaphorical perspective, we can begin to tell the story of the dualistic split in the body and mind of humanity. The unconscious, where all that is repressed resides, became not only the home of all that was considered to be unacceptable, bad or evil, but because it represents the deepest innermost nature of humanity, is also the home of the repressed feminine. The conscious personality was then left to identify with the good and the masculine. The feminine was, therefore, not only associated with evil, but she was wrapped in the external identification with the masculine—which was associated with goodness. As this continued down through the centuries the feminine aspect became more and more repressed and more and more distorted. Indeed, she became monstrous in both proportion and power.

Lilith and Samael, Adam and Eve represent the one thought of duality split into two aspects. Lilith and Samael represent the shadow or unconscious aspect of Adam and Eve, and Adam and Eve represent the conscious expression of humanity. But we also know that both Lilith and Samael and Adam and Eve eventually split off again from each other. Lilith and Samael went their own ways as their stories are told in ancient mythology and Adam and Eve, separated into conscious ideas of gender.

There is wide assumption that the book of Job was one of the first stories of the Bible passed down as oral tradition for many years before it was actually written down. If that is so, then Ha-Kohen's interpretation of Lilith as Leviathan, cited above, must be considered as a viable metaphor. Indeed, it is an excellent poetic metaphor, for she perfectly demonstrates what happens to the feminine aspect of the psyche when she is hidden away in the unconscious. It is apparent that the image of Leviathan springs from the discussion of the first of the ways of God and that Leviathan is something to be greatly feared. If Job's projected image of the divine is like that of an ox who can have his way simply because he is big, and that image brings forth the next image of Leviathan whose name means joining, and whose scales are joined so tightly that nothing can penetrate and the face of the feminine cannot be seen; and further, if the question is raised as to whether or not he can be divided among the traders, then one has to begin to consider the possibility that this feminine aspect has been trapped inside the scales of the mighty power of the masculinized, externalized image of the divine.

This metaphor, therefore, can be seen as the sleeping giant that is the unconscious feminine within Job. She is to be feared because she will put Job in touch with mystery. Mysteries cannot be contained within names for God or appropriations to God. Mysteries cannot be pierced, or owned, or traded, or divided. And when the hard-hearted, tough outer masculine exterior that hides the inner feminine finally crashes down, leaving only the

mystery, that *crashing* leaves us *bewildered*. The word *crashing* as
it is used in 41:25 is the Hebrew word, *sheber* (שבר), which means
breaking, fracture, crushing, breach, shattering, or *interpretation.* It is
rooted in *shabar* (שבר), which means *break, break in pieces, rend
violently, quench, to cause to break out,* or *bring to the birth.* So, even
as we are broken by the crashing down of the hard outer
exterior—which is our interpretation of ourselves as broken off
or separated from the divine—we are also brought to birth.

And the word used for bewildered here is *chata'* (חטא), which
has multiple meanings but the most common are *to miss, to sin, to
miss the way,* and *to make a sin offering, to purify from sin, to cleanse,*
and of the more interesting meanings, *to miss oneself, to lose
oneself.* We can clearly see dual meanings here, for the word used
for bewildered is two sides of the same coin—both to sin and to
cleanse from sin. We do lose ourselves in the dualities of sin and
cleansing from sin, instead of just being able to sit with the
mystery of our own essence.

Moreover, there is also the double entendré we've already
found in the name for Leviathan or the notion of joining, for in
the joining of the scales of Leviathan we are distanced from the
inner experience of the feminine—which will inform us that we
are joined as one with the divine. There is, indeed, a joining that
prohibits the exploration of the inner mystery, and one that
allows it. In recognizing the oneness or joining of all things,
people, places, animals, vegetation, etc., we enter the domain of
the interior world, for we must see beyond the external to its
internal connectivity. But when we join the outer scales of our
identities or personas to keep out any awareness of the inner
world: "When *he* raises up, the mighty fear; because of the
crashing, they are bewildered." The feminine has been hidden
away for so long that even the strongest among us fear her
crashing—her opening, her birthing. And we are bewildered—as
Job is bewildered—when our images of life and the divine open
up to the inner world of the feminine. We miss the way, for the

way is inward, when we seek spirituality from an external base—
i.e., when we fear our own inner world. Without going into
greater depth about the language used in this poetry, we can see
that it is possible that Job was actually being given a unique and
profound message by looking at the nature of his projected image
of the divine. He was being told that he had a faulty image of the
divine because he was not familiar with his own feminine—or
interior world—where he would actually find the divine. And
because he could not previously access that world, he could not
know true spirituality. True spirituality is based completely on an
inner connection to the divine. It is wisdom itself—known to Old
Testament or the Ketuvim of the Tanakh, in the book of Proverbs,
as Sophia—a feminine energy.

In the end, Job acknowledges all that he did not previously
know because his image of the divine had been internalized from
the external, and he finally says:

> I have heard of thee by the hearing of the ear, but now my eye
> sees Thee; therefore, I retract and repent in the dust and ashes
> (42:5-6).

This verse is traditionally translated to mean that Job realizes he
never should have questioned God in the first place and he
therefore humbles himself before the vast knowledge that God is
simply bigger than him, and there's nothing he can do about it.
But if it is true that Job is seeing what he'd previously been
unable to see, an inner divine, indeed a divine Self, an inner I AM
that I AM perpetually I AM, then it makes perfect sense that he
would repent of his earlier ways, and that he would say, "I've
only heard of you before, but now I see." And it is this rendition
of the story that takes all of the glory out of the battle between
good and *evil*, which appears to traditionalists to be the whole of
the story of Job.

The most fascinating part of this wonderful poetic story is in what is changed in the end, for there we see that not only is true comfort and wealth returned to Job, but he also had seven sons and three daughters—yet it is not the sons who are named, but the daughters:

And he named the first Jemimah, and the second Keziah, and the third Keren-happuch. And in all the land no women were found so fair as Job's daughters and their father gave them inheritances among their brothers (42:15).

If we consider the usage of words to be important to sacred texts, we cannot dismiss these words from the meaning of the story. It is very significant that Job gave inheritances to his daughters, as well as his sons, as this was simply not done in that culture. This public gift gives symbolic evidence of the change in Job's mind/soul connection—a psyche which can now receive and comfortably sit within the inner space of mystery—a healthy feminine approach to the divine, which can now manifest externally, as the healthy masculine, in the form of new wealth, new children, new comfort.

It is even more significant that we are given the names for his daughters, *instead of* his sons—again, unheard of in that time and place. Charles Fillmore tells us that the name Jemimah means *"dove, purity; fruitfulness; fertility; love; desire; affection, brightness of the day; fullness of the seas."* And he adds that the metaphysical understanding of that name means "the soul purified from fear, contention, and self-justification, and made gentle, peaceful, loving, fertile for greater acceptance and realization of good" (Fillmore 336). The name Keziah, according also to Fillmore, means *"cut off; stripped off; cassia bark; angular; acute; incisive; decisive; discrimination."* His metaphysical understanding of Keziah is, "the purified soul expressing true perception and discrimination, thus aiding in the detection of error, limited, human thoughts and ideals.... By means of our perceptive and discriminative qualities of mind we distinguish between our true thoughts and our lesser thoughts that are no longer necessary to us" (386). Finally, Keren-happuch means *"radiations of color; prismatic radiations; horn of beauty; horn for paint, paint horn, cosmetic box."* Metaphysically, it means, "the elevating power of light, of spiritual beauty, of Truth, a beautiful soul, expressed in a beautiful character" (385).

Fillmore goes on to explain this about the daughters of Job:

> The daughters of Job represent the soul, or the feminine aspect of the individual character when it has passed through the Job experience and has come out refined and established in the true Christ righteousness (385).

So we see that Job is changed through this encounter with his own unconscious projections, more than through the suffering itself. But as he encountered his projection, he also began to see through it to his own soul, his own I AM. And that encounter created the change. Prior to Job's willingness to actually hear from his own projected image of the divine, he was still lost, still questioning and blaming, still unable to see, through his external lenses, the story of his own life. But after his encounter with his projection and its transformation to the true divine nature within him, he is able to recognize and honor his own feminine—or interior world, the world of the soul, the home of the I AM.

And again if we consider the usage of words to be important to sacred texts, we must also consider what was *not* said. In the end of this story there is no resolution of the argument between God and Satan—a story whose beginning starts with that argument. By all story-telling and writing standards, this argument should be clearly resolved by story's end. We can only assume then that the resolution of the argument between God and Satan is found in the heart and mind of Job. And while God is mentioned in the end, Satan is not. This is significant.

From the traditional perspective, God's entire oration is meant to convince Job that he is separate from God. God is big, right, and basically uncaring about where he lays his huge brutal lumbering feet. And Job has dared to question his judgment? How dare he! God is fierce and uses language that, to traditional understanding, sounds as if he's pounding his fist on the pulpit and looking directly into Job's eyes with the threat of hellfire and damnation right behind him. In fact, this traditional interpretation offers absolutely no loving gesture towards Job at all, but rather appears to criticize him for his audacity in questioning why these terrible things have come up out of nowhere to flood his life. The man has lost everything of any value to him whatsoever, and that based on a bargain between God and Satan. Any human being would be able to show some compassion towards this man. Why not God?

But this traditional interpretation is called into question by the end of the story, for in the end, God requires sacrifice of Job's friends, Eliphaz, Bildad, and Zophar because, though they appear to be saying to Job the exact same thing God appears to be saying to Job, though without the metaphors, God tells them "you have not spoken of me what is right, as my servant Job has" (42:8). This is quite confounding to most traditional readers of Job, and so the book is often put aside as too hard to understand.

But if we look deeper, we see that this purely poetic rendition of an answer from the divine uses metaphor after metaphor to introduce Job to his own shadow. God's very first question to Job, is not a sardonic accusation of Job's arrogance, as is traditionally thought, but an honest and quite loving question: "Where were you when I laid the foundation of the earth? Tell Me, if you have understanding" (38:4). Do we know where we were at the foundation of the earth? Most of us would answer that we were nowhere. That we'd not even been invented yet—not even a sparkle in Papa's eye. But Job is encouraged to think about this with the word *understanding* as it is used in the text.

The word is *biynah* (בינה), and it means *discernment*. It is rooted in *biyn* (בין), which means *acted wisely, cared, consider, consider carefully, diligently consider, observe, learned, look carefully, discern, gain understanding*. Job is being challenged to actually consider, even observe where he was when life began—not just his life, but all of life. Job, like all of us, was *'elohiym*, the *one that is all*. And this is but the very edge of the mirror, which Job's encounter with his own unconscious will use to show him more about who he really is. From there, the metaphors carry the day.

In verse five of chapter thirty-eight, the divine speaks even through Job's projection, saying something like: As you are considering that, consider also this these things: Who laid the cornerstone of the earth, when "all the sons of God shouted for joy?" (v 7); "who enclosed the sea with doors, when, bursting forth, it went out from the womb" (8); "have you ever in your life commanded the morning and caused the dawn to know its place" (12)? These questions direct Job inward, for it is the I AM that is the cornerstone of the earth and this theme is reiterated by the statement "all the sons of God shouted for joy." We are all constituent parts of the I AM, and as such we were all there in the beginning, shouting for joy at the formation of matter! The sea represents the unconscious, born of human womb and needing enclosure lest it consume all of life. And the word *commanded* tells us much about what we are doing here enfolded in matter as we elicit the spiritual experience. That word is *tsâvâh* (צוה), which means *to constitute, to enjoin, bid, charge, send a message*, or *put in order*. Has Job, have we, ever constituted the morning? If we are one with morning, with dawn, we constitute it, we are part of its makeup, and we are alive with it to co-command what it does.

But an even more significant word in that same passage helps us to exactly understand the message to Job: Have you ever commanded the *morning*? The word *morning* in that passage is *boqer* (בקר), which means *morning, break of day, end of night, coming of sunrise*, or *bright joy after a night of distress*. It is rooted in *baqar*

(בקר), which means *to seek, inquire,* or *consider.* Job is being asked if he has ever constituted his own questions.

Job is being shown how to trust the pathway to his own inner terrain and to find there, his own I AM. If Job begins to constitute his own inquiry then he begins to begin. He begins to birth his own awareness of who he really is. He begins to inhabit his own inner being. No longer hated, he comes to see that his projections onto the divine have meant that he has lost touch with his own feminine or inner knowing. He begins to see that he has only heard of the divine by the hearing of the ear, but has not until now really seen or understood the divine—as it constitutes his own essential nature. Now the shadow has been pierced and its holdings understood, and now Satan and the idea of evil disappear.

There is no longer a battle between God and Satan nor one between *good* and *evil.* The shadow, where we store the unacceptable, has been seen and brought into the light of truth, and what was found there was that all of Job's projections onto his God were the same as those projected onto him. God was hated—and I might add, pretty hateful. How could Job love a God who used him as a pawn in a struggle between his own gigantic ego and Satan's challenge? How could a man who believed himself to be so insignificant (40:4) as to be hated, ever really love—ergo, how could God? Righteousness, in its most moralistic sense, is not, after all, love. Job's heart had been as hard as that of Leviathan, sealed up in that morality, which constituted a refusal to go within. The only character in this story who seems to offer anything close to loving kindness to Job is Elihu, the youngest of his friends, who basically says that though Job is suffering, there must be some wisdom behind it. And finally, God, now changed from entirely Job's projection to something more akin to the I AM, is seen as acting through Job as inheritance to his daughters. The divine and Job are now one. And because that is so, Job's brothers and sisters, and "all who had known him" come and eat bread with him, console and comfort him (42:11).

Where were these people before, when Job suffered in his aloneness? Well, actually, they may not even represent real people, for the phrase "all who had known him" is actually one word, *yâda'* (ידע), which carries many different renditions of the transitive *to know,* including *to discern, to perceive, to know through experience* and the most interesting to me, *to reveal oneself.* And the word *brother* is actually *'ach* (אח), which means both a literal *brother* or *relative* and a more metaphorical *affinity* or *resemblance.* Prior to Job's shift in consciousness, his only known associates were his pesky friends who, like him, once also sat at the gate of the village to give counsel in right living. But like his own counsel his friends misguided him. Now, Job can invite all of his knowing into the picture; he can reveal himself to himself; he can come to resemble his truest Self.

What this beautiful story reveals is that the battle between so-called *good* and *evil* is unfounded. These are but projections onto a vast outer world of our own internal split. And the split is not based in an objective reality, but rather in the notion that we are separate from the divine. So, what is the origin of such a notion?

4

The Tree

The tree of knowledge of good and evil, a metaphorical tree, was planted in the likewise metaphorical Garden of Eden for a reason. Most traditionalists do not even discuss why the tree was planted there, but rather spend their time talking about what happened when Eve ate of it. Those who do mention its purpose generally explain that the tree was put there to test humanity. From that perspective, humanity, having just been created by the divine in the image of the divine would need to be tested because—why? We don't really get much satisfaction from traditionalists when it comes to answering this question. It seems rather cruel of a new parent to test his newborn infant. And it seems rather cruel of the traditional God to test his newly created humans. But when we say that to traditionalists the response we get is usually something like, "Our ways are not God's ways." And that's as far as it goes.

But if these sacred texts, in which we find the story of the Garden of Eden and the tree, tell us anything legitimate about our origins, then we have to assume that the story has meaning. And if the story has meaning then everything in the story has meaning, particularly those things which are given so much significance for the rest of human history. This tree of knowledge of good and evil is quite significant to the rest of human history—even traditionalists would agree with that foundational premise. But to them, the tree of knowledge of good and evil was our first venture into sin. And that sin is the origin of all other sins. Their theory is that when Eve ate of that tree, she sinned against God, and in so doing she literally changed the body and mind of all creation from that point forward. Because of her sin, traditionalists tell us, we are all now born in original sin. No one is born innocent. No one can attain anything like a divine walk, for we are all born and will forever exist in original sin, until the inglorious end—unless, of course, there is a divine intervention which will save us from our sins.

But we've been trying to figure this whole thing out now for centuries. We ask questions like, "Why would God create humans who could sin, knowing that they would sin, since He knows all things, stand there and watch them sin and then condemn them for doing the very thing they were created with the capacity to do?" When we ask this to traditionalists the usual answer is that God needed us to prove our love for him by turning from sin and serving God. So, if that is true, then why would he send a savior to save us from our sins, knowing that A) millions would either not know of this savior or outright deny him, and B) even after being saved we would continue to sin? Did his saving intervention somehow prove our love for him? No, traditionalists would answer, it proved his love for us. But, I thought you said that God created humans with a capacity for sin so that they could prove their love for him? And what about all those souls who didn't get saved? Could sending them to hell somehow prove their love for God?

This perception of the story of the tree of knowledge of good and evil leaves us with a God that is pretty inept, for it seems that he has failed miserably to accomplish his original goal. And there's not much hope that that goal will be accomplished—at least not as long as humans continue to sin, which they do whether saved or not. When I hear this story, I want to say, "Poor God." He comes off as a dumbling, who doesn't know much about what he's doing but does it anyway. Barney Fife comes to mind. And trying to make his bumbling look like wisdom is nothing short of a magic act.

So, let's just start with the premise that there was a reason for the tree of knowledge of good and evil to be planted in the same relatively small metaphorical plot of land as the tree of Life. Well, it seems that the first issue of discovery would be the plot of land—the one place that offered two possibilities.

The word used for *garden* is *gan* (גן), an *enclosure* or *garden*, and it is rooted in the primitive word *ganan* (גנן), which means *to defend, cover* or *surround*. So, this place was a safe place, an enclosed place where things could grow in safety. And this place was called Eden, or `*Eden* (עדן), which means *pleasure* and is synonymous with another word of the same spelling, which means *luxury, dainty, delight* or *finery*. That second word originates in the word `*adan* (עדן), which means *to luxuriate* or *delight oneself*. So this was a place of total safety in which we were called upon to luxuriate, and delight ourselves in its pleasures.

Why then would the creators of this wonderful place of abundance and safety, create within it a tree, which offers the potential for evil—which is anything but safe, and as it turns out, anything but abundant? We seem to have no explanation in the text as to why this tree was created, only that it was (Genesis 2:9). That's it. No other explanation is given. Later, in verses 16-17, we learn that:

> The Lord God commanded the man, saying, "From any tree of the garden you may eat freely; but from the tree of the knowledge of good and evil you shall not eat, for in the day that you eat from it you shall surely die."

The most compelling piece of this instruction is that it seems that Adam and Eve would have been permitted to eat of the tree of Life. The tree of Life is that same tree we see much later in the "Revelation to John," which is planted right in the middle of the streets of heaven. Does this mean that had Adam and Eve elected to eat of the tree of Life, they would have gone immediately to heaven? Or, could it mean that they were already in heaven? Heaven is also a place of complete safety in which we may luxuriate and delight in its abundant pleasures, is it not? So, let's assume that this enclosed delightful place called the Garden of Eden is heaven. Again, we'd have to ask, why would *'elohiym* create an enclosed space for heaven which contains the possibility of evil? We are going to have to go deeper.

The word used for the *tree* of knowledge of good and evil is *'ets* (עֵץ), which simply means *wood, tree, timber, stock, plank,* etc. But it is rooted in *'atsah* (עָצָה), which means *to shut.* It does appear that that same word, with the same root, is also used for the tree of Life. So, we must assume that there is some kind of shutting that takes place when one eats of the fruit of either of these two trees.

The word knowledge is rooted in the same word for knowledge we've seen earlier, *yâda'* (יָדַע), which we said carries many different meanings, including *discernment, perception, know by experience* and *self-revelation.* The word used for good is *towb* (טוֹב), which has many meanings as well, most of which have to do with agreeableness: *pleasant, desirable, bounty, benefit, becoming, prosperity* and *happiness.* It is rooted in a primitive word of the same spelling, which renders it an infinitive, *to be good, to be pleasant, to be joyful,* etc., but also seems to add the idea of being right or doing the right thing in *to do well.* And the word evil is, *ra'* (רַע), which means *bad, disagreeable, malignant, displeasing, hurtful, unkind, distress, injury, wrong,* etc. So, this tree of knowledge of good and evil offers us a shutting of some kind that distinguishes between the agreeable and the disagreeable—those things we find pleasant and those things we find to be unpleasant—a definition not too far removed from *the distribution of fortunes,* defined previously as the meaning behind the word devil.

Before we go any further, we need to go back to the Garden of Eden, that enclosed space that is very much like, if not literally, heaven. Why would such a place be enclosed? What encloses it? Well to answer those questions we have to understand what has been happening previously in this metaphorical story of our origins. And what has been happening is that the creators have been making matter where previously there was only formlessness. "The earth was formless and void" (Genesis 1:2) prior to this sudden flurry of activity by *'elohiym*. But in order for a place to be enclosed, neither that place nor its enclosure can be formless or void. Something has to have been formed for an enclosure to exist.

Charles Fillmore helps us to figure out what it is that is enclosed and what encloses it, for he says that from a metaphysical perspective:

This garden is the substance of God or state of perfect relation of ideas to Being.... The Garden of Eden is the divine consciousness (181).

The something then that is enclosed and defended is our consciousness of ourselves as divine beings—and this consciousness is the sphere of our activity as *'elohiym*, and means to last as beauty, pleasantness and to allow us to witness it for a season, an age, an eternity.

And the two different trees within that consciousness, according to Fillmore, "represent nerves, and nerves are expressions of thoughts of unity; they connect thought centers" (663). So, what begins to unfold here is that the Garden of Eden is enclosed within the mind of humanity. In fact, it is his soul, his truest essence, his awareness of himself as a divine being and all genuine activity originates from there.

When we first hear of the tree of knowledge of good and evil, the story of creation has already been told once, and though there has been mention of fruit trees being created, yet there is no mention of this tree or the tree of Life. So, *'elohiym* had already created man, male and female, and blessed and sanctified the seventh day of rest. However:

Now no shrub of the field was yet in the earth, and no plant of the field had yet sprouted, for the Lord God had not sent rain upon the earth; and there was no man to cultivate the ground. But a mist used to rise from the earth and water the whole surface of the ground (2:5-6).

Tradition tells us that chapter two of Genesis is a second version of the creation story, written by another author but included for its depth of understanding. But if that is so, significant portions of the original story are left out, for here the only story is what happened to the trees and what happened to the humans. So, if we assume that the story is a continuation of that told in chapter one then we must conclude that though the trees had been created, yet they had not grown or appeared on the earth. And the next step is that man is brought to life, for 'elohiym:

formed man of dust from the ground, and (then) breathed into his nostrils the breath of life, and man became a living being" (2:7, parenthetical insert inserted).

Like the trees and shrubs, which had been created but which had not spouted or appeared on the earth; so humanity has been created but had not yet been brought to life. Now, humanity is brought to life and *then*:

the Lord God planted a garden toward the east, in Eden; and there He placed the man whom He had formed. And out of the ground the Lord God caused to grow every tree that is pleasing to the sight and good for food; the tree of life also in the midst of the garden, and the tree of the knowledge of good and evil (2:8-9).

So, first 'elohiym moves divine consciousness to the East in the mind of humanity and then he allows thoughts to grow in that mind. The word for East is *qedem* (קדם), which means *east, antiquity, front, beginning, in front, ancient time, aforetime, earliest time*. It is rooted in *qadam* (קדם), which means *to meet, come or be in front, confront, go before, receive, to lead, to anticipate*. So our consciousness of ourselves as divine is now moved to the place in the front or beginning of our journey here. In other words, time is now a feature of human consciousness. There is now a past, a beginning, where divine consciousness was all that was.

So *'elohiym* brings life into form, but gives our consciousness of ourselves as divine beings a place, an enclosed place in the human psyche. It is put away into the past, in memory, so that now we must become conscious of it before we can know it. Because that is so, now it is possible for humanity to think itself separate from that consciousness, thus the tree of knowledge of good and evil—the thought of separation—is created. And so it is that Eve, the representative of the feminine inner realm of humanity, ate of the tree of knowledge of good and evil.

But Eve did not sin, as is traditionally believed. As we can clearly see here, it was *'elohiym* that moved our consciousness of ourselves as divine beings into an enclosed space of time in human consciousness. If our consciousness of ourselves as divine can be placed in the past, then what of today? Today we can consider another option than the one that is now in the past. We can consider the possibility that we are no longer divine. Here we began the brave creative process of joining form with formlessness, through the difficult journey of duality. As form we are wholly new to the history of the universe. Before us there is a vast history of formlessness. And so, we are here to creatively experiment with this completely new reality of form. And as we know, all truly good scientific experiments start with a null hypothesis. In this case that null hypothesis is that formlessness is divine, but form is not.

Right now and since this ancient shift in our consciousness, we think that matter is separate from the divine. We think that matter and all that exists within matter, including thought, emotion, and things like courage, fortitude and love, exist as separate from the divine. That's what we've been totally living into for centuries.

But some of us, including quantum physicists, doctors, healers, therapists and just regular Joe's are beginning to question that. Due to the increase in technical skills and the immediate access to worldwide communication we are connecting with each other in an as-if fashion—as if we were one. There has been such an increase in the frequency and depth of our conversations about quantum reality that the possibility that we are not separate from each other or from the divine is now becoming a feasible reality for many. As time goes by, more and more of us will come to understand this original paradigm of existence and we will all return to the Garden of Eden, our own internal heaven, with the completed knowledge of good and evil having merged form with formlessness. That knowledge is this: There is no good or evil, there is always and has always only been divine beingness.

The tree of knowledge of good and evil was meant to bring us to the hypnotized trance state in which we saw ourselves, our lives and all of earth's existence as separate from the divine. When Eve took the fruit of that tree, encouraged by the metaphorical serpent, she internalized that dualistic trance state, making it seem to be the only truth. And because she and later Adam no longer saw themselves as divine beings, they could not stay in the Garden of Eden, for that place was now shut out of human consciousness. This was the shutting that occurred. The metaphor clearly explains how it is that the soul-connecting chakras were shut or closed and why it is that we have such trouble opening ourselves to them again.

The separation is explained to the intellect by a grand battle between what has come to be called *good* and what has come to be called *evil*. In the hypnotized trance state of duality, we believe that the divine is good and man is evil. We believe that we are limited and time bound and that at the end of our lives we die. Just as *'elohiym* promised, when we ate of the tree of knowledge of good and evil, we began to experience death. But according to the tree of Life, which still exists in that enclosed place in the human psyche, we are one with the divine and no one dies, for how could the divine die?

So, why did the serpent encourage Eve to eat of that tree? According to traditional thought, the serpent is a slithery Satan, the tempter, the deceiver, the liar. But actually there is no lie, no deception and no temptation in the serpent's statements. Here are his comments from chapter three of Genesis:

And he said to the woman, "Indeed, has God said, 'You shall not eat from any tree of the garden?'" (v 1).

And the serpent said to the woman, "You surely shall not die! For God knows that in the day you eat from it your eyes will be opened, and you will be like God, knowing good and evil" (vs 4-5).

The first statement is a simple question, and the second is the ultimate truth: we do not die. The third one is troubling to most people for it promises that Eve will be like God knowing good and evil. But actually, when we know the *true* nature of good and evil, we are like God, our eyes are opened and we do see ourselves for who we really are: divine beings in whom there is neither good nor evil.

The process is a circle. We came here as divine beings without form. And we created ourselves anew as form. But our form was at first simply dust of the ground, and the divine changed our consciousness of ourselves to include time and moved our awareness of ourselves as divine beings to the unconscious receptacle of the mind called Eden. Then life was breathed into form. Form was filled with divine energy—but the mind could not see form as divine. So the mind—fully empowered with creative abilities—created the option of living in form as if it were separate from the divine. And that is exactly what we were put here to do. Why? Because if we do not fully explore all the options inherent in the creation of a totally new paradigm of existence, we will never fully know the truth of that existence. Form was a totally new way for the divine to exist. And it had to fully answer the question of its nature before it could fully understand itself as form that is also formlessness. We are still in that creative process of defining form. Once our journey here is complete, we will know fully who we are as divine beings in form. We will be like God, knowing the whole truth that good and evil do not exist and never have.

The serpent, therefore, did not lie, nor did he deceive or trick or tempt. So, is this serpent really a symbolic form of Satan? Down through the centuries the serpent has been seen as many things, and often its symbolic meanings are contradictory to each other. The serpent then is healer and an emblem of eternal life, the kundalini energy that rises up through the spine to open the chakra system, and a trickster who tempts, buffets and even wounds us. Again, I refer the reader to the wonderful book, *A Woman's Encyclopedia of Myths and Secrets,* by Barbara Walker, for a very thorough rendition of the mythologies of the serpent. But for now, what we need to know is that the serpent has been seen as both good and bad.

So, the traditional interpretations that tell us that this serpent is Satan in disguise might need to be called into question. But one of the passages in the Bible that seems to add merit to the traditional view is found in Genesis 3:14-15:

And the Lord God said to the serpent, "Because you have done this, cursed are you more than all the cattle, and more than every beast of the field; on your belly shall you go, and dust shall you eat all the days of your life; and I will put enmity between you and the woman and between your seed and her seed; he shall bruise you on the head and you shall bruise him on the heel."

If God always knew that Adam and Eve were going to be "tempted" of that "devil," the serpent, and have to be driven from the garden, then why did he need to punish the serpent for doing this? If the serpent is not evil, then why does God appear to be so angry with it? Well, if we believe that the Garden of Eden was within the mind and soul of humanity and that the trees of knowledge and Life were also to be found in that same place, then we have to assume that the serpent is likewise within the mind and soul of humanity.

If the serpent really does represent kundalini energy, then he is the door to the opening of the chakra system. The chakra system, made up of various centers of consciousness in the body/mind of humanity, represents soul energy in different areas of human endeavor. Kundalini energy is said to run up and down the spine of the body opening the chakras located there. The doors to the chakras were all wide open when we, as 'elohiym, created the first visages of formlessness as form, but as we've seen, both the tree of Life and the tree of knowledge represent a shutting. If we'd chosen the tree of Life we would have shut out the possibility of living in the trance state of duality, but since we chose the tree of knowledge of good and evil, we shut out the possibility of eating of the tree of Life, of living fully conscious of who we are as divine beings, at least until we come full circle into that knowledge through the necessary journey of duality. This means that our conscious experience of the chakras was also closed, which means that kundalini energy was made inaccessible to the conscious mind. So, instead of living from the spine, where the chakras are found on the body of matter, kundalini energy must now live from the belly—from the hunger for soul, and from the need to digest the concept of duality before we can complete the circle. Interestingly enough, another symbol represented by the serpent is the Uroboros, or the circle of life, the snake eating itself, a symbol for eternity.

But there are some other even more interesting things to be found in this passage. The fact that there will be enmity between the serpent and the woman—the feminine energy, the inner terrain of humanity—makes perfect sense if we realize that we've been trying to live from an external frame of reference since the time when Eve partook of the tree of knowledge. If the serpent represents our quite natural kundalini energy, and Eve represents the inner and receptive world, which would take us directly to that soulful kundalini, then this statement that there would be enmity between the woman and the serpent makes perfect sense, for it is telling us that the doorway to the inner world is now blocked. When we incorporated duality into the mind and body of humanity, we shut down the chakra system, thus relegating our deepest awareness of who we are to the unconscious. The idea of this duality experience was to allow us to fully experience it—which we could not do if we were fully acquainted with ourselves as divine beings. Becoming aware of ourselves as divine beings is a feminine—or internal—experience. Duality wants to keep us out of touch with the internal so that we can believe that we are separate and distinct from the divine and fully experiment with that notion over many lifetimes. So, putting enmity between the seed of the serpent and the seed of the woman means that, because duality has now been incorporated into the body/mind of humanity, all humanity thereafter will believe itself separate from the divine and will act accordingly. And so we have. We have lived our lives and formulated all of our customs, activities, politics, cultures, etc., from an external rather than an internal perspective. We do not know ourselves as one with the divine, but rather, if we think of it at all, we see ourselves as trying to accomplish some kind of connection with the divine, who is otherwise, absent from our lives. We see our fortunes as somehow correlative with this notion that we have been left out of the world of all things divine.

And it will not be until we turn and look at the serpent raised up on a stake, as described in Numbers 21, and see that the serpent represents both our poisoning and our healing that we will become fully conscious of who we are. It was our own kundalini energy that called us to participate in the Grand Experience of duality—because that is what we came here to do. We came here to define form as divine energy, by first defining it as separate from the divine, as our null hypothesis for the Grand Experience with duality. When the experience is complete we will have all the knowledge there is to be had about separation from the divine and good and evil. The journey will be complete on that day when we turn and look, and the looking itself will be our healing, for we will see that we have never been separated from the divine—we just *thought* we were.

And the statement, "he shall bruise you on the head and you shall bruise him on the heel" has caused great consternation among theologians for centuries. Many have connected it to the death of Jesus, as prophecy regarding his conquering Satan at the point of his death on the cross. This is difficult to determine, but there does appear, at first glance, to be a switch in pronouns in this address to the serpent, from "your" and "her" to "he." With further study, we find that what has been translated as "he shall bruise," is actually *Qal*, a syntactical use of language representing the most simplified form of action—so we cannot be certain that there is an actual change in pronouns. *He shall bruise* is two words *Qal shuwph*, which essentially means that an action was done by someone. In fact, *Qal* is quite often used for past-tense verbs, as in he sat, he ran, she talked. So the futuristic sound of "he shall" should also be questioned.

The word *shuwph* (שׁוּף) means *to bruise, crush, gape upon, desire, seize, strike out,* and *to fall upon.* The word *head* is *ro'sh* (רֹאשׁ), which derives from an unused word meaning *to shake.* The meaning of *ro'sh* is *head, top, summit, upper part, chief, total, sum, height, front, beginning, choices, best, division, company,* or *band.* The word *heel* is *'aqeb* (עָקֵב), which means *heel, rear, footprint, hinderpart, hoof, rear of a troop,* or *footstep.* That word is rooted in *'aqab,* a primitive root word, which means *to supplant, circumvent, take by the heel, follow at the heel, assail insidiously, overreach, hold back* or *attack at the heel.*

What we see clearly here is that the translation to the literal meanings, *bruise, head* and *heel,* leave out several potential metaphorical meanings that have to do with *seizing upon, because one desires, the chief or first* and *the last* or *final part of something.* So, if we put that all together, another possible translation might be:

And I will put enmity between you and the woman, and between your seed and her seed; which will desire and therefore seize your beginnings and your ends.

Duality has, indeed, supplanted the fact of our truest divine nature with its perceptual reality. We do not know ourselves as divine beings, but rather as simpletons disempowered to rule our lives. All of our beginnings and all of our endings have, indeed, been seized by that perceptual trance state, which inserts itself into our minds as reality. And, to continue with that metaphor, all of our creations are birthed in pain (v. 16). And the last part of that verse tells it all, as God speaks to the woman: "yet your desire shall be for your husband, and he shall rule over you."

The word *desire* there is *T⁰shuwqah* (תְּשׁוּקָה), *desire, longing, craving, as of a woman a man, or a man a woman, or as a beast to devour.* What is unique about his particular word for desire is it's metaphorical *stretching out, reaching out to obtain.* The word derives from the primitive root word *shuwq,* (שׁוּק), which means *to be abundant, to give abundance to,* or *to overflow.* And the word we commonly translate to be *husband* is `iysh* (אִישׁ), which means *man, male, human being, person, servant, mankind, champion, great man, whosoever,* or *each.* The traditional and literal translation of this verse indicates that the woman will desire to serve her husband and that the husband shall rule over the wife. This was her just punishment for bringing original sin into the world.

But another look at the deeper and metaphorical meanings, where the woman represents the internal and the man represents the external, yields something more like this:

> The internal shall turn itself outward, shall overflow its internal boundaries, deeply desire and live only for and in the external world, and be ruled by it.

The idea that the literal woman should be ruled by a literal man, specifically her husband (the word *husband* not even being found in the original text), turns out to be completely false. Duality has turned us inside out, so that we crave only the external to fulfill us, when our truest fulfillment lies within us. Our abundance, our joy, our peace, our truth is found within, and then and only then should it be carried into the external world by the masculine energy. But we see here that the masculine energy, the external energy, now warped by the duality trance state, has overwhelmed the internal, so that we hardly even see it anymore.

The transition from consciousness of divine oneness to the duality trance state was almost complete, yet one more thing was to be understood. In vs. 17-19, God informs Adam that because he also ate of the tree of knowledge, he would toil and strive to get the earth to produce for him, and even then it would often only produce thorns and thistles. Unlike the days in Eden, when the earth provided freely, even growing of its own divine accord without rain, now humanity would have to work and sweat for its food, for as long as we live in the duality trance state we do not see that abundance is within us, and because it is within us, can be manifested externally as well.

A few other things happened to Adam and Eve after they ate of the tree of knowledge of good and evil. The first thing that happened was that they realized that they were naked, and they "sewed fig leaves together and made themselves loin coverings" (3:7). Later, after *'elohiym* had finished prophesying their future as it would look from the duality trance state, and that induction into that trance state was utterly complete, then "the Lord God made garments of skin for Adam and his wife, and clothed them" (v. 21). Most traditionalists regard the nakedness of Adam and Eve as a temptation to sin. They were naked and must be clothed because it was no longer proper for them to be naked. And we know that they covered their loins, so that's their genitalia, right? Not according to the word used, which is *chagowr* (חגור), which means *girdle* or *belt*, and is rooted in the primitive word *chagar* (חקר), which means *to gird, gird oneself, bind* or *put on a belt*. And the word for fig leaves, *tsela`*, is of foreign, i.e., not Hebrew, derivation, so it is difficult to really know what is meant by this term. But a study of the words used in the Bible for girdle or loins does not have to do with one's genitalia, but one's heart, one's chest and one's abdomen. Putting on a belt or girdle had to do with guarding oneself.

The term for naked in these verses is *'eyrom* (עירם), the adjective *naked*, but rooted in *'aram* (ערם), which means *to be subtle, shrewd, crafty, beware, take crafty counsel, to be or become shrewd*. The thing that was missing, prior to their eating of the tree of knowledge of good and evil, was the physical body form. Adam and Eve did not know prior to their induction into the duality trance state that they'd been living in a subtle body—an etheric body, a body that very probably had the appearance of a physical body, but was not yet fully formed as physical body. They were now inducted into the duality trance state and yet their bodies were still subtle bodies. That nakedness—that awareness of subtle body—must have been very frightening to them in the duality trance state, in much the same way that a ghost would be frightening to us. So they had to guard themselves by trying to put on something physical to cover the subtle body.

'*Elohiym* then created a body form for humanity—they "made garments of skin for Adam and his wife" (3:21). Here, for the first time, Adam and Eve were given the flesh and blood bodies we know today—or at least a flesh and blood body that would evolve to those we know today. Later in *The Revelation to John*, we see that these same garments are called *worthy*, because they have completed the task assigned to them, as part of the creative endeavor. Because '*elohiym* was now living in matter, in form, humanity was uniquely assigned the task of bringing form to full awareness of its divine nature. The assignation was done by giving us freely physical incorporation in which to live out this Grand Experience with duality. We would do this by experiencing every single drop of what it is like to live as if we are separate from the divine. We can do that because we live incorporated in what appears to be a finite, limited and temporary structure, which seems, for all practical purposes to be separate from its formless divine nature.

The object of the game here is to unite form with formlessness. Quantum physics is now helping us objectively see what the soul has known since the beginning, that form is actually formless. That every object considered to be form is, in fact, made up of so many tiny particles that it is objectively formless. Einstein's Unified Field theory is becoming more and more of a potential reality, as we uncover more and more of the interweave of form with formlessness. And this will be the ultimate outcome of our journey here, that we will be able to see clearly that form is just another version of soul. Body will come to know itself as divine—rather than just something to be dumped at the end of a lifetime. Soul will no longer be seen as contained within a body, but body will be known as a constituent part of soul.

Adam and Eve, as those first metaphorical examples of early humanity, were creations of the soul, for the purpose of bringing form into being. But in order for form to come fully into being, it has to know itself as beingness. Our brave journey here is to bring that knowledge into full consciousness. For centuries and even now, we have not known body as part of the divine. In fact the body has been considered to be the source of our downfall. It is what makes us sin, it is what gets sick, it is what dies. That is the fulfillment of the prophecy given in the beginning that, because we cannot see who and what we truly are, matter can die, and because it can, it rules us. Matter has become our source of existence, rather than soul. We rely on money, food, air, shelter and clothing to take care of us, instead of relying on the soul. But as time goes by, and we evolve into greater and greater awareness, we will come to see that those external things are unreliable, and only the soul can be counted on to provide for us, for it is and always has been our only true source. Just as in the Garden of Eden—a metaphor for heaven within us—all was provided for effortlessly, so it is that when we arrive at full consciousness of who we really are, of what matter and our body form really is, we will see that actually we have always been likewise provisioned—we just didn't see it. This body form is our garment, which is worthy, and once we know this fully, we will then be permitted to take that second option and eat of the tree of Life. And the universe will evolve to take on its next creative endeavor.

5

The Split

Because duality became the order of the day, we split ourselves off from some aspects of ourselves in order to live in the dualistic mind-set created by the duality trance state. This meant some parts of us went into the unconscious—which represents the biggest split-off: that between consciousness and unconsciousness. But only within the past two-hundred years has the unconscious become a topic of conscious discussion and research. And, of course, the more light we shine on the unconscious, the more conscious we become.

But what do we mean by *being conscious*? Consciousness is personal responsibility. It is the recognition that we are each individually and all as a collective, able to fully respond to life in all of its challenge and glory. It is the willingness to be present with a feeling until it reveals its fullest message. It is the willingness to notice one's actions and look compassionately for the motivation for that action. It is the ability to consider one's own thoughts and beliefs and question their validity. It is all there is of true power, and the only thing there will ever be of genuineness. Any genuineness that comes by accident comes as a Freudian slip. Beyond that, one must be conscious to be real and one must be real to be conscious.

Unconsciousness on the other hand is all of the material that lies dormant, latent, or unknown within and about the self. For eons the majority of us have been very comfortable not knowing much about ourselves, and it seems that whatever patterns developed did so without our thoughtful intention. We lived most focused on the external world without much thought at all about what was going on within, unless a feeling either overwhelmed us with its power or we acted in ways that we later regretted. When we were overwhelmed by a mood or a feeling, we said that we were either "beside ourselves," "insane," or the more modern term "having a nervous breakdown." And if we did something we regretted, it was confessed as sin to be forgiven by a higher power, rationalized, or simply continuously regretted. It was rarely explored for its motivation. We just don't have much of a history of non-judgmental self-reflection, which would help us understand why we do the things we do. Inevitably any self-reflection concluded in either a goodness or a badness.

This was in part due to the duality trance state, for it has been very easy for us to place our behaviors and thoughts into the two preordained categories of *good* or *evil.* So if we did something we regretted we needed simply to know that we'd done something bad or *evil,* and that was that. Or, if we believed in confession for forgiveness, then we knew we had to confess. Later, when we repeated the same deed, we might feel worse yet, but only repeat the same responses. We rarely bothered to ask ourselves why we did the things we did, which if pondered long enough and deep enough might have helped us to come to know ourselves at deeper levels and to take greater responsibility for our actions. Thinking in terms only of *good* and *evil,* led us only to judge our behavior and try to eliminate it through moralism, punishment, or confession—usually to no avail. So, thinking in terms of *good* and *evil,* only perpetuated our unconsciousness. In fact, thinking in terms of *good* and *evil,* is the shallower of the all of the possibilities inherent in self-examination.

So, as we first began to study the unconscious our terminology for it tended to fall into the same shallow thought patterns. Thus, Freud divided the human psyche into three commonly known domains: the domain of the ego—which consisted of our everyday conscious behavior and thought; the domain of the superego—which judged and moralized so that the ego would behave itself; and the domain of the id—which was the wild amoral part of the psyche which took over from time to time and acted quite immoral. And, of course, sexuality was considered to be one of those areas in which we could cross over into wild abandon if we weren't careful, so Freud's interpretation of the unconscious id presented in the form of dreams was typically related to sexuality.

When Carl Jung, who had been a follower of Freud, finally broke away from him altogether, it is commonly thought that this was largely due to these very limited versions of what was going on in the human psyche. He felt that there was much more to be found there than just that near black and white version of humanity described by Freud. His discoveries led him to the conclusion that the unconscious was made up not only of repressed material—or material we've judged to be unacceptable to conscious experience—but also of both a personal unconscious and a collective unconscious.

As I interpret the personal unconscious, it is made up of personal attachments, complexes and latent and otherwise unknown aspects of the individual mind. And the collective unconscious is made up of collective archetypes that come from our connection, in fact our oneness with the rest of humanity, and yet these have a very powerful personal draw for the individual. There are many of these by now well-known archetypes, such as the masculine and the feminine, of which we've already spoken and will again. The most important and powerfully magnetic of these archetypes, however, is the archetype of the Self. Jung and many others have taught that it is this archetype that is birthed from the union of all of the aspects of psyche into wholeness.

Therefore, if we consider a wider more expansive version of the unconscious than that held by Freud, we have to discuss concepts that run much deeper than the two categories of *good* and *evil* can even begin to cover. The concepts of *good* and *evil* cannot even come close to the depth of the kind of union it takes to create wholeness. In fact, it seems clear that such a union would alchemically dissolve these opposites into wholeness. But we also know that in order to come to a place of such union, one would first have to differentiate the various parts, in order to put them into their appropriate place within the whole.

It is in that same way that our journey through the duality trance state will allow us to differentiate before we integrate. The split between the unconscious and the conscious worlds is a duality that will ultimately evolve into differentiation. As we evolve we will become more and more conscious of the duality, seeing it as our own psychic split rather than as a reality, thus differentiating the two. Perhaps we are even coming into that age now, in which our differentiation becomes a conscious choice we make, rather than just a continuation of the split between consciousness and unconsciousness.

This kind of differentiation means that we look at, name, place and come to know the variant ways of being within ourselves in order to marry them in a union that creates wholeness. On the collective level this means that we come to name and see as projections, the various aspects of humanity such as the warring aspect, and the peaceful one, the power aspect and the powerlessness one. On the individual level, it means much the same, so that we get in touch with the desire to control and the desire to be controlled and merge them in love and understanding; we get in touch with hate that hates because it loves, etc.

But the split between consciousness and unconsciousness has affected every aspect of our individual and collective lives. We have split the collective oneness into alienated individual and societal units, which cannot, at least in our current mindset, be merged. We have divided into religious units—which dare not merge. We have split off from our resources, so that some of us have resources and some of us don't. We have split our own psyches into compartmentalized and estranged units of emotions, behavior, thought and belief.

In most cases, the unconscious has the greater part of the psyche. So great, indeed, that the ocean is frequently used as a symbol for the unconscious. So, if we go with that symbol, then the conscious mind is a swimming pool, compared to the ocean of unconsciousness. There is a tremendous reservoir of information about ourselves from which we have over the centuries become more and more alienated. That alienation is necessary to the Grand Experience we are having with duality. We have to differentiate before we can integrate. We have to see form as separate from the divine before we can see it as constituent to the divine. But now, as we study consciousness, we are challenging ourselves to go deeper and that process means that we might have to learn to breathe under water.

If we take up that challenge, we are going to have to become comfortable in the realms of the unconscious. Indeed, many are finding, through such practices as meditation and Yoga, that there is a great deal of peace to be found in the midst of other more painful things drawn forth from the unconscious. How can this be so? Well, it can be so if one of the things that we have pushed away, compartmentalized and even called blasphemy, is our truest nature as divine beings. That repression was absolutely essential to our taking on the duality trance state. But through meditation and other such inner-world experiences, many are at least touching the hem of that garment.

Were we to fully know ourselves as the divine beings we are, there would be no need for a duality trance state, nor for consciousness and unconsciousness, for all would be conscious oneness. But because we still live in the duality trance state there is a deep well of information to which we are not privy about ourselves, including both our truest nature, and the games we play to keep us out of touch with that nature. But the games we play, more often than not, have to do with protecting our minds from an image of ourselves with which we feel we cannot live.

And mostly what we want to protect ourselves from, in this dualistic mindset, is an image of ourselves as bad or *evil*. Most of us want to believe that we are good people. Maybe we occasionally do bad things, but we are good people. And that's where the games start. We repress those thoughts, feelings, recognitions and resonances with which we can judge ourselves to be bad people.

And the games we play to keep ourselves from considering the possibility that we might be less-than, bad or *evil*, include the following and more:

- Smoke and mirrors: In this game I throw up a veil of smoke or fog to keep you from seeing what I have done, to basically confuse the issue and you entirely, so that you cannot convince me of my badness. And then I hold up a mirror—usually by blaming you for the whole thing—so that all you see is yourself. So, now I've confused you so well that you are already questioning your own perceptions of me, and then when you are most vulnerable, I blame you.

- Shadow-dancing: This is a game of mental abuse in which I pretend to have the ability to peer beyond your persona deep into your unconscious. Instead of taking personal responsibility for what I've done, I begin to project onto you. You're just crazy. That way anything you say about me can just be attributed to your craziness. It's not a problem that I cheated on you, you're just crazy. It's not a problem that I'm gambling away all the money, you are just crazy. Because I'm unconscious of how my own irresponsibility is "crazy" I can just project that "craziness" onto you. And the worst thing about this one is that it works like a charm.

- Bait and Switch: In this game, I acknowledge that I've done something wrong, but I'm not real sure what it is. You know me, I'm just a lout and you can't trust me to do anything right. So, I'll apologize maybe more than once. But my apology is meant to make you shut-up. If you continue to tell me how you feel after my apology, I'll sit humbly by, wishing you would just stop nagging me. And then later—after you've decided that I understand—since I haven't done anything about the problem, and since I've never really admitted to myself that I did something hurtful, I'll subtly bring it up again blaming you for it. You took the bait, and then I put the whole problem back into your lap.

- Denial: In this game, I simply deny that I've done anything to offend or hurt. My intentions are always good, so I must not have really done anything bad. I may even say things like: "I didn't mean it the way you took it." Or, "I didn't mean it." Or, the most lame excuse ever invented, "It just happened." With denial I never have to take personal responsibility for my interactions with others, because I'm really a good person and they just don't understand me.

- Playing dumb: Here is where I get to look like I'm in denial, but really, I'm just denying. I pretend not to know what I'm up to. Or, I pretend not to know what you are talking about, or I pretend that I'm just a little dense. The object of the game here is to get you to stop looking at me.

- I win; you lose: With this game, the object is to make sure that I win, at all costs. I want only to win the argument, so that I look like I'm *right*, even if it's blatantly obvious to any onlooker that I'm completely out in left field. My pride is at stake and I must leave this encounter with my pride intact.

- Victim: When I play victim, I don't have to take responsibility for my behavior, my behavior is someone else's fault. "IF you hadn't done so-and-so, I wouldn't have had to do so-and-so."

- Lie: This one is just an outright lie. You catch me with my hand in the cookie jar, and I'll just tell you that I didn't have my hand in the cookie jar, or if I did, it was because Sally or Joe needed a cookie really badly. I'll make up entire fictions to keep you from ever knowing that I did what you just caught me doing or what you suspect me of doing.

- Name-calling: One of the best games to play when we are trying to assure that no one sees what we're up to is to call them a name. The names can range from "Selfish" to much more obscene names, but the object of the game is to make you the problem.
- Punishment: You caught me lying, and you and I both know it, though I'm not saying it's so. Now, I'm going to have to punish you. So, for the next few weeks, I'll be cold, indifferent and refuse any signs of affection from you. Or if this happens at work, I'll find a way to get you in trouble with the boss. You'll learn.
- Indifference: I don't care what you think of me. I don't care that you think I spent too much money without honoring our agreement to talk about money before we spend it. So, if you catch me, I'll just shrug my shoulders and keep on rockin' and rollin'.

Each of these games, and more, has as its primary intention, the blinding of my own sensibilities to any recognition that I might have to consider whether or not I'm really a bad person. But we can see clearly here that the issue is not my morality at all, nor my worth. Rather the issue is my identity. I cannot abide the notion that I am a bad person. So, I'll lie, cheat, steal, mentally abuse or whatever else I have to do to keep you and thus me from considering that perception of myself. If the issue were really one of morality—would I commit immoral acts to avoid immorality? In fact, these games only serve to further the split between the conscious and the unconscious realms of reality. And they are based entirely on the duality trance state.

There are also people, however, who identify as bad or *evil*. These are people who, as we've suggested, typically grew up in homes in which the only way they could find any place at all for a distinct identity to exist was in the place of badness or *evil*. In extremely religious homes, for example, children are quite often taught not how to behave, but who to be. They are not loved for their uniqueness; rather their uniqueness is frightening to parents who see sameness as moral and uniqueness as bordering on *evil*. Everything the child does is judged as some degree of good or bad. No other categories exist. This child may be rigidly disciplined and, in fact, such discipline is probably the only way in which he is noticed at all. Therefore, the child may identify with badness as a way of finding a unique and palpable image of himself. If he is good, he'll just blend right in with everyone else in the family — trying to look, walk, talk and think just like the parents. But *this* child's blending in is tantamount to becoming non-existent. This child needs a sense of self just as much as he needs a sense of connection — which actually means that he starts off pretty healthy. But in this home the only way he will find both connection and a sense of a separate identity is to be bad. And as the connections become dull or expected and/or his sense of himself is blurred, he'll need to up the ante and become more and more ill-behaved over time in order to keep both his connection (even if only through arguments or fights) and his sense of self. People who grow up with this bad-guy identity will play the same games as above, but the games are meant to show you how bad they can be, and to keep you from seeing that they have a heart or care anything at all about you or anyone else.

All children need to find an identity. In fact they spend the first several years of their lives looking for mirrors in their environment. They want to look in these mirrors and find a clearly defined sense of self. And children tend to take on responsibility for things adults do that otherwise would make no sense — because taking such responsibility, while purely imaginary, allows them to believe that they can do something about it. So, if the child is abandoned or the primary caregivers only respond with silence or literal absence, the child may believe herself to be bad in some intrinsic way that makes people go away. Or, if the parents are always cautioning him with a subtle demand for goodness in the extreme the child may sense that he is intrinsically bad, or why would they need to keep cautioning him. Or, if parents are those who can't be wrong, then the child may pick up that wrongness for them as a way of staying connected to them. These are the mirrors the child is looking in by which she will make up her mask and costume, i.e., her identity. Identity allows us to believe we are alive. Without an identity, we do not feel that we are really here.

But what has the need to feel alive to do with morality? Not a thing. And yet, we continue to see those who identify with badness as evil—which of course is exactly what they want us to do. And those who spend their lives trying to avoid any notion of themselves as bad—what of them—are they really bad people trying to be good, or do they just believe in the duality trance state so much that they cannot see beyond it to define themselves separate from it?

But of course this mask and costume, this identity is not who we really are, it is just who we need to be to survive in this particular family-of-origin and/or society or culture. Who we really are has been relegated to the unconscious so that the external family and its needs can be met and so that the child can belong somewhere in this world. If parents only knew that simply mirroring the child's authentic unique self would allow the child to grow into his essence and bless the world with that beautiful beingness, we might raise a generation of mind-blowing children. But because we live in the duality trance state, just the very idea of mirroring our children's authenticity sounds a little too much like letting them get away with it. So, we don't.

Because of this duality trance state, when we first ventured into the human psyche to try to understand it we did so using the same tribal consciousness of duality we'd always known. So, for Freud there was this great battle between the feral id, and the moralistic and judging superego, in which each was battling for control of the poor conflicted ego. As we've said, Jung disagreed.

But then, until recently, no one paid much attention to Jung. In fact, it's historically been difficult for those who are the leaders in the mental health field to separate morality from diagnosis. It was not until 1986, for example, that homosexuality was removed from the Diagnostic and Statistical Manual of Mental Disorders (DSM)—which is universally used to give diagnoses. Because homosexuality was, prior to that time, considered to be a sinful and mysterious way of life, it was put into the DSM as a diagnosis.

Even today, many still refer to those with an Antisocial Personality Disorder, or a sociopath as incurable, simply because we think of them as evil—in fact more or less pure evil—and who can cure that? Yet there are those researchers who are providing single case studies in which those with antisocial personality disorders demonstrate significant changes in dysfunctional behavior after specifically designed interventions. But these studies are still not being done with enormous frequency, nor is the Federal Government putting a lot of funding into grants to do this kind of research—research which would, if effective treatment were to be found, virtually empty our jails. We believe that evil defines a person and therefore cannot be healed. Certainly there are many who would choose to remain in the familiar world of sociopathy if given a choice, but that doesn't mean that no one who identifies with it, can find another more healthy and authentic way to live.

Thusly, the mental health world is facilitating the psychic split between consciousness and unconsciousness, though that is something of which the mental health world is largely unconscious. And thus, the splitting continues. But there have been a few who have studied human development, who concentrated at least part of their energy on the study of the meaning of moral development. These include Jean Piaget, Lawrence Kohlberg, and Carol Gilligan and while they disagree on the some significant details, and while their studies have been called into question in several ways, they agree that there are stages of development which basically start with fear of punishment and evolve through the stages to a more universally principled approach to life.

What remains unclear from these studies is what is meant by *universal principles*. For example, is it possible for universal principles to dictate a life in the same way that morals would? I have actually worked with some people who declare themselves to be non-religious but highly principled people, and who stand so firmly on that identity that they will end up harming themselves in some distinctly unprincipled ways in order to prove that identification valid. What, for example, happens when a highly principled man marries an extremely unprincipled woman who lies, manipulates and plays games with his heart, by flirting with other men and even cheating on him? Well, it is a universal principle that one should love one's wife, right? And that one should sacrifice for those one loves? And that one should forgive? In the name of his principles this man may go down in the annals of fools everywhere who tolerate the intolerable and accept the unacceptable to their own demise.

Actually, in this fictional example, this man has an identity, an identity that informs him that he must always be good no matter the results. And whether or not he has a religion, his principles have become his life. In fact, he believes that his very survival depends on the absolute maintenance of these active principles of living. He is literally nothing without them. But, as we can sadly see, he is also nothing with them. His wife has completely negated his existence, right in his face, and he has his actionable hands and feet tightly tied firmly behind his back with the rope of principle. He believes that it is unfair to leave this woman who has been left by parents and other men so many other times. He simply will not be one more person who abandons her. He has his principles after all. In fact, after all is said and done, that is all he has or ever will have. But then, after all is said and done, he is quite proud of that fact.

Studies of morality are limited by the fact that they do not tell us anything about that amoral stage of development, which is present prior to the influence of authority figures and societal pressure to conform. By the use of the term *amoral* here I don't mean Freud's id. Nor do I mean unprincipled, unethical or unscrupulous. What I mean is *lacking the moral codes that are later learned through interaction with authority figures and society, yet fully equipped with unconditional love and an authentic Self.* And it is this amoral stage, which I believe has much to tell us about who we really are, if we could just find it in our memory banks. But whether or not we ever remember this place, we do understand that morals are taught and learned. In fact, it is this reality that had parents of previous generations believing that they could and should mold their children. Much of our understanding of parenting in general comes from our ideas and beliefs about morality.

It is our job, as parents, or so we think, to teach our children "right from wrong." And of course these ideas about right and wrong are relative to the beliefs of the parents. If a child grows up, for example, in the home of a white, rightwing radical, gun-toting racist, then right might mean something like killing off all of the darker races. And wrong might mean tolerating them. I made that deliberately extreme to make the point that right and wrong are definitely relative. But regardless of the values assigned to *right* and those assigned to *wrong*, we tend to believe that it is our job, our right and our prerogative to teach our children that they *must* follow our morals.

If you want to find out just how strongly we value this job, right and prerogative, just try to interfere with a mother fiercely spanking her child in the grocery store. Not only does she think she is right for spanking her child, but she will tell you in no uncertain terms, that this is *her* child, and she will raise him as she sees fit. And she will look at you like she thinks you are off your rocker for even thinking about interfering. But consider this: which is right—fiercely spanking a child, or interfering with that fierce spanking? If we were to take a poll of the answers to that question, we'd probably get a 50/50 response—which informs us of all we know about *right and wrong*. It is definitely relative.

Yet, in spite of its apparent relativity, we continue to believe that there is some kind of universal morality, which not only defines our separation from the divine, but which, if everyone could find it, would allow us to finally end the battle between *good* and *evil*. So, not only does this duty to teach our children right from wrong appear in every single home in the world, but it also appears in our schools. In America, if you want to know how much it appears, just ask any teacher, in the public and even many private schools, to give you a ratio for the amount of time she spends disciplining compared to the amount of time she spends teaching her subject matter. The best case scenario is 50/50. But most of the time, it's going to be something like 80/20— with discipline taking the highest end. But, of course, once No-Child-Left-Behind started, the ratios would have to include how much time the teacher is spending preparing the students for standardized tests, as opposed to how much time she is spending on really educating students. Best not to get me started here.

Most teachers would say that they are principled. And many would add to that they come from a certain religion. All would most likely say that they believe in *right* and *wrong*. And many teachers feel that it is their duty to "instill moral values" as they teach. Of course, more and more our students are living out the shadow side of this instillation. They are showing us, clearly showing us, that what we are doing in our schools isn't working.

With increased suicide, homicide, drug use and abuse rates skyrocketing in and out of our schools, even reaching down to kids as young as 5 and 6, it is clear that the school system is failing not only our kids but all of us. If all of the horrors from Columbine to Virginia Tech haven't taught us anything—what will it take? Yet, we just continue to do the same old thing harder. Why? My theory is that we are afraid that to do anything different from what we are doing would be immoral.

You see, we get habituated to a thing, and it slowly takes on the tenor of a moral. We are trying to teach these kids right from wrong—this is clearly a moral obligation. So, if it's not working, it's not the fault of the system, it's "these kids today!" or perhaps their "lazy parents" that are to blame. Let's see. Maybe we can say it's the immorality of the higher divorce rate, or the fact that mothers are now working—to many a questionable morality—or maybe it's just the ever-decaying morality of the species which will finally have us destroying ourselves in an earth-shattering explosion of ultimate evil.

We dare not consider the possibility that our kids can teach us how to teach them. That within them lie dormant the interests that can be utilized as a jumping off point from which they will learn all of the other less interesting things, which they will learn. We dare not consider that they came here already prepackaged with an authentic Self that can come to full term and deliver them to the doorstep of adulthood, if we will but begin the process of enabling them to find it and use the information they find there for educational purposes. We dare not consider that, for example, an intense interest in science can be used to teach reading, writing and arithmetic; or an interest in bugs, or kites, or even sports. No, that might involve dispensing with the moral duty to teach right from wrong. It might even mean that compassion and the motivation to do something about it are also prepackaged in the authentic Self—which eliminates our need to teach *right from wrong*—for compassion and the motivation to do something about it are, according to Jesus, all there is of morality. But we'll talk more about that in the following chapter.

Today's studies on morality tell us even more than previous moral development research. According to recent research regarding moral responses, as reported by Nancy Ryerson in the article entitled "Virtuous Reality: Why your moral compass is more pliable than you think" in *Psychology Today* Magazine, (July/August 2011), a number of things can impact our moral decisions—none of which have much at all to do with morals, including, smells, changes in lighting, antiseptic wipes and whether the eyes are closed or open. According to that research:

> Even seemingly trivial things like faint smells or changes in lighting can rejigger our compasses by reminding us of meaningful metaphors; in fact, our minds may naturally base abstract concepts like morality on simpler, body-based experiences (32).

Therefore, when we smell a harsh smell we may be more likely to make harsh judgments, or if we have just cleansed our hands we might lean more toward a judgment of immorality on a controversial issue. Can we say then, that moral judgments are accurate?

The truth is that our moral codes keep us split off from who we really are. How do they do that? They inform us of how we *should* act, what we *should* think and how we *should* feel. So all of our effort goes into doing that, or into rebelling against that, and we don't put any energy into finding out who we really are. There is certainly adequate reinforcement out there for staying completely out of touch with who we are. For many there is even an intense fear of finding out who we are, because who we are is inherently evil—or so we think. Still others identify with this so-called evil and make a life out of it. The truth is, however, that when we do this we are all homeless. We make our little cardboard shelters out of a moral code we try to live by or rebel against, instead of inhabiting our deepest selves. We live outside of ourselves in the superfluous territory of *should*. But if we only knew who we were, we would find that all of those shoulds are completely unnecessary, for we are fully empowered divine beings who know exactly how to initiate our own behaviors, thoughts and feelings without the false valuation and judgment of these codes.

6

The Judge and The Condemned

The split operates on the basis of two. Not one. Two. But each of the two are interdependent upon the other. There can be no condemned if there is no judge. And there can be no judge if there is no condemnation. So, when St. Paul, supposed author of the New Testament book of the Christian Bible said to be a letter to the new church in Rome, (Romans 8:1) wrote, "there is therefore now no condemnation for those who are in Christ Jesus," what he also meant was that there was now no judge.

But that's not how it is traditionally seen. For regardless of what we think that Jesus or any of the other great Master-Teachers did or didn't do while they were here on this planet, we still believe mightily in both the judge and the condemnation. For if there is no judge and no condemnation, then there cannot be good or evil. But since there is still good and evil—at least in our estimation—there is still a judge and still condemnation. Additionally, those who hold a fundamentalist view of what Jesus did while he was here believe that the phrase "those who are in Christ Jesus" in the passage in Romans 8:1, is exclusive to a few born-again Christians. But exclusivity is but another element of the duality trance state in which oneness is denied.

In the Western world, and even in some of the Eastern traditions, that denial is based largely on the concept of *sin*. Sin is considered to be disobedience to the law. In fact, in some Eastern religions the religious law is also political law, and so sin is severely and publically punishable. But sin is also considered to be punishable in eternal ways, in many Eastern and Western religions. In some Eastern traditions, sins in one life are presented as bad karma in the next life. In Western thought many will go to hell because of their sins, and others, because they are forgiven, or have completed the right ritual, will go to heaven.

I would say that the concepts of heaven and hell, as we currently understand them, came about *because* of our concepts of sin, not vice versa. We needed to believe in the possibility of an afterlife reward or punishment in order to accommodate our ideas about duality. And we are going to say more about that in just a few moments. For now, we are going to elucidate this concept of sin as disobedience to the law. We'll continue to use Western sacred texts to do this—again, not because we cannot find it in Eastern texts, but because we've been taught that Western texts do not tell us that we are divine. Our exploration here, will elucidate the Master-Teacher's messages in a way that clarifies, that he taught the exact same message taught by the Buddha, the Bhagavad Gita, early Gnostic Texts, and others, i.e., that we, like Jesus, are divine beings.

The Western version of the law is not only the Ten Commandments, but all of the Hebraic law that came about as a result of the disobedience of the Hebrew peoples and their leadership. And it is further based, according to tradition, upon the laws which seemed to be laid out by Jesus. So our example comes from the latter. Jesus gives a long sermon in chapters five, six and seven of the Gospel of Matthew, traditionally referred to as the "Sermon on the Mount." Many traditionalists consider this sermon to be an eloquent exposition of the state of the mind of man, as well as a list of laws which must be obeyed if one is to consider oneself to be a good Christian. But if, indeed, that is the purpose of his speech, one might wonder why he starts off in Matthew 5 like this:

You are the salt of the earth, but if the salt has become tasteless, how will it be made salty again? It is good for nothing anymore, except to be thrown out and trampled underfoot by men. You are the light of the world. A city set on a hill cannot be hidden. Nor do men light a lamp, and put it under the peck-measure, but on the lampstand; and it gives light to all who are in the house. Let your light shine before men in such a way that they may see your good works, and glorify your Father who is in heaven. Do not think I came to abolish the Law or the Prophets; I did not come to abolish, but to fulfill (vs. 13-17)....

For I say to you, that unless your righteousness surpasses that of the scribes and Pharisees, you shall not enter the kingdom of heaven (v. 20).

From the perspective of non-duality, it is clear that this passage is telling us about who we really are. We are the salt of the earth, the light of the world. But because we do not believe that we are these things our salt has no taste and our light has been hidden. It is important to note two things: 1) Jesus is not just speaking to the disciples here—he is speaking to multitudes; and 2) he does not say that these people could *become* the salt of the earth and the light of the world. He says that they *already are* the salt of the earth and the light of the world. So, if sin is such an issue to Jesus, how is it that all of these people, at least some of whom were probably "sinners," were considered to be the salt of the earth and the light of the world? And if he thought that we were all hopelessly driven to sin—as most traditionalists teach—then why would he ever tell us that our righteousness should surpass that of the Pharisees—who were the law keepers of his day?

Looking into the meaning of the word *righteousness*, might help us to answer these questions. The word is *dikaiosuvnh* (δικαιοσυϖνη), which is a general term that means *man as he ought to be*, but it is rooted in *dikaios* (δικαιοϛ), which means *observing divine laws, innocent, guiltless,* and several other like terms. But the most interesting of those terms is this one: *only Christ truly.* That word is further rooted in *deiknuo* (δειϖκνυμι), which means *to show with the eyes, to evidence or proof of a thing.* So what Jesus most likely meant when he used that word was that we were to show ourselves to be *only Christ truly,* indeed, prove to ourselves that that is who we actually are, and in doing so become who we ought to be. If we are only Christ truly, then *like Christ* we are fully aware of ourselves as divine beings. If we are only Christ truly, then we are *truly* aware of ourselves as divine beings. If we are only Christ truly, we are *only* aware of ourselves as divine beings. In Buddhism, this would be the same as becoming fully, truly, only aware of the Buddha nature. To the Bhagavad Gita, this would mean becoming fully, truly, only aware of Divine Self.

But Jesus says even more by comparing this consciousness to the consciousness of the Pharisees. In his day, these were considered to be the most moral people alive. Yet Jesus called them "hypocrites," "white-washed tombs" (Matthew 23:27) and "vipers" (Matthew 3:7), because their righteousness was not *only Christ truly,* but rather an external exposition of the law. In other words, they obeyed the law with their actions but their hearts were still living as if separate from the divine. Worse than that, they also expected from others what they themselves could not accomplish. What Jesus suggests when he says that we cannot enter the kingdom of heaven unless our righteousness exceeds theirs, is that we must know ourselves to be divine before we can live in the realm of the divine. We'll say some more about that shortly.

But he also says here that, he didn't come to abolish the law, but to fulfill it, and that:

> For truly I say to you, until heaven and earth pass away, not the smallest letter or stroke shall pass away from the law, until all is accomplished. Whoever then annuls one of the least of these commandments, and so teaches others, shall be called the least in the kingdom of heaven; but whoever keeps and teaches them he shall be called great in the kingdom of heaven (v. 18).

And these are the verses that most traditionalists focus on, when it comes to understanding this chapter in its context. But these verses are followed by:

> For I say to you, that unless your righteousness surpasses that of the scribes and Pharisees, you shall not enter the kingdom of heaven (v.20).

What Jesus is saying then, is that the righteousness that is only Christ truly *is* the fulfillment of the law, but that the law must remain in place until we pass through to the other side of the duality trance state. In fact, the law is a derivative of the duality trance state, which is what must be completely fulfilled. We must walk all the way to the other side of duality, to the place in which we can clearly see that it doesn't exist, before we will fulfill it, and the law. And he says that in several other places in the gospels as well. Until we know ourselves to be divine, we will be striving to fulfill the law by trying hard to be *good* so that we won't be *evil*.

And then he begins to make comparisons between the Law of the ancient Hebrew texts, and the realities of the inner man. Here are some of those statements, again from chapter five of Matthew.

> You have heard that the ancients were told, "You shall not commit murder" and "Whoever commits murder shall be liable to the court." But I say to you that everyone who is angry with his brother shall be guilty before the court....(vs.21-22)

> You have heard that it was said, "You shall not commit adultery"; but I say to you, that everyone who looks on a woman to lust for her has committed adultery with her already in his heart. And if your right eye makes you stumble, tear it out, and throw it from you; for it is better for you that one of the parts of your body perish, than for your whole body

to be thrown into hell (vs 27-29).

And it was said, "Whoever sends his wife away, let him give her a certificate of divorce"; but I say to you that everyone who divorces his wife, except for the cause of unchastity, makes her commit adultery; and whoever marries a divorced woman commits adultery (vs. 31-32).

Again, you have heard that the ancients were told, "You shall not make false vows, but shall fulfill your vows to the Lord." But I say to you, make no oath at all, either by heaven for it is the throne of God, or by earth, for it is the footstool of His feet, or by Jerusalem, for it is the city of the great King. Nor shall you make an oath by your head, for you cannot make one hair white or black. But let your statement be "Yes, yes" or "No, no"; and anything beyond these is of evil.

You have heard that it was said, "An eye for an eye, and a tooth for a tooth." But I say to you, do not resist him who is evil, but whoever slaps you on your right cheek, turn to him the other also (vs. 33-39).

You have heard that it was said, "You shall love your neighbor, and hate your enemy." But I say to you, love your enemies, and pray for those who persecute you in order that you may be sons of your Father who is in heaven for He causes his sun to rise on the evil and the good and sends rain on the righteous and the unrighteous (vs. 43-45).

Therefore, you are to be perfect, as your heavenly Father is perfect (v. 48).

These verses are traditionally interpreted to be yet another set of laws laid down by Jesus for us to follow. For example, there are many today, who still believe that if they divorce, they are causing their spouse to commit adultery, and if they remarry they themselves are committing adultery, and further, if they marry someone who has been married before they are committing adultery twice. And there have been many over the centuries who have literally tried to remove hands, eyes and other sin-creating body parts, or who beat themselves with a cat-of-nine-tails, or scraped their skin bloody or did other atrocious things to the body in order to make sure that it didn't sin, in an effort to follow these laws. Interestingly enough though, there are fewer people who believe that they should literally turn the other cheek, or give away their shirt or give money to those who want to borrow from them.

But if we take these verses to be a new more strict version of earlier laws, then what are we to do with this story, found later in the same Gospel?

> And one of them, a lawyer, asked him a question, testing him, "Teacher, which is the great commandment in the Law?" And He said to him, "'You shall love the Lord your God with all your heart, and with all your soul, and with all your mind.' This is the great and foremost commandment, and the second is like it, 'You shall love your neighbor as yourself.' On these two commandments depend the whole Law and the Prophets" (Matthew 22:35-40)

Mark adds a bit more clarity to the story, for in Mark's version, when the lawyer asks Jesus that question, he answers first with:

> The foremost is, "Hear O Israel! The Lord our God is one Lord; and you shall love the Lord your God with all your heart and with all your soul and with all your mind, and with all your strength." The second is this, "You shall love your neighbor as yourself." There is no other commandment

greater than these (Mark 12:28-31).

In Mark we see *why* Jesus believes that these two are the greatest of all commandments: for the Lord our God is ONE. Our power to love comes from our union with the divine. All of the heart, mind, soul and strength are ONE divine energy, and are capacitated with that same divine power to love. Further, we are also one with our neighbors, and that same capacity to love enables us to love them as we love ourselves.

And it is based on this same premise that Jesus discusses the law in the verses cited above from Matthew. When Jesus says, "You have heard it said..." he is talking about the externalized version of the law. And when he says, "but I say to you..." he is talking about the human heart and soul. What he is trying to do over and over again in this lengthy sermon is to show people what genuine betrayal is really all about. We don't betray the law when we behave differently from the law's intent. Rather we betray the law when we act, think and feel as if we are not *only Christ truly* or I AM that I AM.

From a traditional perspective, what Jesus seems to ask of us in this sermon is impossible. He wants us to never have a hateful feeling, never lust, never divorce, never make a promise, turn the other cheek when someone hits us, give away our clothes, walk the extra mile, love our enemies and he even says that we are to "be perfect, as your heavenly Father is perfect" (v.48). How could he possibly expect that of us?

He can expect it of us, because we are *only Christ truly.* The fulfillment of the law comes when we see clearly who we are— as Jesus did. The Lord our God, the divine is ONE—we are not separate from the divine, nor is the divine separate from us. The evidence of *only Christ truly* is within us. And all of our striving to obey the external laws only makes us into white washed tombs. We might look good on the outside, but inside, we are dead, for we have yet to come alive to our essence as *only Christ truly.*

With tongue firmly planted in cheek, Jesus is mocking the rigid obeisance to those external laws. He is clearly saying that if they really want to obey the law they must take it to its ultimate home—the inner human. In his mockery he is basically saying that no matter how much we try to obey these laws, we will not be able to do it. He is demonstrating the impossibility of the duality trance state, so that he can give us the answer to every moral dilemma: we are *only Christ truly*. But what we have done with his wonderful sardonic speech is make it into yet another impossibility. And we judge ourselves now by this impossible standard—and tell ourselves that, of course, it is impossible, but we should strive for it anyway.

All condemnation is based entirely on our understanding of our rules. We suspend condemnation when we live from *only Christ truly*. There can be no condemnation if all is ONE with the divine. But rather than knowing that we can live from *only Christ truly*, we are our own judge, jury and executioner. We bare the marks of our punishments all day long in our words, our thoughts and our deeds. How many things do we unconsciously prohibit, simply because we think we do not deserve these things? How many times have we surreptitiously sabotaged relationships because we thought we didn't really deserve them? How many obstacles and blocks have we created to our creativity and joy because we do not feel worthy of them? How many ways have we unconsciously chosen to suffer because we just can't allow ourselves to rejoice when there is still so much suffering among others?

We are the salt of the earth but we do not know this, so instead we are trampled over by the urgent riot of humanity, split off from such awareness. We are the light of the world, but we hide our light because we don't believe it is possible for us to be the light of the world. That is where Jesus started this sermon. And he ends it with "be perfect as your Father in heaven is perfect." In other words, be who you are! You can love the divine with all your heart, mind, soul and strength, because you *are* the divine. And you can love your neighbor as yourself, because your neighbor *is* yourself. And this knowledge is the whole law. But even so, we still seem to reduce this amazing reality to a battle between *good* and *evil*—where evil is always ahead.

So, what does the inner judge and condemner feel like? According to Jesus, it feels like death. The term "white washed tomb" is not used lightly. That other option we ignored in the Garden of Eden was the thought of eternal and abundant Life—with a capital L. And while obedience to the law allows us to white wash the external—or make it *look* "righteous," if we are not eating of the tree of Life, we are not consciously alive. We are consciously dead, while Life energy has been consigned to the unconscious. We may go through the motions of living, but if we are not using soul energy as the source of that consciousness—we are consciously dead. In other words, if we are not fully surrendered to soul, we are not operating from Life energy. We are operating from the energy of duality—for we are still eating of the tree of knowledge of good and evil.

And here's what that energy produces (Genesis 3:16-19):

...in pain you will bring forth children; yet your desire will be for your husband, and he will rule over you. ... Cursed is the ground because of you; in toil you will eat of it all the days of your life. Both thorns and thistles it shall grow for you; and you will eat the plants of the field; by the sweat of your face you will eat bread, till you return to the ground, because from it you were taken; For you are dust, and to dust you shall return.

T.S. Eliot's *Wasteland* comes to mind. In the dualistic trance state, we think we are striving to survive, to stay alive, but actually we are striving to bring forth life from death. In the beginning, when

133

humanity lived in the psychic state of the Garden of Eden, there was no effort involved in provision. But above we can clearly see that once the duality trance state took over, there was a complete reversal, so that there would be a lot of effort, but very little provision—but only because we believed more in the effort than we do in the provision.

The inner judge has us judging our effort, instead of expecting our provision. The inner judge tells us that there is separation between us and our provision, that we must put forth great energy, and maintain an ever-accelerating effort in order to earn our keep. This is based in another of our codes: "You gotta' work for a living." Think about that statement for a moment. We have to work for a living, but watch out because too much work means no life. Since working for a living means keeping ahead of life's necessities, however, we feel we must keep up an ever-accelerating pace. Yet it is that pace that keeps us from enjoying the living we are creating by working so hard. Or worse, we'll keel over in a dead faint one day from exhaustion. This code offers but another double-bind. If we don't work we have no life, but if we do work, we'll have to work so hard that we'll have no life. Add that to the fact that there are still too many of us that believe that joy and work are oxymorons, and we can see the growing enormity of this problem. But the origin of this thinking is in duality: We absolutely believe that life itself is dependent on our efforts to get money to put food on the table.

To the mind caught up in the duality trance state it seems insane to think that we don't supply our lives by our own efforts. But to the mind awakened to its truest divine nature, to *only Christ truly*, to I AM that I AM, to the Buddha nature, to Divine Self, all effort is effortless effort—for the flow of divine energy carries both us and our provision. But when that inner judge is banging his gavel, silencing the truth, numbing the thoughts of awakening, we fear that we must continue to sing for our supper. And so we bargain: IF I work really hard, THEN I will keep the wolves away from my door. And so it is that we are condemned by our own inner judge.

And that's just a code! With regard to these so-called laws of the New Testament, purported to have been laid down by Jesus, who said he came to fulfill the law; the inner judge puts us in terrible and sometimes even life-threatening positions. I have literally known women—yes even today—who stay married to extremely abusive men, simply because they are being taught that if they leave their husbands, they are both causing their husband to commit adultery and will be committing adultery themselves if they marry someone else, and thereby they are in danger of hellfire! Some even appeal to family members to set them free, to help them get away from their abusive spouses, only to be told by mothers and fathers that they will not take them in, for to do so would be to support their "sin." So it is that the inner judge was ingrained in us by both the duality trance state in which we all participate, and by the parents who raised us to believe that this inner judge *should* dictate our actions, thoughts, and beliefs.

We fear living without a direct access to this inner judge, for we give him the credit for our power to control our behavior. Evil people that we are deep down inside, we are certain that without that criticizing and judging voice within us, we would be wild, rebellious, sex-crazed, murderous people. We need him on those walls—as Jack Nicholson so aptly told us in *A Few Good Men*. For outside those walls is the threat of hellfire in most Western religions, or the threat of bad karma in others. That inner judge keeps us from "sinning." But of course, he doesn't really, for even those people who use the inner judge on a daily basis to control their actions and thoughts, will confess that they "sin" frequently. But if I ask these people about the power of this judge, they will give him credit for keeping them from the bigger "sins," rather than just the "little sins" of omission, bad attitudes, and unloving thoughts, etc. And yet, if we look at the verses above, we might have to recognize that it is these inner "deeds" that are the issue of Jesus' sermon. And if we believe the traditional interpretation, they are just as *bad* as the outer deeds that others can see and judge.

We engage in all manner of double-speak when it comes to this thing of the inner judge: We need him, we hate him; society would fall apart completely without him, but he keeps us from trusting ourselves; he is bad, he is good; he keeps us from the bigger more venal sins, but he is a constant and incessant inducer of guilt, etc., etc. And the traditional interpretation of Jesus' lengthy sermon on the inner and outer man seems to make him absolutely essential—and yet, even then, even then, we cannot attain to what that sermon is traditionally interpreted to mean: We must be perfect.

Ha! Perfect. Who can do that? No one. And we all know this, at least intellectually. Yet many of us spend all day every day insisting that we should strive for it anyway. Others of us resent the word tremendously and all of its connotations, so that we spend most of our days finding ways to rebel against its meaning. And many others of us land somewhere in the middle rebelling some and striving for goodness some. The word perfect, as it is used in that text, seems to be self-explanatory, for it tells us that we should be perfect not simply in human terms, but as our "heavenly father" is perfect. And since traditionalists teach that God is absolute perfection, well, what are we to do? But the word *perfect* as it is used in this text is *teleios* (τελειοζ.), which means *brought to its end, finished, mature, full grown,* and it also means *wanting nothing necessary to completeness.* That's quite a bit different from our common definition of perfection—which means *never, ever making a single solitary mistake or "sinning."* The word is rooted in *telos* (τελοζ), which means *end, termination, the limit at which a thing ceases to be, the last in any succession or series, eternal, that by which a thing is finished, the end to which all things relate.* How does a person live in the eternal, and at the end to

136

which all things relate, be brought to completeness, be mature, full grown and the last in any succession while living right here on planet earth—for that is what we are being challenged to do?

We can do this if we suspend our dualistic ideas about good and evil, beginnings and endings. The best way to think of the meaning of this word is to use the phrase *the end to which all things relate*—except we should probably change the word *end* to the word *outcome*. The outcome to which all things relate is the knowledge of ourselves as divine beings. We come to know ourselves as *only Christ truly*. So, when we are being challenged to be perfect, we are actually being challenged to live into that outcome to which all things relate—live into ourselves as divine beings. We will not be perfect in the sense that there will be no "sin," because so-called *sin* has never been the issue. The issue is not whether or not we are *good* people; the issue is whether or not we know who we really are. And that has always been the only issue.

When being good or not ceases to be the issue, then we are able to see who we are and begin the mystical process of allowing the divine Self to be initiator of our behaviors, thoughts and feelings. This is not something we have to wait to have; it is something that is relative to its own outcome. In other words, there is no end, because there was no beginning—everything always has been and always will be one with the divine. The only thing that is missing is *knowledge* of that truth. So, we are not on a journey to become better people. We are on a journey of *knowledge*—and we will say much more about this knowledge later. But for now, suffice it to say that this term *perfection* means coming to know what is already known.

But most of us think of perfection relative to *goodness* or *badness*. And we make those concepts relative to futuristic outcomes, ultimate consequences. There's bad karma, and there's hell to be considered. And then there is the heaven for which we all long. To many, regardless of religion, heaven is that place to which we referred above—a literal place to which those who are saints, or who have been forgiven or saved from sin will ultimately arrive—but only after death. It is a literal place in the future. A place that we can only imagine here on planet earth. A place which is filled with glory and bliss, where there is no sin, no sorrow and no suffering. A panacea for all of the things over which we seem to have no control here on this plane.

The major source for our thoughts about heaven is in our sacred texts—or at least in our interpretation of them. In Buddhism, there are several temporary heavens—but they are still a part of the illusionary reality called *samsara*, in which we cycle from one life to another seeking to move beyond the cycle. So, if a man lives a good life, he may reincarnate into a heavenly life in which there is no suffering. But when he finally evolves through the karmic cycle to the point where he no longer needs karma there is another heaven to which he may go upon attaining enlightenment. In Hinduism, there are six heavenly planes where the gods reside. In the Hindi Vishnava traditions there is also a highest heaven above the other six, where those who have attained what they call *moksha*—or release from samsara—live eternally. In Islam the Qur'an speaks of an afterlife in Eden where those who do good deeds go to live in pleasure and bliss. In Jainism, there are several layers of heaven that offer different rewards to different souls. In Rabbinical Judaism there is very little said about an afterlife, though they do refer to a new earth on which humankind will reside after the resurrection of the dead. But they do believe that humans are rewarded after death for their deeds. The Kabbalah speaks of seven different heavens that correspond with the seven psychic centers of the body known to many Eastern religions and much of New Age/New Thought as chakras. And in Christianity heaven is a place to which those who have been reborn into a new spiritual relationship with the resurrected Christ, or those who have lived good sincere lives will go after death.

But as we can see, some of these refer to heaven as something that happens after death and others refer to it as something that can occur even as we live this life. In most of them, however, there is a consistent theme of reward that is pleasurable and that ends suffering. It is my belief that when we place this end of suffering in the afterlife it is because of the duality trance state — because we simply cannot imagine a planet earth in which suffering does not occur. And we simply cannot imagine that human kind would be "good enough" to live life here on this plane without doing something *wrong* or *bad*.

In Western traditions, and especially since each person is believed to have only one shot at life, the end of all suffering can only occur once we have left this mortal coil. But in all cases the end of suffering is the ultimate goal of heaven. Unlike some of the more complicated Eastern systems, the Western is quite simple. You do good or get forgiven and you go to heaven when you die; you do bad or refuse to get forgiven and you go to hell. Simple, black and white — very Western. The only problem is that I am hard put to find this anywhere in the Bible. Here are some of the ways that Jesus described heaven:

The kingdom of God is not coming with signs to be observed, nor will they say, 'Look, here it is!' or 'There!' For indeed, the kingdom of God is in your midst" (Luke 17:20-21).

The kingdom of heaven may be compared to a man who sowed good seed in his field. But while men were sleeping, his enemy came and sowed tares also among the wheat, and went away. But when the wheat sprang up and bore grain, then the tares became evident also. And the slaves of the landowner came and said to him, "Sir, did you not sow good seed in your field? How then does it have tares?" And he said to them, "An enemy has done this." And the slaves said to him, "Do you want us, then, to go and gather them up?" But he said, "No, lest while you are gathering up the tares, you may root up the wheat with them. Allow both to grow together until the harvest; and in the time of the harvest I will say to the reapers, "First gather up the tares and bind them in bundles to burn them up, but gather the wheat into my barn" (Matthew 13:24-30).

And:

The kingdom of heaven is like a mustard seed, which a man took and sowed in his field; and this is smaller than all other seeds, but when it is full grown, it is larger than the garden plants, and becomes a tree, so that the birds of the air come and nest in its branches" (Matthew 13:31-32)

And:

The kingdom of heaven is like leaven, which a woman took, and hid in three pecks of meal, until it was all leavened" (Matthew 13:33)

There are many more, but that will suffice for now. The first of these statements is not a parable but a very direct statement that the kingdom of heaven can be found within us. The single word for the phrase *in your midst* is *entos* ($\varepsilon\phi\nu\tau o\omega\zeta$), which means *within, inside or in your soul*. So, once and for all, let us suspend the notion that heaven is an external place to which we go after we die—for here, without the use of parable Jesus clearly tells us where we may find heaven.

But then Jesus also speaks about heaven in parable. Each of these parables speaks not of place but of process. The first speaks, from a metaphysical interpretation, of the fact that the kingdom of heaven was a part of our origin. The man *sowed* good seed. We were originally planted in the Garden of Eden, which we've already described as our internal awareness of ourselves as divine beings. But because of the duality trance state, tares grow along with the wheat, and these tares must eventually be weeded out, differentiated, and thrown into the fire. We'll come back to that fire in a moment. But there is this growth and this gathering up that speaks of process, and since we know that the kingdom of heaven is within—we can also know now that this process—this evolution—is within us. There is an origin, a growing of wheat and tares, the growth of each, a decision about what to do about them, and a gathering of wheat and tares, i.e., a process or evolution. And it is this evolution that describes the kingdom of heaven.

The second parable above tells us that the kingdom of heaven may only be experienced as a tiny spark of awareness within us, but eventually it will grow so big that even the birds of the field will be able to build their nests therein. The birds of the field represent transcendent thoughts that will eventually be able to inhabit that tree. Is that tree the same tree of Life, which originated in the garden of Eden—a place we've already discovered to be a state of awareness in which we know who we are as divine beings?

And the third parable tells us that the kingdom of heaven is like leavened bread, which even when divided, will grow until all is leavened. This is a strange analogy, given that the Jewish people ate only unleavened bread, and that they thought it a sin to eat leavened bread. But that is precisely why Jesus used this analogy. He meant to say that what we expect to be true will not necessarily end up being true. Is it possible that what appears to be sin to us, is just another way in which the kingdom of heaven is evolving within us? Can even our sins be our teachers? For most that idea feels like quite a stretch. But what we learn from this parable is that this kingdom is constantly growing. Not only that, but even through our divisions, the kingdom of heaven continues to grow within us!

It is important to note that in this same chapter of Matthew, from which we collected the above parables, Jesus also explains why he speaks in parables (13:13-15):

> Therefore, I speak to them in parables, because while seeing they do not see, and while hearing they do not hear. In their case the prophecy of Isaiah is being fulfilled, which says, 'You will keep on hearing, but will not understand; you will keep on seeing, but will not perceive; for the heart of this people has become dull, with their ears they scarcely hear, and they have closed their eyes, otherwise they would see with their eyes, hear with their ears, and understand with their hearts and return, and I would heal them.'

These parables are metaphors, which should be interpreted as metaphors. When we interpret these parables literally, we hear and see without hearing and seeing. And it does appear that this is exactly what we have done with the words like *heaven* and *hell*. If we look at the root language of the word Jesus used for *heaven* it is *ouranos*, (ουϕϕρανοωζ), *the vaulted expanse of the sky with all things visible in it, the universe, the region where the clouds and tempests gather, where thunder and lightning are produced, the seat of the order of things eternal, where God dwells and other heavenly beings.* Nothing in that definition says that heaven is a place we go after we die. As we've seen from Jesus' parables, heaven is within us; it is a growing evolving process within us. And if we put that together with the meaning of this word we find that this growing, evolving process within us is also *the seat of the order of things eternal* in our lives. This means that our lives are constantly being ordered by our souls, by divine Self, by I AM that I AM, by only Christ truly, by heaven within. But that's not all, we also see that from this growing, evolving seat of the order of things eternal, all things are visible. All things includes both duality and oneness. And so it is that the word is further rooted in *oros* (οροζ), which means *a mountain*—another place of strong and majestic transcendence from which we can see all things.

So, heaven is not an external place at all, but rather, an internal place in which, significantly, both wheat *and* tares grow, in which both visibility *and* clouds originate, in which we originate, and in which we evolve, as the seat of the order of things eternal makes decisions about our lives. And this process allows us to see all things. And ultimately heaven will completely overtake the mind of humanity so that even our most transcendent thoughts can inhabit that earthly consciousness. In other words, heaven is our evolving awareness of who we are as those divine beings we were originally, when we, as *elohyim* recreated ourselves as form. The evolution is in the recognition of form as divine beingness.

Heaven encompasses our entire evolutionary process. It enfolds us, so that we are never without it. It is the very soul of who we are. But unlike our previous versions of the soul as a small part of us, this soul is actually analogous to the egg white—while the life in duality is the yoke that will grow into fully evolved awareness. Rather than being a tiny pinpoint of spirit through which we might ultimately find truth—it is the truth that always surrounds and encompasses us, even as we lie to ourselves. Rather than being a part of the human psyche, which can be damaged and must need healing—it is actually the ultimacy of who we are—that though we may not know who we are, we nevertheless, are. The soul is our divine nature, and heaven and soul are synonymous terms.

But that damned fire, right? Jesus is said to have interpreted for the disciples a few of these very parables, and to have told them that:

the enemy who sowed them (the tares) is the devil, and the harvest is the end of the age; and the reapers are angels. Therefore, just as the tares are gathered up and burned with fire, so shall it be at the end of the age (Matthew 13:39-40, parenthetical comment inserted).

Taken literally, these terms intimate that there might really be such a thing as hellfire. But let's look again. First, traditionalists tell us that here Jesus is prophesying about the so-called *end times*, in which there will be a great divide between the righteous and the unrighteous with the righteous going to the literal place of heaven, and the unrighteous going to the likewise literal place of hell. But the phrase *end of the age* is much more significant. The *end* is *sunteleia* (συντεωλεια), which means *consummation*, and it is rooted in that word we saw earlier in Jesus' Sermon on the Mount when he said that we should be perfect, *teleo* (τελεωω), *to complete, fulfill* or *finish*. And the word age is *aion* (αιφωων), *forever, unbroken age, eternity, universe, age*. It is rooted in *aei* (αει), which means *perpetually, incessantly, invariably, at any and every time*. So, Jesus is not talking about end-times, but about a consummation that goes on perpetually, even incessantly.

We begin to get the hint here that eternity has nothing to do with time, in much the same way that heaven has nothing to do with place. Time and place are dualistic concepts about which eternity and heaven know nothing. Rather eternity is the energy of ever evolving consummation. We must remember that Jesus — and all of the other great Master-Teachers — did not operate in a world where time rules. They operated on the soul plane, where time does not exist. Master-Teachers operate in the perpetual *now*. So, when Jesus speaks of a perpetual consummation — what he means is that in the perpetual *now* whatever acts as a tare inside of us is perpetually being consumed or transformed in the all-consuming divine nature I AM.

But later in this same chapter Jesus continues to explain his parables to his disciples and it appears again that he is telling us of the torment of eternal hell. Read the following and weep:

The Son of Man will send his angels, and they will gather out of his kingdom all stumbling blocks and those who commit lawlessness and will cast them into the furnace of fire; in that place there shall be weeping and gnashing of teeth. Then the righteous will shine like the sun in the kingdom of their Father. The one who has ears let him hear (Matthew 13:41-42).

The most important sentence in this paragraph is the last one. Remember that Jesus told us that he spoke in parables because those who heard do not really hear, and those who could see do not really see. He is speaking here to those who can hear. Not to those who hear while not hearing. And the use of that sentence means that he has just spoken again in parable. And yet, if we know the root language, he is actually speaking much plainer than we have previously thought. The word used for *furnace* is *kaminos* (καωμινοζ), which is *a place for smelting, for burning earthenware, for baking bread*. That's pretty plain. The word does not indicate eternal punishment, but change, transformation—in that smelting is the process of producing a metal from its core; burning earthenware finishes the process of creating the plate, bowl or vase; and when we bake the bread we finish the process started with a recipe. But there's more. *Kaminos* is rooted in *kaio* (καιωω), which means *to set on fire, light, burning, to burn, to consume with fire*. How many fundamentalists refer to themselves as *on fire for the Lord*, yet in another compartment of their brains they use fire as having only to do with eternal punishment?

This furnace is a furnace of fire, *pur* (πυ'ρ), while the burning up or consuming by fire is *katakaio* (κατακαιωω), *to burn up, consume by fire*, rooted in *kata* (καταω), which means *down from, throughout, according to* or *toward*, and in *kaio* as above. This burning that transforms by consuming is thorough so that when it is done, a total consummation has occurred. And just so, our completion, referred to earlier in Jesus' Sermon on the Mount, is a consummation—a total consummation so that we are completely transformed.

Three very important things we should know about this consuming fire:

1. When this Gospel was written, there was no other form of light besides fire.
2. In Hebrews 12:29, God is described as a consuming fire.
3. In 1 John 4:8, we learn that God is love.

When we put all of this together, we may conclude that if God is both consuming fire and love, and fire is not only consummation but light, then God is all-consuming love and light. This means that the perpetual consummation that is occurring within us is one that gathers up aspects of ourselves in order to consume them in this love and light.

What is even more significant, if we open our minds to the metaphor is this: He tells us that all stumbling blocks and those who commit lawlessness will be gathered *out of his kingdom*. Out of is *ek* (εφκ), which is a primary preposition denoting origin—*out of, from*. In other words, the stumbling blocks and those who commit lawlessness were living *in* the kingdom of heaven when they were gathered. This means that the stumbling blocks and those who commit lawlessness, like those tares, are growing right alongside the wheat *within* the kingdom of heaven. And "just as the tares are gathered up and burned with fire, so shall it be" in the perpetual consummation. In other words, these stumbling blocks and law breakers exist *within* us as individuals, and they are being ever consumed in the all-consuming love of the divine nature in which they already exist. And they will be gathered together (or joined, perhaps even married?) to throw them into this furnace of fire in which they will be smelted (made into metal from their core essence), made into beautiful earthenware, and baked as bread. In other words, they will be transformed into their deepest, truest essence—divine nature. And though these parts of us may go unwillingly, kicking and screaming (weeping and gnashing of teeth), nevertheless, they will be gathered as a part of the perpetual consummation and transformed into their essence as divine beingness.

Isn't it so that we are often transformed into more awareness of oneness, by the very experiences that were created by the duality trance state? How many times have we grown more compassionate and wiser by being put through a fiery furnace of trauma and betrayal? How many times have we known life to be all the more meaningful because we'd come so near to death? This is the perpetual consummation that brings us to completion again and again, lifetime after lifetime, reincarnation after reincarnation. It is the process known to the Gnostics as divinization—a process which carries us through the duality trance state, allowing us to encounter each aspect of ourselves that remains stuck in dualism, resolving the issues therein little by little, reincarnation after reincarnation until we become more of who we originally were. But rather than simply returning to our original state, we will carry form with us, so that it is equally transformed into awareness of itself as divine. Not only that, but we will also carry with us the experiential knowledge gained through our encounter with duality. And that knowledge will alter the universe entirely. When the entire journey is complete for the collective humanity, both body and mind will forever after know itself as both form and divine.

But since it will be asked, we must pursue this notion of hell just a bit further. Later in the book of Matthew, Jesus uses another parable to describe heaven in which a person got into the King's son's wedding feast without wearing wedding clothes. The king tells his slaves to: "Bind him hand and foot, and cast him into the outer darkness; in that place there shall be weeping and gnashing of teeth" (Matt. 22:13). First, it is important to note that this is the son's wedding—not the King's. In other words, the parable implies that it is *our* wedding that is taking place as sons and daughters of the divine. This wedding, variously referred to as the union of opposites, the great wedding, the *hieros gamos,* the integration of humanity, the union of form with formlessness also happens perpetually in the eternal now. And such a sacred union abides no fakery. So, this man—who represents the part of us that is not prepared for such a union—is bound and thrown into the outer darkness where there is weeping and gnashing of teeth.

Traditionalists translate this binding and this outer darkness as a very personal and eternal hell. Since this darkness is an "outer" darkness, it seems to be the kind of darkness that can only be had outside of the kingdom of heaven. But let's look further. First the binding is important. The word *bind* here is *deo* (δεϖω), a root word that means *to bind, fasten, to put under obligation,* or *to bind as a husband to his wife.* We'll come back to that in a moment. The word *outer* is *exoteros* (εφξωϖτερο∫), rooted in *exo* (εξο), *without, out, out of, forth, outward, strange, away.* And that is further rooted in *ek,* which we previously knew to be a preposition denoting origin. So, it seems at first glance that the part of the human psyche that is not prepared for the wedding feast is then bound as a husband to his wife and taken back to his origins. Bound hand and foot, meaning totally bound so that there is no wiggle room. Indeed, we might all do a bit of gnashing and weeping when we are so bound by our own souls to experience something difficult that prepares us yet further for the wedding feast of our integration.

But let's take it one step further. The word used for darkness is *skotos* (σκοϖτο∫), *darkness, of night darkness, of darkened eyesight or blindness, or ignorance respecting divine things,* or *persons in whom darkness becomes visible and holds sway.* It is rooted in the primary word *skia* (σκια), which means *shadow, shade caused by the interception of light,* or more literally, *an image cast by an object and representing the form of that object.*

Where in the human psyche do we find our origins? In the

unconscious—or the shadow. We know the truth of our existence and our divinity there. So, this man is obligated by the fact of his already known union with the divine to explore his shadow material and come to terms with who he really is. Here in the darkness of the unconscious, illumination is possible. We see the darkness for what it is and we become enlightened—for a shade is only caused by *the interception of light*. So, when this unprepared aspect of us is sent into the shadow it is only meant to allow us to see, where previously we were blind; it is meant to give us knowledge where previously we were ignorant. There is nothing punitive and certainly nothing eternal in the translation of these words.

Many fundamentalist and traditionalist Christians talk about the *spark of the divine* within us. And they refer to God as *One God*. Taken literally, this means that there is only one God and it is the Christian God, but taken metaphysically, it means that God is a God of oneness. There is no divide in God. So, if that is true and it is also true that we each carry within us a spark of that oneness, how then will some of those sparks be sent off to an eternal separation in the form of hell?

While the concept of hell, as it is traditionally understood, has persuaded many a man, woman and child to go to church, temple or mosque, accept Jesus Christ as personal savior and lord, try to live a good life, sacrifice self for others, etc., it is entirely fear-based, and sadly (at least for those who so need it) utterly false. Just as there is no literal and personal devil, there is no hell in which he lives awaiting our arrival. This translation of the beautiful concepts introduced to us by Jesus (and several of the other great Master-Teachers) is entirely reductionist, for it reduces eternity down to a small, dualistic, painfully inaccurate version of life here on planet earth. Is God really so small and insignificant that he could create a world which is so utterly failed—even an eternity which is so utterly failed?

But what about when Jesus actually uses the word *hell*, as in

the above text when he tells us that "it is better for you that one
of the parts of your body perish, than for your whole body to be
thrown into hell" (Matthew 5:29)? The word used there is *geenna*
(γεϖεννα), which describes Gehenna or the steep, rocky Valley of
Hinnom, located southwest of Jerusalem, separating Mount Zion
to the north from the "hill of evil counsel" and the plain of
Rephaim to the south and used as a garbage dump. It is rooted in
the Hebrew word *gay* (גּיא), which means *valley, steep valley, narrow
gorge;* which is further rooted in *gevah* (גּוה), *pride, a lifting up;* and
that word is further rooted in *gev* (גּו), *the back, back, midst;* and in
ga'ah (גּאה), a primitive root meaning *to rise up, grow up, be exalted
in triumph, to be lifted up, be raised up, be exalted;* and *gab* (גּב), *convex
surface, back, back (of man), mound, convex, bulwarks, breastworks,
brow, eyebrow, rim. Geenna* is also rooted in *Hinnom* (הנּם), which
means *lamentation.*

Other than the word lamentation, we see nothing in any of
these meanings that indicates a sorrowful separation and
certainly nothing that indicates a place of eternal punishment.
What we do see is place that was used as a garbage dump, which
had a symbolic meaning of lamentation. But we also see a rising
up, and growing up, an exaltation and a triumph. How can this
be? On the back of humanity—behind his experiencing
consciousness and his convex or externalizing consciousness—
near both his heart chakra and his 6th chakra, or third eye (near
his eyebrow), is the ultimacy of our work here on planet earth.
We are growing into ourselves, but we do not always recognize
this, so that behind our lamentation, often unconscious to us, is
our growth and our triumph. Behind what seems to be worthy of
burning in the garbage dump is our growth, our rising up into
the upper chakras of consciousness. Again, we see only
evolution. We simply must begin to elucidate what was meant
here by these words heaven and hell before we can begin to really
let go of the duality trance state.

But let's take one more step now. Traditionalists have also

taught us that the word *Father*, as used so often by Jesus, defines God as a distant and external masculine figure-head of creation, who judges us harshly, while telling us he loves us; who needs us to serve him, though he is omnipotent, omniscient and omnipresent; who needs us to worship him above all else for he is jealous of anything we might put before him; and who demands our utter perfection, even though he put the tree of knowledge of good and evil in the Garden of Eden, knowing we would choose to sin against him. To those of us in the mental-health field, this description aptly defines a personality disordered and abusive individual. So, when Jesus refers to *your heavenly Father*, or *Father*, traditionalists insist that this personality disordered entity is Jesus' point of reference. But actually the word used most often in these references is *pater* (πατερ), a root word which carries a multitude of meanings, including *generator or male ancestor, father of the corporeal nature, natural fathers, both parents, the founder of the family or tribe, progenitor, originator and transmitter,* and *author.* So, in fact the term used by Jesus in this phrase refers us back to our origins. We might translate it best as *source.*

So, when Jesus tells us in Matthew 5:48 above, that we are to be perfect, even as our heavenly Father is perfect, he is actually telling us to return to full awareness of our source, of our original essence as divine beings, *elohyim.* He was saying that we are already complete — in just the same way that he said we were already the salt of the earth and the light of the world. He was telling us to remember who we are. And that can be done right now!

So, while we think that Jesus came here to tell us that we are sinners who need him to intervene for us, to pay the penalty for our sins, perhaps he was actually saying something quite different. Perhaps when he went over all the old laws with "You have heard that it was said" and then added, "but I say to you…" he was telling us that we'd misunderstood the whole thing.

Perhaps when he referred to the anger or lust in a man's heart, he was trying to tell us that the inner human was the most important aspect of a life. Perhaps he was telling us that the inner human cannot be legislated with external laws, and because that is so, the law was empty and useless before the enormity of the inner human. And once we could see that, perhaps he gave us the correct path—the simple solution to all moral dilemmas: remember who you are! *Perhaps his life—as a man clearly identified with his divine essence—was much, MUCH more important than his death.*

But because we are living entranced by duality, we look more commonly to his death to save us from sin. If he is telling us that we can return from the blindness of duality to see our origin in divine Self, however, then *good* and *evil* were not even close to what he was referencing when he spoke to us about right-eousness and completion. But we are so busy with the duality trance state that we are constantly judging ourselves and others along these lines of *good* and *evil*. And because we are, most of us think that our great Master-Teachers were using that same line of reasoning when they spoke to us. Perhaps this is why they used parables.

But we do find the word *judgment* in many of the sacred texts. In order to continue to expose a similar message to that found in Eastern texts, we continue looking at the root meanings of words used in the Western texts. For example, here are a few of the ways that Jesus used the word *judgment*.

John 3:17: For God did not send the Son into the world to judge the world, but that the world should be saved through Him.

John 5:22-23: For not even the Father judges anyone, but He has given all judgment to the Son, in order that all may honor the Son, even as they honor the Father. He who does not honor the Son does not honor the Father who sent him.

John 5:26-27: For just as the Father has life in Himself, even so He gave to the Son also to have life in Himself and He gave Him authority to execute judgment, because He is the Son of Man.

John 5:30: I can do nothing on My own initiative. As I hear, I judge, and My judgment is just, because I do not seek My own will, but the will of Him who sent Me.

John 8:16: But even if I do judge, My judgment is true, for I am not alone in it, but I and the Father who sent me.

John 9:39: And Jesus said, "For judgment I came into this world, so that those who do not see may see, and that those who see may become blind."

John 12:32: Now judgment is upon this world; now the ruler of this world shall be cast out. And I, if I be lifted up from the earth, will draw all men unto myself.

From the traditional and dualistic perspective on the word judgment, these verses could be very confusing, because on the one hand, they tell us that the Son (which could refer to either Jesus or all of humanity) did not come to judge the world. But then in several other texts we are told that all judgment has been given to him. How can this be? It can be, because saving the world *is* judging the world. Because duality has taught us that judgment means condemnation of some sort, and because Western traditionalists would have us believe in an eternal damnation that comes about as a result of divine judgment, we tend to believe that these concepts of saving and judging are as separate as we are from the divine.

In order to understand what was really meant by the term judgment as it was used in this text, we have to understand the phrase *day of judgment*, which was also used many times in the gospels. In fact the words, *judgment, day of judgment* and *justice* are all the same Greek word in the texts, except that one is a noun and one is a verb. *Krivsiß (Κρισισ)*, a noun, means *a separating, sundering, trial, contest, selection, judgment, opinion, or decision, a condemnation or sentence. Krino (Κρισνω)*, a verb means *to separate, or choose; to approve; to be of opinion, to resolve or decree; to pronounce an opinion.* We can see that the overall and most common theme of these two words is *decision*. In order to separate, try, select, choose, approve, resolve or decree, we have to make a decision. And very often in order to make a decision, we have to separate out various components of an issue, we have to differentiate, and then we can integrate. The integration includes approving of our decision and resolving the issue. So, more than anything else, we can be certain that when we see these words, a decision is being made. And, according to John 12:32, above, we also know *when* this decision was made. It was made while Jesus was here, "now."

The judgment day occurred when Jesus was here making his decision to live fully conscious of his divine Self, thereby overcoming his own duality trance state and making it possible for us to believe that we could do the same. This is what he meant when he consistently encouraged his listeners to believe in him. And this is exactly what he meant when he said, "And I, if I be lifted up from the earth, will draw *all* men unto myself." He lifted himself up beyond the duality trance state, he transcended it, and thereby *all* humans can see who they are. He spoke of this seeing, when he said, in John 9:39 above that his choice would enable the blind to see and the seeing to become blind. Those who see are those who see only duality. They will need to be blind to duality in order to transcend it. Those who are blind are those who do not see who they really are. They will need to see this, in order to transcend duality. And both things will happen to each individual as he evolves into full awareness of who he is. And this is the whole judgment, this seeing—a topic about which we will yet have much more to say, but one which is also referenced above in our description of heaven as the eternally evolving and consuming awareness from which we can see all things.

Again, we can find this same message, that we are divine Self, in the Eastern and Gnostic texts. But precisely because Western traditionalism, based entirely in duality, has removed the idea of divine Self from their translations of the texts of the Old and New Testaments, we must clarify them here. In fact, to traditionalism, the very idea of divine Self is worthy of intense judgment, the judgment of blasphemy—considered to be the worst sin of all. Traditionalists tell us that we are somehow taking something away from the divine, by acknowledging that we are divine. But we can clearly see in the above verses that we—as the "son of man"—have the same power of discernment as Jesus, and that we are to be honored even as the divine source is honored (John 5:22-23). Wasn't it he who also said, "You are gods" (John 10:34)?

It is important to consider the possibility that maybe we've misinterpreted these messages from one of the Masters as a result of the duality trance state itself. While we may blame the church, the translators, the political environment of the time in which the texts were translated and organized or any other number of things; the reality is that none of those things would have been in place without the duality trance state. So, without condemnation, I offer these new (to the Western world) paradigms of heaven, hell, judgment and human evolution, in order that we may begin to decide to stop judging and condemning ourselves and learn to inhabit heaven now.

7

Evil

Imagining ourselves to be fully united with our souls is like imagining that there is no gravity. We have an extremely difficult time with this concept. More difficult than that, however, is imagining that there really is no such thing as *good and evil*. Just try to have a conversation with anyone—religious or not—about this and you will see with what hostility such an idea is met. The most fascinating part of this response to me, however, is not in the emotion that comes with it, but in the fact that the argument does not try to prove goodness, but evil.

We are ready at every turn to look for it, and to find it. And so it is that the beginnings of these arguments usually cite historic *evil* leaders, typically the classic dictators, as proof of human evil. And since the more modern dictators and commanders of genocide are largely unknown—simply because we don't want to know about these horrors—evil leaders from the past are generally cited. Hitler is generally the first one to come up in the discussion. He commanded the death of millions of innocents, based on his *evil* nature.

It is difficult to argue with these things, for who doesn't have compassion for the millions who were imprisoned, starved, raped and murdered by the orders of this madman or by those who considered his hatred of the Jews or other populations to be tacit permission to misuse and abuse. And who doesn't have compassion for those who survived to tell about it, or for the families of those who suffered such intense inhumanity. And so it is easy to slide into the shallow end of the pool and simply say that Hitler was *evil*—of course, he was. What else but evil could commit such acts? But a deeper look at both Hitler and the complex context in which Hitler was allowed such power reveals something far more important.

Volumes have already been written psychoanalyzing the painful, humiliating, confusing childhood of this man, of the cruelty of his father and of the ways his libidinous dependence on his mother was encouraged, thus increasing his narcissism and hatred for his father. But don't worry, I'm not going to say that the poor fellow was doomed by his early environment to commit his atrocious deeds. That said, it does help us to understand that he'd probably developed a sociopathic bent long before he became the Führer. But what happened during Hitler's reign of terror was not just about Hitler's mental problems. It was much bigger, much more insane, and tells much more about the state of humanity than do any of the stories of his singular *evil*. In order to understand this we are going to have to come to understand what went on before, during and after the time of his rise to power, which serves not only as context, but as a driving force to the entire holocaust.

For example, what happened to the population of a nation that it could so ignore the insane and profane ramblings of this man, as he spoke to the masses? How was this missed? Didn't someone say, "You know, that guy sounds really nuts?" Why is it that so many were willing to do his bidding, even after they saw him, literally, frothing at the mouth?

What we know about the historical context that led up to the holocaust is that the end of World War I left the populace of Germany desperate and its economy on the brink of collapse. We all know that desperate people do desperate things. But there was more to it than that. It is well-known fact that the Treaty of Versailles left everyone unhappy. And the Germans felt that they took the brunt of the penalties distributed by that treaty. They were asked to pay in war reparations more than they could afford since they were already greatly in debt. So, they went into hyper-inflation mode and unemployment skyrocketed. The people ended up bearing the brunt and there was so much tension that it erupted into literal fighting in the streets. On top of that the political foundation of the country was very unstable with many of the populace believing that Germany would be the next to become communist. All manner of fracturing occurred and gang-like, agenda-driven parties sprang up with their own platforms, mostly having to do with restoring law and order. Many reasoned that order could only be restored if the people who created the chaos were punished. Many believed that the Jews were basically liberal, socialist and communist subversives who, from the home-front, had betrayed the frontline German militia during the war by pulling back support and otherwise sabotaging the effort—thus leading to Germany's current state-of-affairs.

Those historical facts are known to most, but what we most often do not consider when we ask whether or not Hitler was evil, is the fact that this context served as an emotional backdrop to Hitler's rise to power and subsequent atrocities. Not only were the people feeling utterly defeated, but having come from such a previous place of national pride, their new subordinate place in global affairs seemed all the more bleak and hopeless. What is the general manner of dealing with things about which humans feel so hopeless? The choices left to us in hopelessness are either depression or repression. And if we must get on with life, repression is generally the option of choice, albeit unconscious choice. In this case German society felt that going on meant regaining their previous superior position and its sense of entitlement. In order to do that, they had to repress huge amounts of psychic material—mostly the shame of their current insubordinate position—into the unconscious, making it what we call shadow material. The battle in the collective psyche of the German people was the battle between pride and shame. They repressed the shame in the name of pride—national pride, collective pride. Most commonly shadow material becomes the material of projection. And we can clearly see here that the

German nation was ripe for such projection.

So, when Hitler frothed at the mouth in his rage against the Jews, both in his book and in his speeches, instead of confronting the leader with his blathering, what did this society do? Since he appeared to be offering them hope to deal with the problem of shame (which in the unconscious triggers that ancient archetype of *evil*) they quickly and easily transferred this shadow material onto Hitler. He was to carry their shame for them and to remove it. He became the hope of retribution. Instead of using collective power to build back their country and raise their consciousness to new levels of heightened humanity, they did the shadow-dance. The shadow-dance is one in which we pass on shadow material to another and continue to dance with them as if nothing has transpired between us. Once the material is passed on, the original carrier is now free of it, and the new carrier must either find someone else to whom to give it, or identify with it and live it out in some way—or both. In this way, the collective could raise their self-image by becoming a Master Race through the transfer of personal and collective power on to this little raging man. They wanted a Utopia to compensate for the hell they thought that they had lived through—and he was just the man to give it to them. Hitler was being unconsciously assigned all of the people's power to deal with shame.

So what happened? Hitler's individual shadow, now enlarged by the projected and received collective shadow material, took on more and more of that power as he became more known and as more people passed shadow material onto him, until finally it became an identity: "My name is legion" (Mark 5:9)! Hitler's unconscious, which certainly was filled with his own personal shadow material—a mix of self-hatred and inflation similar to that of his country—was now asked to take on the shadow material he had collected from the masses, shadow material which matched his own. He could now be both the shame and the inflated desire to rescue from it, as a way of saving the collective from having to identify with it. And because no one can bear the enormity of such a powerful internal conflict between shame and rescue from it, he was then compelled to pass this huge shadow material on to another collective—the Jewish people and later anyone else who seemed to look like shame or like they had the power to shame others. How else does one person carry the shadow of a population, unless he is also able to pass that shadow on to another population? The Germans and later the rest of the world were largely unaware of the genocide that was taking place. And that is how the shadow-dance works. Out of sight. Unconsciously.

As we can see, Hitler had some leanings toward acceptance of this mass shadow anyway due to his inflated image of himself, empowered by his intense and ugly unconscious shame. *Mien Kampf*, published twice between 1933 and 1939, as I interpret it, shows clearly that he had merged in himself a kind of scapegoat plus political-hero complex. But the heinousness of Hitler's crimes did not occur in a vacuum. They did not just occur because Hitler was "nuts," or *evil*. They occurred because he was allowed to *be* nuts and evil for the masses, and was allowed to pass on that crazy evil to another mass of people. This is not merely an example of trusting the wrong person. It is an example of empowering *any* person to take on the shadow of a whole population.

What would have happened if his followers had said, "Did you hear what he said?", or, "Did you see what he did?" to others loud enough, often enough and with enough passion for the masses to begin to recognize the smallness of this man's character? And why didn't that happen? We have certainly seen examples of a population taking back their country from a malicious dictator recently in the revolution that deposed Ferdinand Marcos and in the death of Muammar Gaddafi. And we now know that there were some people who could see what Hitler was up to, and some who even made attempts to stop him.

But the majority was unmoved. They were unmoved because they all thought he was huge. They needed to believe that he was huge, for only hugeness could eradicate cultural shame. But he wasn't huge. He was just carrying around their huge power. Yet if they had taken back their own power, Hitler, bereft now of his mission, probably would have taken back his own shadow and killed himself a lot sooner.

So, was he evil? Well, if he was he certainly was not alone—in fact if we call him evil, we must, based on the facts cited above, also call the entire nation evil. But what if he didn't do those things because he was evil? What if he and others who joined him did this because *en masse* we have the capacity to pass around our unconscious yet fully empowered shadow material in a way that unleashes it on other masses of people? What if he was allowed to be the very essential ingredients of what we would call evil, because no one else in that collective was willing to own his or her own shame and do something about it? What if the problem isn't evil at all, but shame?

If we bring that first question down to the more personal, we must address other questions. For example, how many times have we feared a boss's power so much that we did not say to him, or to our peers, "This is unacceptable?" How many times have we allowed him to stand on our toes while yelling in our faces, either figuratively or literally, his own vituperative shadow material? How many times have we tried to slip around him to accomplish our own goals? How many times have we attempted to manipulate him to gain our own small modicum of power?

And why? Why did we fear a boss's authority so much that we could not say to her the truth or at least say it often enough to our peers until a group of us began to see and act on it? Why have we allowed her to abuse us and rule us by fear, when we are so clear about not being abused in other areas of our lives? Why can't we just act on truth instead of sneaking around her to do our jobs? Why do we feel we must manipulate her to gain power, instead of just gaining more personal power?

Are we evil? Are we good and the boss evil? Remember the adage "You can't fight city hall?" Well, *there* is a clear projection of power. We elect these guys, but we can't fight them? Something's wrong with this picture. We can fight them. We just don't *believe* we can. The reason is that we have projected our own power onto them. They now have the power to control our lives, but we *gave* it to them. Both literally and spiritually.

We have personal power to control our own lives, to live in a safe world and to assist in gathering together our peers to make this happen. We just don't exercise it often enough. We let *them* use it for us. We put them in office, often knowing little to nothing about them, and then we go back to our daily living, thinking of them only when they do something we hate. Then we sit around griping about dirty politics and cracking jokes on politicians, but they still have all the power, because we continue to give it to them. This is very similar to what happened with Hitler, absent democracy. The people gave him all of their power to find a solution to their problem of shame. In a different cultural and historical background than that which we now have in America—would we do the same?

But this argument is rarely-to-never heard by those who are trying to prove that evil exists by the merits of this singular man's atrocities. No, they can see the damage created by *evil*, they can see the abuses, the assaults, the crimes, the objectification of other humans, and they see how others' *evil* impacts them. Any argument with that reality is considered to *be* evil. It is interesting, however, when I ask these same people to come up with a like argument for good, they have a harder time with that. It seems that the only thing that proves that there is a battle between *good* and *evil*, is the evil we see.

Why is that? My theory is that we tend to want to see ourselves as good, regardless of what we've done, and anything that is against us and our efforts is seen as evil or the enemy. So, proving good doesn't really prove that there is a battle between good and evil, but the presence of evil does. But really, if there is such a battle going on, wouldn't it be important to find out who and what is the enemy of evil? And yet when I put this question to those who want to prove the existence of that battle to me, I typically get no answer at all. A wave of the hand and a complete dismissal usually follows.

In fact, what we are doing in arguing to prove this battle is trying to prove that duality is real. Like coming from a dysfunctional home to which we return repeatedly, both metaphorically—through adult relationships—and literally, we find the trance state to be a familiar place. Familiarity has a strong pull. I can't say we like it, but like a moth to a flame, we return to it again and again. And so, we need to prove that duality is truth, in the same way that we tell ourselves that the husband who is beating us only does it because he had such a bad childhood—he can't help himself, and he needs us to stay and fix him. In the same way that we deny our substance abuse, we deny anything that says that duality is not true. And so it is that we need to prove evil, not only in the external world, but also in the internal world.

As we were each and all being raised, we were being systematically taught that we should do certain things in order to be *good* people and that if we did certain other things, we would be *bad* people. Recently, over the past 30 years or so, parents have been being more or less taught that they should teach the child that what he has done is bad, but not that *he* is bad—for prior to that, little Johnny was told that he was a *bad boy* if he did certain things. But though some parents have learned to change the language, the feelings, connotations, voice inflections and body language that go with the new words, haven't really changed all that much. And because little Johnny is a child, he is reading more of those nonverbal cues, than he is hearing the words that go with them.

And so, each time a child is taught that something is a *no-no* or that it is *bad* or that she shouldn't do so and so, she is reading the fear in our eyes, the inflection in our voices and the hopes draining ever thin for her perfection. Some children will develop entire identities out of these mirrors, but others will simply be programmed—as we all have been—to understand that they are *good* if they do certain things, and they are *bad* if they do certain other things. Of course, none of what is said here is meant to imply that we should suspend discipline for our children, but rather to illustrate how we pass on the duality trance state. Children who are disciplined from a neutral position are taught to live from something other than duality. But since most of the population of the world still lives in the duality trance state, we pass it on to our children. And they incorporate our teachings way down deep inside so that mostly they experience goodness or badness as a vague feeling. And that vague feeling can actually become self-definition for some. Self-definition is identity. It's how we define ourselves.

That vague feeling is a bit like *free-floating anxiety*, a term invented in the 1970s and 80s as a label for unexplained anxiety. You can't really put a name to that feeling, you don't really know why you carry that fear in the pit of your stomach or hovering around your solar plexus, but there it is. It inhales and exhales like the tides, and it runs your life as if you are caught in its undercurrent. Similarly, the vague feeling of badness tells us that somehow we are or have been bad but we aren't sure what we did, said or thought that made us have this feeling of being dirty or bad or wrong. We may attempt to rid ourselves of that feeling by trying really hard to be good, but it always seems to be chasing us—so that we must do more and more good in order to replace that vague feeling of badness with another vague feeling of goodness. The other option is to identify with or define ourselves by that bad feeling—so that we must act out the badness to prove our existence. At bottom, the vague feeling of badness is one of deep-seated shame, and though we don't know how we came to it, it seems to tell us who we are. Most of us try really hard to hover somewhere around the middle so that we don't have to risk feeling too holy or too bad.

Nevertheless, this feeling is all that is necessary to get us to behave as others would have us to behave. All they have to do is look at us, for that vague feeling of badness to overtake us, so that we are compelled to do some compensatory *good* deed. For example, if Mary has plans for a nice Saturday, but her narcissistic mother wants Mary to come and take care of something for her, Mary, having been raised to believe that she is somehow responsible for her mother's well-being, may wish fervently to keep her own plans and say "no" to her mother. But that vague feeling threatens to overwhelm, and Mary, having had no more external trigger than her mother's call, caves to do her mother's bidding. Later, she is furious with herself for having caved, but the feeling is a siren call to crash into the rocks of the distant isolating island called shame. What Mary doesn't know is that if she would begin to disobey this siren call, even if it means tying herself to the mast of the ship of her own desires, the vague feeling will eventually lose its power. In fact, the more she caves to it, the more power it has, so that ultimately it controls her life choices.

Mary has been taught that her worth is dependent on her ability to serve others. She has incorporated this belief so deeply into the very marrow of her bones, that acting out her good deeds has become a rote response to just about anything that comes along. Others think that Mary is a truly good person. Mary thinks that others who don't follow her codes are really pretty bad people. But actually what is going on is that Mary believes that her survival depends upon her worth and her worth depends upon her ability to serve others. Survival became attached to worthiness because her parents used both overt and covert language to tell her that they needed her to *be good* for them so that they could be okay. Mary instinctively knew that if her parents were not okay, she would not be okay either — in fact she knew that her survival was dependent on their okay-ness. So, as a very young child, she began to emotionally take care of her parents, as they relinquished their responsibility to take care of themselves. Now, doing good deeds is a reflexive response to everything.

Yet Mary also harbors a lot of so-called *negative* feelings. She's angry and resentful of others who constantly seem to need her. And she hates herself for having these feelings because she knows that they are evidence that she is actually a bad person after all, even when she is trying so hard to be good. What she doesn't know is that these negative feelings are actually quite positive, for they are telling her that what she is doing is not really true for her. They are telling her that she is doing things that do not match her authenticity. And if she would listen to the messages behind these feelings, she could start living more authentically, more true to her real nature, rather than to this identity she's concocted to survive her parents' ineptness.

Other times, when because of our upbringing we've identified with the bad or evil side of the polarity, this siren calls us to secretly act out its urgings. In this case, Henry might carry that vague feeling with him until it begins to itch to come out into the open where he can see it. That feeling of deep shame calls him to act in secret but shameful ways — which he can definitely recognize as shameful. These actions may have escalated over the years to become more and more shameful, as he needs to prove to himself that he exists, by affirming that he is bad. For example, he might start secretly getting more and more involved in pornography, or he might steal things from his company, or he might start having secret and somehow profane and/or solicitous sexual liaisons. Or, in the case where Henry has been taught that "sin" is an ever-present potentiality, he may simply tell little secret lies, or find ways to eavesdrop on others' secret discussions, or secretly spit in the soup of a customer, either metaphorically or in the real. These seemingly small acts will be enough to activate shame for the person who is oversensitive to the potential for "sin." Either way, shame is not only activated, but validated so that Henry proves to himself that shame is the truth of his existence and is caused by certain actions. Each time it is activated Henry can also prove to himself that he exists—he has an identity—without which he is certain he would not exist at all.

Other times the siren calls us to act out in ways that validate it, grow it *and* also expose it to others. In this case, Henry becomes uncomfortable with hiding his shame. So, what he'll need to do is ritualize the exposure of his shame in a way that almost worships it. He may spend exorbitant amounts of time planning and plotting how he will show others the validity of his shame and invite them into it, or he may spend less time planning but still get fascinated with the idea before he acts on it. The planning and plotting, the fascination with what he's about to do, gives him a high and a concomitant sense of shame. In fact, he is high *on* the shame. When he literally exposes himself to others on the sidewalks and highways of the world, he does so only after getting a kind of high from the idea of such exposure. The time spent, however long or short, in imagining the doing, is a part of the ritual experience that worships shame, inviting others into that church of shame to worship with him. So, his mind plays with his options: Will he open his car door and flash someone; will he walk down the street and flash someone; will he masturbate on webcam or cell phone imagery; will he set up a customer service call on which he will masturbate; will he stand in his window naked? And then there's the act itself, in which he gets a thrill out of both his own shame and the reactive shame of his unwilling and often unwitting participant. And then there's the aftermath of the action in which he can live on his shame high for a while, until the cycle starts again.

Most people would say that Henry is evil—or they might use other more obscene terminology to describe him. But really, what has more than likely happened here is that Henry identified with shame many years ago, when he was a preverbal child. He was imprinted to shame. And as we've said about people who identify with the bad or evil side of the polarity, he quite probably did this as his way of surviving in a home in which he was otherwise invisible—and was, therefore, uncertain that he even existed if he did not become the bad person he sensed they needed him to be.

In the case in which there is a great deal of secrecy, or secrecy followed by exposure we might typically see this same pattern in childhood in some way. So, for example, let's say that Henry donned the cloak of invisibility over his evil or badness when he was so little that he can't even remember it. He knows he's evil because they have either overtly or covertly communicated this to him and he knows his parents hate his evil, so he hides it from them. But his parents are highly moralistic and feel that it is their job to stay aware of what Henry is not only doing, but thinking and feeling as well. So, for periods of time they badger him to expose his thoughts and feelings to them. They need to be sure that he is not morally corrupting in silence. They worry that he might be harboring some secret sin and are certain that it is their job to exorcise it from him. So, after being nagged for a while about what he is thinking, he gives them what they want—some small evidence of his sinfulness. Now he is satisfied because not only has he relieved himself of his burden, but he has punished them for their rejection of his authenticity in favor of this evil mask and costume he carries for them, *and* he has maintained an identity that allows him to assure himself that he is really alive. And of course, they punish him for his sin and then, thinking that they have done all that is necessary, they leave him to his invisibility again. The punishment is affirming for Henry because it assures him that he is real, for his identity got a reaction from his parents.

The fact is that these parents need Henry to carry that evil mask and costume for them for some reason. They certainly don't want it and, because of their hyper-moral stance on life, they cannot abide the thought that they themselves might have some "evil" lurking around inside of them, so they project all of that onto Henry and he gets the honor of carrying it for them. He really wants them to just love him for who he actually is—a soul looking for an identity here on planet earth. But when he looks in their faces, he sees only this projection. So, he comes to believe that this is who he is. As he grows he begins to do the very things they always suspected he was capable of and they punish him, often severely, for it. The more he hides it from them, the more they need it to out—so that they can be relieved of their projection—and so, they try to cajole and guilt it out of him. And the cycle continues.

In this particular identity, Henry sensed that sexuality was something that was really taboo to his parents, and so was compelled to incorporate it into his identity as a way of proving his badness and thus the fact of his existence. But he must also hide it for fear of their wrath. And as he does this his rage at his parents grows. They abandoned the real Henry in favor of this projection and while he might never know how to put that into words, he knows it and he hates both them and himself for it. So, as he becomes an adult this need to hide his growing compulsion is in conflict with his need to express his growing rage by putting his compulsion in their faces. And he can temporarily assuage this inner conflict vicariously now by first hiding his compulsion then exposing himself to others.

We can clearly see now that Henry is not evil, but he has totally misconceived and distorted his image of himself in order to survive in a home in which his authenticity was completely abandoned. Of course, this is only one example of how such distortions occur. But does this mean that we should feel sorry for poor Henry and excuse or overlook his behaviors? No, it only means that calling him evil is a very shallow and self-aggrandizing way of looking at it.

Calling Henry evil keeps us from having to look at both Henry and ourselves in ways that will allow us all to heal. Henry won't be healed by knowing himself to be evil. This will only compound his shame—enabling him to continue to escalate his behavior. But if Henry could ever realize that this identification is not his true Self, he could be healed. Henry has a Self that lives unrecognized and barely audible underneath this cheap mask and costume of the bad Henry. If he can find and begin to rely upon that Self, he will no longer need the other false one.

Calling Henry evil also gives us a sense that we are somehow different from him, and thus protected from his behavior. We build a psychological wall that keeps all the Henrys out there, so that not even the thought of them can come in here, where we live and breathe. Further, calling Henry evil allows us to see ourselves as better than Henry—so that by comparison, we end up feeling pretty good about ourselves. In other words, calling him evil doesn't even come close to scratching the surface of the truth about the cycle of shame in which we all live.

What we can see from this example is that there are two very important aspects of shame and its need to prove itself valid: 1) hiding the shame and 2) exposing the shame. In both of these ways the shame can prove itself to be a valid identification. If I spend considerable time and energy hiding my shame, some either small or large part of me is identifying with it. When I expose my shame I'm either pleading for help with my overwhelming identification with shame, or I'm seeking to expand that identification. In most instances it is a little of both. So, if I expose it, I'm both finding an unconscious way of demonstrating to myself and others how overwhelmed I am, thereby asking for help; equally relieving myself of it as it is expressed outwardly; and simultaneously hefting an enormous "up yours" to the parents who denied me any other identification. Since most of us feel ashamed on some level for feeling rage toward our parents, and since the exposure of our shame is yet more shaming, after such an exposure we will go back into hiding and the identification with shame will grow.

In the case where the identity is one of goodness, that goodness is compensation for that vague feeling of badness, and shame grows relative to anything we do which can be considered selfish (even down to thinking about the self), or otherwise bad. As in the case of Mary cited above, she will never expose her shame to others other than to humbly claim her right among the citizens of sin in this world. For example, she does not ever tell her mother of the shame that compels her to keep on doing what her mother wants rather than doing what she needs or wants. Rather she will hide it and cave to her mother's demands telling herself that this is the *right* thing to do. But later she may blow up on someone else—thus enabling the increase of her shame. This cycle will run her life until and unless she comes to recognize—not how weak, bad or shameful she is—but the cycle itself. When she can see the cycle as one which continues to confirm an identity, an uncomfortable one at that, she can begin to draw appropriate boundaries with her mother and take her life back from the devouring monster her mother has become.

The majority of us, living in that middle ground between badness and goodness, are quite willing to accuse others. But we are far more cautious about revealing those things we perceive to be our own faults. We will hide them, sometimes even from ourselves. We will keep them a secret, boxing them up like some unused piece of clothing in the very back of our psychic closets. We absolutely must not ever tell anyone about our shame—unless it is through some kind of confession. But for most of us, even if we know that others can totally relate and our life depends on confessing our shame to someone, we will still hesitate. If you want to see this fact in action all you have to do is talk to an alcoholic who refuses to continue to attend AA because it might mean she'd have to confess her shameful deeds to someone. She will go back out and use exorbitant, even lethal amounts of her drug-of-choice rather than confess to her shame.

But the cycle of shame runs even deeper than that, for if we ever do confess to something about which we feel ashamed—an action that is purported to free us from it—the confession only acknowledges and supports our shame. In other words, we don't recognize the power that shame itself has over us; we only acknowledge that we've done something "wrong" and that we *should* feel ashamed. This is the duality trance state in action. We don't realize that we are in a fatal cycle of shame, for if we did we'd have to recognize that shame serves only one purpose in our lives—self-destruction. Shame's only mission is to put us into one of these cyclical and desperate trances. We are hypnotized further into the duality trance state every time we obey the siren call of shame—whether it is through hiding, exposing or confessing. The very term confession implies that we've done something worthy of shame, which should be told to another and forgiven. While telling significant others the deeper and more hidden aspects of ourselves creates greater intimacy, if it is seen as simply confessing, it generally is only meant to assuage the desperate feeling of shame. But realizing the cycle in our own lives assists us in moving beyond shame, indeed, moving beyond the entire duality trance state.

Mostly, however, we stay on the cycle—whether in big or small ways—identifying by degree with either goodness or badness, because we believe that the cycle is correct. Whether we hide, expose or confess our shame, we are simply growing our connection, even our identification with it. And what is worse, we think that the correction of this cycle will be in our bowing to shame and obeying its urgings to feel bad, shameful or guilty about our actions, rather than to get off this nightmarish merry-go-round entirely.

In fact, there are many otherwise loving and wise people who still insist that there is a kind of shame and/or guilt that is essential to our well-being. They tell us that our feelings of shame remind us of our separation from God and call us home. And they tell us that feelings of guilt are necessary to inform us of our wrongful deeds. In fact, it is not just traditionalists who tell us this, but many New Age/New Thought leaders are also telling us that there is such a thing as "good guilt."

Let me be very clear here so that there are no misunderstandings. This book does not and cannot agree with that stance. Guilt always brings us to shame. There is simply no other place to which guilt can carry us. And shame has to do with how we see, not our deeds, but ourselves. Guilt tells us we've done something bad. Why do we do bad things? Because we are bad people, badness is in us—ergo our shame. Shame tells us that we *are* bad. And shame further convinces us that there is, indeed, a treacherous battle between good and evil going on and that there is really no way to win it—for just look at this mess I've made, how else could I have let myself do this thing but for the fact of my utter separation from the divine?

So, if feeling guilt and shame isn't helpful, then what do we do when we know we've done something harmful or hurtful to ourselves or someone else? Is there a more authentic and balanced emotional response to these actions? Yes, there is. It's called *compassion*. When we've done something to harm self or others, if we are open to it, we feel compassion for ourselves and/or others. This feeling is a form of passion and it pushes us to act—to act in rectifying ways or in ways that make amends and correct our actions in the future. Compassion is one of the strongest and most enlightening of our emotions, for it is quite direct in its push for action. Why, if we trust our compassion to guide us, would we need guilt and shame to help us to self-correct? But we do not trust our compassion because to trust the human heart is to assume that it is good, and we already know that it isn't good, so why would we trust it. No, better to trust guilt and shame to do for us what we refuse to do for ourselves.

In fact, shame and guilt blur compassion. They keep us tied to a narcissistic position in which our guilt and shame paralyze us or have us going about repentance in some kind of self-flagellating way. They do not bring us to a place of compassion. They keep us wallowing in the vanity of our own image. "Oh my God, I've done something bad, I must be a bad person!" Where is the compassion in such a vision of ourselves? In working with individuals in therapy about this issue of guilt and shame I very often find that instead of feeling compassion for either ourselves or the one(s) we have hurt, rather we feel embarrassment—another form of shame—for having been so stupid. So, we spend the next 2 weeks, 2 years or 20 years, telling ourselves how stupid we were for doing that and how we are never going to be that stupid again. Yet, because we have not yet had compassion for ourselves we have no clue as to why we did that stupid thing— thus we are all the more likely to do it again.

Further, if we've done something harmful or hurtful to others, instead of spending our time and energy feeling guilty and shameful, wallowing in our self-imposed, self-absorbed prison, wouldn't it be better to recognize our compassion and empathy for how *they* might be feeling? Wouldn't that compassion and empathy urge us to make contact, make amends and self-correct? No, we don't need guilt and shame. We need awareness and compassion.

In that same vein, all of our judgments toward ourselves or others are but shallow misinterpretations of reality. If we say, for example, that Hitler was evil—then we miss what was going on in the minds and hearts of the people who put him in office and kept him there. We miss the lesson of shadow-dancing. We may entirely miss the wonderful gift that this horrific time in our history has to give us. While we may say that we've learned the lesson and that these things could never happen again in our modern-day world, all we have to do is look around at the many countries in which it is happening right this very moment. We have yet to figure out that shadow-dancing is the cause of many of our global issues. We have missed the major lessons that bias, genocide and dictatorship, even power issues in general have to teach us, both about ourselves as individuals responsible for our own destinies and as collectives responsible to and for our worlds.

We fear, however, that if we stop judging we will also lose our powers of discernment. If I can't call you evil, then I might allow you to harm me. But recognizing the unconsciousness, or the manipulative and/or harmful energies of another human being is not the same as judging them as evil. Yet it still gives us the ability to choose what we are going to do with that information. In other words, we don't have to call the guy evil to recognize that he's trying to harm us.

We have come to believe in the magical thinking that calling him evil somehow casts a spell over him so that he can't come into our worlds. He becomes part of an amorphous *they*. And *they* are not allowed in our worlds where we go to church, temple or mosque and follow the rules. We will keep *them* out of our worlds through our judgments. *Those* immoral people go to the bars and crack houses, and stay out all night on the streets, whereas *we* don't do those dreadful things and so *we* are safe from *them*. Thus our judgments provide us an illusory wall that allows us to go no further into the depth of the problem than to give it a name. We've called it evil, isn't that enough?

So, we can see that our judgments are more based in fear than in morality. We want a method by which we can keep ourselves safe from things and people we don't understand. These same people have often seen more suffering than we can even imagine, but we don't take the time or energy to reach down into the depths of ourselves for compassion. No, we've built our wall and that's what we came here to do. Judgment allows us room for such illusions to fester and grow. And simultaneously, since we are all one, and each of us impacts the collective, we all take on just that much more shame.

On the other hand, we *do* need to recognize when someone is trying to harm us. I have worked with so many clients, listeners, and readers who think that if they are using discernment, they are judging and they've been taught not to judge others. So, in the name of righteousness, they are putting themselves in harm's way. They tell me that they think that they ought to give others the "benefit of the doubt," a phrase largely misconstrued to mean something more like *let them take advantage of and abuse me.* The benefit of the doubt means, "Oops! I'm judging, better stop doing that or I might have to think of myself as a bad person! So let me just give them credit where no credit is due." Just so, we tolerate the intolerable and accept the unacceptable from others. People who refuse to accept and utilize their own powers of discernment often live entire lives holding resentful bile behind their teeth, criticizing themselves for their resentments, and failing to recognize those very resentments as their savior. If they could see that resentment as a voice of authenticity—informing them that they are choosing to do, say and tolerate things that are not really true for them—then they could move past these lose-lose relationship dynamics.

Now if we look back over the last several paragraphs we will start to see one of the most hypnotizing of all of the double messages we get from believing in duality. We are to see shame and guilt as painful but worthy emotions that have a message to give us, but we are not to see anger or resentment as painful but worthy emotions that have a message to give us. Again, we can see that the weight is being put on the *evil* side of the good/evil polarity presented to us in the duality trance state. Anger and resentment are bad because—why? Guilt and shame are good because—why? We've not stopped to ask these questions, and why? Because to ask these questions seems to us to be betraying the very fabric of our connection to other human beings.

But if we stop to ask and answer all of these questions then we discover that the reason that guilt and shame are good and anger and resentment are bad is because guilt and shame remind us that we are bad and anger and resentment remind us that we are bad. Both sets of emotions lead to the same psychic place! We need to feel like bad people, in order to confirm that yes, indeed, we are separate from the divine. And why do we need to confirm that? The weight of the evil side of the good/evil polarity presented to us in the duality trance state offers us all kinds of secondary gain:

- We get to maintain our loyalty to a system of beliefs that connects us to others, without whom we fear we would feel alone and even abandoned.
- We get to use judgment of others to provide ourselves with an illusion of safety.
- We get to hide our own shame and guilt-inducing but insidious behaviors behind a blanket of deception that keeps us believing that we are still good people—but not so good that we could call ourselves divine, because to do so would separate us from those from whom we are trying to separate ourselves through our secrecy.
- We get to maintain our myriad fears as our primary modus operandi, because to not be afraid is to be even more afraid.

Can we see the convoluted complexes here? We can wrap our minds around this insanity, but we can't wrap our minds around the concept that our essence, our truest self is divine? The fact is that we need evil. Yep. There it is. We need evil to keep us stuck in the above miasma. And the best that it will ever offer us is the sitting in the bottom of the bucket with all the other crabs. Have you ever seen a crab try to climb out of a bucket full of crabs? It won't happen. Why? Because the other crabs will pull the little runaway back down to be with them again.

And so we remain seated at the bottom of our bottomless buckets and pushing ourselves back into the repetitive cycles of shame. Apparently, we plan to keep doing this until enough of us get it that the choice is not between good or evil; the choice is in whether to throw out the entire duality trance state and see ourselves for who we really are—or not.

8

Good

Since, in our most common paradigm of life, duality reigns weighted most heavily on the evil side of that polarity, goodness is very often defined by its lack of badness. In other words, when things are not so bad, they must be good. When people are not so bad, they can be called *good*. It is difficult for us to describe a good person, without at some point inserting that he doesn't do bad things.

Goodness, just like badness, is mostly defined within us as a vague feeling. We feel good when we've done something good. Very often in speaking to clients, they will tell me that they've done something that they resent having done, and I ask them, "What was the first feeling you had, when you finished doing it?" Oh, they can answer that one very quickly: "I felt good." "What does that mean?" I ask, "Did you feel good as in peaceful, or joyful or loving or calm, or do you mean that you felt like a good person?" More often than not, they tell me that they felt like a good person. So, what has happened in these cases is that the client did something out of a compulsion to feel like a good person, but simultaneously, she was building resentments, because she did not really desire to do this thing that she did — purportedly in the service of someone else and out of a sincere desire to serve.

That compulsion to feel like a good person is huge. And very interesting. How does one feel *like* a good person, unless one has a very clear and internally resonant definition of what a good person is? Feelings arise in response to an idea or supposition we have, or in terms of a simple authentic generation of emotion. Feeling *like* something is the former, not the latter. Feeling *like* a good person comes about as a response to a notion about what a good person would or should do. It is not authentic, simply because it is an imitative response. But it is also not authentic because it is based in an effort to do something which one expects *will* generate that feeling. In other words, it is contrived.

Many of us, not all of us, but many of us need to generate that feeling frequently so that we can allow ourselves to believe that we *deserve* to be here on planet earth. That's another concept largely associated with the term *good*. We have come to believe that we must *deserve* our lives. This concept is birthed directly from the loins of the duality trance state. Those same people who largely believe in a literal Garden of Eden, in which the first humans were provided their food, drink and supplies without ever having to work for it, insist that now we do have to work for it. And the work is all about striving to be good. If we do that well enough, then we deserve good things to happen for us. If we don't, well, we should not have those good things.

Of course, that all goes topsy-turvy when we realize that many of the best things go to the people who are stealing from others, selling drugs to others, and committing all manner of great *evil*. But that's easy to rationalize, we just sigh and say, "Well, that's the way of the world" —the world which is ruled by the devil.

The concept of deserving is one of the hardest beliefs to dispute. We have all—regardless of religious persuasion or lack of same—been weaned on this one. But what it really means is that many of us absolutely will not allow ourselves to have and really relish in a pleasant experience until we sense that we deserve it. Of course, the concept of *deserving* is relative to our backgrounds and conscious, unconscious and archetypal associations. So what it takes to give us the sense that we deserve the good thing varies. But we are definitely looking for a sense of it— another vague feeling.

The other part of this equation is the sense of what is and isn't a *good* thing. So, for some a million dollars is a good thing, but for others, desiring a million dollars is too materialistic and we should not even be thinking of such things. For some having a baby is a good thing, for others it is an unwanted thing. For some marriage is a good thing, for others, no, they don't want any part of it. Confounding this is the fact that what is defined as a *good thing* can change as we evolve into our lives.

Regardless of all of these confusing definitions and messages about life, we are, most of us, striving to attain whatever good thing we desire. We may desire it for a multitude of reasons, none of which may be authentic, but nevertheless we are still striving for it, in fact we are almost compelled to strive after it. There is an entire chapter dedicated to sorting out the fine distinctions between authentic desire and inauthentic desire, in the book *The Law Of Attraction: The Soul's Answer to Why It Isn't Working And How It Can*. So, I will not detail that same information here, except to say that the inability to make those distinctions further complicates our definition of the word *good*.

So, now let's go back and try to sort some of this out. Let's start where we started: goodness is mostly defined in terms of its feeling content. Ever wake up in the morning in a foul mood? Ever wake up in a good mood? What is the difference? Feeling. Moods are feelings that dominate our thoughts, words and behaviors. Who knows what we dreamed in the night that caused us to wake up feeling either good or bad, but that's how we woke up, so that's how we feel. On a day in which we wake up in a good mood, or even later find ourselves in a good mood, we are more likely to do good deeds for others, without complaint. On another day, when we are in a bad mood, someone might ask us to do the exact same thing, but we either won't do it, or we do it grumbling. What is the difference? Feeling.

We didn't do those good deeds because we were highly moral people who live principled lives dedicated to serving others. We did those good deeds because we felt like doing them. But if someone were to ask us if we should do these same good deeds on a day in which we don't feel like doing them, most of us would answer that yes, we need to check our attitudes at the door and just suck it up and do it. And if we do that, for just few minutes after we do it, we feel *like* good people. Why is this? It is because we have certain ideas about what good people do.

As we said, these ideas may vary but these associations lead us to believe that we are good people *because* we did x, y, or z. Good people do x, y, and z and so when we do them, that makes us good people. When I work with people who are making these associations, I frequently ask them, "So, if you didn't do x, y, or z, that would make you a bad person?" Well, it wouldn't necessarily make them bad, but it wouldn't make them good—that's for sure. But if we pursued this line of reasoning we'd have to say, "How do you know?" How do we know that doing x, y, or z makes us into good people? Most people, if asked to run down this rabbit hole, will cite some rule, code or text that tells them that doing x, y, or z makes them into a good person. Of course the text, code or rule doesn't say *specifically* that doing those things makes them good, but it gives a general idea, so I guess that works, yes?

So, let's take that a step further: If we didn't have the text, code or rule to go by, how would we know it was good to do x, y, or z? Many people would respond to that question with something like "But we do have the rule, text or code, so that question is too hypothetical to answer." But if we push, ever so gently, most would have to admit that it is this vague sensation, this feeling *like* a good person—based on associations we've made with what goodness means—that is the most convincing of all.

We are looking for that feeling. We want to carry that feeling around with us all the time. And if we could, regardless of what we did, we'd still feel like good people. I'm thinking that probably Mohammad Atta and his cohorts, who flew the planes into the Trade Towers and the Pentagon, had that good feeling about sacrificing themselves for their fundamentalist cause. Of course, we'll never know, but given the fact that we often sacrifice ourselves for some good deed we really don't want to do, in fact hate doing, but which promises to make us feel like good people, I would not be surprised at all.

So, in much the same way that we can define ourselves as bad people based on a vague feeling of shame, so it is that we can define ourselves as good people based on a vague feeling of goodness. And many indeed have sacrificed entire lifetimes, seeking after this feeling compulsively. Let's take Jerry, for instance. Jerry thought it was her mission to take care of her addicted child, Thomas, by allowing him to live with her instead of going to treatment and a halfway house. Jerry told herself that she was being much more loving than anyone else in the family. They just wanted to abandon poor Thomas, but she was loving and kind and was willing to sacrifice herself for the needs of her child. In fact, Jerry divorced her husband and Thomas' father because he was insisting that Thomas—a 25-year-old man— should not live with them, but should go to treatment and get some help for his problem. But Thomas didn't want to go to treatment, said there were bullies there and thugs and he could not be around those people. Yet Thomas hung out with dealers, who were largely bullies and thugs, many times a week, and he stole from his mother on a regular basis to get enough money to buy marijuana and other street drugs from these bullies and thugs. She'd get mad at him for stealing but chalk it up to the notion that he needed some form of independence, but poor thing, he couldn't work because he was too sick. So, when he stole from her, she'd lecture him and cry, but then forgive him, because she understood him. No one else really understood poor Thomas. And she never stopped to consider the fact that he might be lying to her about his reasons for not wanting to go to treatment. Mainly this was because she needed to feel like a good person.

In fact, Thomas was addicted to prescription drugs—"his

medicine" according to his mother. And he compulsively came up with one illness after another, visited one Doc-in-the-Box after another to get his prescriptions. And when he couldn't get those, he used street drugs—and later began to use street drugs in combination with his prescription drugs. Jerry went to church every week and served in some important positions in the church, but never told anyone at the church about Thomas. In fact, Thomas had her keeping all manner of secrets for him. Actually, Thomas was not only stealing from his mother, but also verbally abusing her, and on occasion, she thought he might actually even hit her. But then she'd tell herself that she was being foolish and that love conquers all fear, so she should just get over it. Still, she knew enough not to tell anyone else, because they'd just tell her to abandon him and she was a woman of love and she would not do that.

But as Thomas' addiction got worse and he ended up overdosing several times, her family intervened to tell her that she was actually helping him to die. They talked to her repeatedly trying to get her to give it up and get him to treatment, but she insisted that she was going to love him out of it. Yes, okay, maybe he did have a problem after all, but love conquers all, right? Eventually he even began to get high in front of her, to the point of passing out. And she'd just either try to walk him to his bed, or cover him up and leave him there till he slept it off. She told herself that if he died, he'd be better off, because, poor thing, he just couldn't help himself. They'd told her he had a disease, hadn't they? So, he was just a helpless victim of his disease and all she could do was love him through it. Thomas eventually did die of an overdose. And Jerry? What did Jerry do? She went around telling family that he was in heaven now, a better place—he'd suffered so, and she was glad that he was better off. Of course, she never told anyone in the church why or how he died. And many of her friends unwittingly reinforced her behavior by telling her how selfless and giving she was.

Jerry told herself that she was being a good person because she felt like a good person. And she felt terribly guilty for ever having a single resentful thought about poor Thomas. Further, she thought that "turning the other cheek" meant tolerating the intolerable, accepting the unacceptable, and attempting to do the impossible. She thought it was her job, here on planet earth, to sacrifice herself for others. She was not to tune in to the voices screaming within her to look at reality. She was to love and to continue to love, even when love had turned to a huge, nasty ball of resentment sitting on her chest at night keeping her from breathing. She was to stuff her anger and refuse to see the danger to herself and her son, all in the name of love. And once she figured out that he really did have a problem, she believed that "God put this situation in her path," and she (not Thomas) was supposed to deal with it. She was just supposed to forgive him his abuse and continued thievery, and she was supposed to cure him with her love alone. She told herself and others many times that she was on a spiritual journey and that these were her lessons along the way. And some of her listeners even believed her. These things made her feel "good about herself," whereas imagining confronting him with his addiction, abuse and thievery made her feel guilty. Besides, he didn't want to go anywhere for help—in fact, he swore to her that he didn't need help—all he needed was for her to keep being the only one in the world who "understood him." And then, he died of being so understood.

In fact, what was really going on with Jerry was that she needed Thomas to stay dependent on her. She'd unconsciously decided long ago that Thomas was her only reason for living. And when he became an addict and his father started confronting him and trying to get him to go to and then stay in treatment, she felt really threatened that she was going to lose her son's loyalty. The truth is that she was in an emotionally incestuous relationship with her son, in which he began, in her mind, to take the place of her husband. So, if he got clean and sober, he'd probably grow up, move out, get a job, get a wife and children and become an independent person. But she couldn't have that. If he did that she would have no reason to live. So, she allowed his manipulations and put up with his abuse and theft, and ultimately helped him die, because that was far better than the other option—which was to recognize that she was lonely and empty and needed a life of her own. After he died, she could live on the sympathy of the members of her church and be seen as a righteous, giving and loving person, who had experienced a tragic loss. Even though she was now alone in her home—as she would have been if she'd encouraged his recovery and he'd managed to grow up, and become independent—she was still living off of the fumes of his absolute loyalty to her even to the bitter end. In fact, he was not loyal to her at all. His loyalty was only to his drug-of-choice and she was just one of the ways he was able to continue to get his drug-of-choice.

Or, what about Alice, who spends her adult life babying her adult daughter and trying to manipulate her into coming back home to live with her, and bring her children, so that she can raise her children too? She calls this love, and anyone who doesn't agree with her way of loving just doesn't understand how powerful her love for her daughter is. Loving her daughter this way makes her feel like a good person, and when she has resentful thoughts over the fact that she "has to" wait on her daughter hand and foot, she feels terribly guilty. Her daughter, having been raised this way and therefore, not having any way of knowing that her mother is a psychic vampire who really wants to take her blood and live off of it, believes that her mother's love is the only true example of love. She spends her life demanding that others love her this way too: waiting on her hand and foot, giving her every single impulsive desire, fixing it so that she will not ever have to face a single hard thing in life. Alice says to herself that the tremendous load of work she is doing justifies everything else that she does. Hopefully, her daughter will eventually figure out what's going on, and break free of her mother's attempts to subtly and seductively control her. Time will tell. But Alice, like Jerry, is getting her daughter to fill in the blanks in her own life.

Or, how about David, who has given up his life, because he couldn't fix his father's life? His father died in an automobile accident. He was driving under the influence and passed out at the wheel, taking not only his own life, but that of two other people in the other car. David feels responsible. He feels that somehow he was supposed to get his father to stop drinking and if only he'd been able to do that, both he and his victims would still be alive today. David sits in his house, refusing to eat, has quit his job, rarely speaks to his wife and children and is consumed by this thought. David is living out of a faulty belief that if he moves on with his life, he is betraying his father— whose life he was supposed to fix. He believes that this thing that he is doing is the best he can do for his Dad. His wife thinks that he's just grieving, and that eventually he will get over his grief and move on. But David refuses to take medication or seek help—because he believes that to live his life means that he's getting to do what his father didn't get to do—and it's all his fault. The thought of getting up and living makes David feel terribly guilty, and even though giving up his life is hard, doing so makes him feel like he's finally successfully doing for his father what he couldn't do while he was alive. This is David's very distorted version of love—and he thinks he's absolutely right to do it this way.

David got raised by his father to believe that he was responsible for taking care of him. This is a very hard pill for a young child to swallow, and children who are put in this dynamic develop all kinds of distortions around such an assignment. David was hypersensitive to every tiny movement of his father, thinking that each movement meant something, and he was supposed to figure it out and make it okay. And he was rewarded for his sensitivity with a close relationship to his father. So, as children typically correlate reward with the rightness of a given behavior, David became programmed to believe that he was absolutely responsible for his father. What David didn't know is that most alcoholics or addicts seek out someone on whom they can become very dependent so that they can continue to use substances without consequence. And as David, as well as Jerry in the story above, continued to block the consequences to his father's addiction, his father's addition got worse, until he finally—after several other DUIs—killed himself and others.

David believes that his father's death and the death of those he killed are his fault because he didn't fix his father—he didn't make his father happy enough, didn't take good enough care of him. If he had, he thought, his father wouldn't have been an addict. But actually, David is responsible to some degree for his part in what happened—but not for the reasons he's outlined in his head. Rather he is responsible for not getting out of the way of the consequences. Who knows whether or not his father would have continued in his addition if David had stopped trying to fix him? His father could have just moved on to find another caregiver—and that is the most likely option. But David continued to make sure Dad didn't experience any consequences of his addiction, by bailing him out of jail, lying for him, covering up for him and trying desperately to get his Dad to be pleased with what he'd done for him. Of course, Dad was never really pleased; he just wanted another drink, please. But even as an adult and even after his wife and other's tried to tell him, David refused to see this—and for that, and that alone, David is respon-sible. Yet, David is too busy still, taking responsibility for his father's life, to take responsibility for his own. And until he does that, he will continue to stay stuck.

One less dramatic example is that of the dutiful daughter, Helen, who always does her duty, even though she really hates doing it. Helen is constantly about the business of doing good, taking on responsibility for others' happiness, feeling guilty and obligated when they are sad, doing far more than can be done in a single 24-hour period by most, simply because to stop and rest would mean feeling guilty. But her parents raised her to be a "good daughter," which means that Helen had to be there to make sure they were comfortable and happy at all times. Of course, she's never considered this to be a problem at all, for not only did she receive affirmation and approval from her parents but she's received loads of praise over the years for her goodness and her self-sacrifice.

But one day Helen arrives in a psychotherapist's office with high blood pressure and a stern warning from her doctor about the potential for a heart attack. She's depressed and angry and only hates herself all the more for these feelings and she can't imagine why a loving God would let her get sick, when she's been so good all of her life. Over time spent looking internally instead of focusing externally, she begins to learn that she feels guilty all of the time and is pressured by guilt—not love—to conform to its demands lest she feel all the more guilty later. She begins to see that she has lived a life of trying to serve others, not because she really wanted to serve others, but because doing so made her feel temporarily like a good person. Of course, that feeling didn't last very long, because the feeling of being really bad at the core kept creeping back in, so that she was again compelled to do something good in order to be certain that she maintained her self-image as a good person. She cannot say "no" to anyone, ever, and if she even thinks of it she begins to feel guilty. She feels resentful and used all of the time, and cannot understand why she cannot make these terrible feelings go away. The truth is that Helen has been being slowly devoured by her compulsive drive to feeling that vague sense of goodness, however temporary. In fact, Helen is just as addicted to that feeling as the drug addict is to his high. And yet, the world looks at Helen and declares that she is the very model of selflessness and righteousness.

These are all fictitious composite examples of how we get love and righteousness mixed up with blindness. These people would all say that they did the right thing in trying to save, salvage or serve another. And the results are or are very likely to be quite similar: some form of devastation. And they all did what they did in search of that vague feeling of goodness. Yet, as we can see, the games they were playing have nothing to do with love or goodness at all. Even in David's case, in which he was only playing the games he'd been taught to play, he continued his denial of what was going on way into his adulthood, and gave up responsibility for himself, his wife and his children, all in the name of that game. And yet, he feels like a better person for giving up on his own initiative, and would feel terribly guilty if he got up off his duff and began living. These people have convinced themselves that guilt is the way to manage a life. And they can only get that vague feeling of goodness when they are not having that vague feeling of badness given to them by their master, guilt.

Even in Jerry's case, in which her own distorted needs were actually running the guilt that she felt, the guilt nevertheless kept her in line. Poor Thomas needed her. And she couldn't even imagine sending him to treatment, or kicking him out of her house for stealing her things, because there was this foreboding guilt looking her in the face and staring her back into compliance. If she could have ever moved beyond the guilt, she might have seen the games she was playing. But guilt held her utterly hostage. And it helped her son give up his own life.

Now, obviously I've cited some of the most dangerous examples. Not everyone's search for that vague feeling leads us to the precipice of death in such dramatic ways. But you can see that even in the case in which Alice's daughter was getting all those wonderful perks by staying stuck in her mother's guilt trap, the daughter was still not likely to recognize the consequences of her choices until and unless she found herself involved with someone who would call her on her programmed narcissism. And since the daughter now believes that her mother's way of loving her is the only true form of love, and that basically her mother is the only one who will continue to give it without confronting her with her narcissism, she is more and more likely to do what her mother's wishes for her to do, giving up her own authentic life to be babied by her mother. And even in the case where Helen was serving others endlessly, the object of the game was to feel like a good person, even if it made her sick to do so.

This definition of love and what is considered by many to be unselfishness are two of the most efficient methods of manipulation on the planet. Think of the soothing and "love" given by cults, as one outstanding example. And just throw the word *sacrifice* into the mix and you have arrived at the most righteous of righteous ways to get that vague feeling of goodness. Thus, the bargains we make with ourselves go something like this: *IF* I demonstrate complete unselfishness, *THEN* I can call myself a really good person. And *IF* I take that one step further by demonstrating sacrifice, *THEN* you cannot ever call my actions, thoughts, words or feelings into question—because if you do, I can always throw out the trump card: I've sacrificed.

Since the days in which we sacrificed to the gods so that they would give us a good strong wind for the sail, a good crop or a good season, we've believed that sacrifice is essential to our relationship with higher powers. And we've interpreted many of our religious texts to include sacrifice as a part of our current understanding of how we should interact with higher powers. Not only are we to sacrifice to prove our love of said higher power, but we are taught that the son of God came and sacrificed his life for us on the cross so that we could be forgiven our sins. And we continue to believe this in spite of the fact that before Jesus was ever born the God of the Old Testament and the Father of Jesus, said: "For I desire mercy, and not sacrifice; and the knowledge of God more than burnt offerings" (Hosea 6:6). And Jesus, himself quoted this very passage again in Matthew 12:7, when he said: "But if you had known what this means, 'I desire compassion and not a sacrifice,' you would not have condemned the innocent."

That last statement made by Jesus was made in the context of a discussion with the Pharisees when they accused him of breaking the Sabbath laws. He told them that David went into the temple and ate of the shewbread — breaking the law to do so. And he reminded them that the priests profaned the Sabbath in the temple and were yet held blameless. And then he made the most interesting statement of all, just before the above statement. He says: "But I say to you, that something greater than the temple is here" (v.6). This profound statement basically assures us that the law, the temple and all of the accoutrements of religion are nothing by comparison to the I AM within each of us.

But just as the Pharisees accused Jesus, as one of our best representatives of the I AM nature in all of us, we accuse ourselves. And so it is that we are looking for that vague feeling of goodness and that powerful feeling of guilt to be our only guides. And so it is that sacrifice, not mercy, has become the biggest trump card of all when it comes to convincing ourselves of our goodness. The more we give to others, especially at our own expense, the more we can convince ourselves of our worth. And the more we allow guilt to keep us within its reign, the more we can assure ourselves that our worthiness is still intact.

Further, the fact that we are seeking to sacrifice ourselves in the name of proving our worth makes it very easy for others to manipulate us using our same terminology. "If you loved me you would…" that's a good one; or how about, "How can you say you love me when you…" Or, the trump card of all trump cards, "I've sacrificed all of this for you and this is how you treat me?" When I worked in three different rehab units in the past, I heard these kinds of statement used all the time against truly loving parents and spouses who were simply trying to offer the correct assistance to their family member. "If you loved me you wouldn't leave me here with all these homeless people!" "How can you say you love me when you lie to these people and tell them I've done all those things I never did!" — things which, of course, they did do. But I also heard it on the other side of the equation: "I've sacrificed all of this time, energy and money on your addiction and you won't even try, you won't even TRY to get recovery!" Yeah, it works when you work it.

The truth is that if we stopped to check in with ourselves we'd find that a multitude of our efforts to be good, particularly those in which we are sacrificing ourselves, were really just attempts to manipulate others into liking us, respecting us or even doing what we'd like for them to do. Some of the examples given above demonstrate a literal sacrifice of years of life in order to "take care" of someone who was using them — all in the name of being seen as a good person, a righteous person, while covering up the emptiness that creates solicitous attachments. Very often when these issues are explored in therapy, what we learn is that when a person carries, deep down, a feeling of inadequacy or wrongness, they try to eradicate it by doing many good things. The bigger the good thing, the greater the hope of erasing that vague inner feeling of badness. So, sacrifice works really well here. As we saw in Chapter 2, however, sacrifice is just a game we play with guilt or the vague feeling of badness. Just so, good deeds are often just a compensation for bad feelings.

But some would say, well why not? I mean if you are feeling like a bad person — why not go out and do something good for someone else. Get your mind off yourself and get busy serving others! And for some who live in self-pity and a victim identity, this might actually be somewhat therapeutic. But many people who carry around that vague sense of badness actually think that they are feeling self-pity anytime they even think of themselves in any compassionate way. Why? Because thinking of the self has been labeled as *selfish* and therefore *bad*. So, telling these persons to go out and do good deeds, means repressing still further their usually massive resentments and manufacturing feelings of love so that they can go and do their duty. But when we think in traditional terms of *good* and *evil*, we tend to also prescribe very black and white forms of healing with a one-size-fits-all capacity.

Yet, it isn't true that all so-called *good* deeds come from some duplicitous motive. Very often the deeds that are called *good* come from sincerity, compassion, love and other genuine emotions and thoughts. The problem with this, however, is that we don't call these deeds *compassionate deeds*, or *loving deeds*, or *genuine deeds*. We call them *good* and we refer to the people who do them as *good* people. They are good because they do good deeds. Of course, we often don't know what else the good people are doing. It is possible for people who are hit men for the mafia to do kind, generous, compassionate deeds, at least from time to time. But if we see them doing *good deeds* and do not see them doing *bad deeds*, we assume that they are *good people*.

In fact, this is very often how it is that the con artist can get us to give him or her money. They do good deeds and we assume that their character matches their deeds. We put our trust in the strength of that assumption and they take us for every penny we've got. We think in these black and white terms because we are hypnotized by the duality trance state. We likewise get ourselves in trouble frequently by trying to be "nice" to people even though those people are not being so "nice" to us. Not only do we think we must "turn the other cheek" but we also believe that being "nice" is a way of proving ourselves to be good people. We don't use our discernment or our intuition—which could be screaming at us to avoid trusting someone or avoid someone all together—because doing so might be seen as not "nice."

And we really don't want to "hurt their feelings." I can't say how many times I've worked with a client who stayed in an emotionally, verbally, or even physically abusive relationship because they didn't want to "hurt their feelings" by leaving, speaking up or otherwise taking care of self. Hurting someone's feelings is considered to be damaging to them, and so we should always be ever-so-careful not to hurt anyone's feelings. But in fact, we don't have the power to hurt anyone else's feelings. That's right. A person's feelings belong 100% to that person. When we make a decision and act on it, they have various options for how they are going to perceive that decision and action. Their perception is going to create their emotional response. So if the person perceives that you've done something hurtful *to them* when, in fact, you've only done something *for* yourself, that is the perceptual option they chose. They could always choose another.

But, we say, they can't help it, they were programmed to perceive things that way. Yes, and so were we programmed to believe that we had the power to control other people's feelings so that we can *make* them angry, or hurt, or afraid, when actually we have no power whatsoever over their feelings. Unfortunately, however, our programming does not give us an excuse. We are still 100% responsible for our own feelings. And the thing is that if, for example, Tom perceives that I have hurt him by deciding to stick with my very appropriate boundaries, then that pain alone might be enough to make Tom consider the possibility of looking at it differently. Whereas, if I let my boundaries go because it might hurt Tom's feelings, Tom won't get that chance to consider that other possibility. In actuality then, when I hold myself hostage to the idea of hurting someone else's feelings, I'm denying them the right and privilege to figure out what might not be working for them, by fixing it before they even get the chance. And this is *good* because—why?

Our efforts to be good are no more than that: efforts to be good. They say nothing about our genuineness, our compassion or our love for self or others. Our efforts to *serve* others by trying to do good deeds, don't serve until and unless they come from genuineness. And they don't come from genuineness when they are driven by this need to be good. They only come from genuineness when they are driven by truth, compassion and love. Where there is resentment hiding in the background or a belief that we *have to* do this deed, there is no genuineness.

What's more, people know the difference. At least on an intuitive level if not consciously, we know when we are doing something out of obligation and duty and when we are doing it from genuine love or simply the joy of doing it—we feel this. And while the recipients of our dutiful service may be glad that the need was taken care of, they don't feel loved or genuinely supported. It's a little like leaving a stink bomb behind every good deed. The recipient of the good deed gets the deed, and then they get the stink. Whereas, when they know that we are genuinely coming from compassion, love or the joy of giving, they feel that, and they receive the gift at a deep level that, at least temporarily, transforms them—or allows them to peek behind the veil of the duality trance state, if only for a moment, to receive all the unconditional love that is there for them.

Is it possible then, that our so-called *goodness* is actually blocking the real blessings that could come from our interactions and encounters with others? I think so. In all the ways cited above and more, the effort to be good is often made up of blindness that also enables others in their blindness. So is goodness really good, or is it bad? Well, actually it is neither. It is simply one of the ways in which we are coping with the blindness created by the duality trance state. And all too often it has nothing whatsoever to do with that righteousness we spoke of in Chapter 6 as *only Christ truly*.

9

The Well

There are several stories in the Christian and Hebrew Bibles in which a well figures prominently. In Genesis 24, we see that Abraham's servant, who was sent out to find a wife for Isaac prayed and waited by the well, also called the spring, to meet Isaac's wife-to-be, Rebekah, who turned out to be the love of his life. Isaac's son, Jacob, also met his future wife, Rachel, at a well, from which he'd rolled away the stone to give drink to the sheep she shepherded (Genesis 29). Moses was introduced to his wife as a result of an encounter at a well, in which he rescued his future wife, Zipporah, from the shepherds who were driving she, her sisters and their sheep away from the well. He sent the shepherds away and watered the sisters' sheep. Later he was introduced to their father and given Zipporah to be his wife (Exodus 2). There were also many early stories of battles over wells, for Israel is a dry country, where the rainy season is very short.

And in the New Testament we have the story of the Samaritan woman whom Jesus met at the well. This story is significant for two reasons, 1) Jesus spoke to a woman, and 2) Jesus spoke to a Samaritan woman. In his day, as most of us know, women were second-class citizens with no rights, but Jesus treated her as a person equal to a man, by giving her information as from a Rabbi to a student—which was unheard of at that time. Also in his day, the Samaritans were considered by the Jews to be unclean because of early associations with Israel's enemies. So, he was not supposed to be associating with her at all. But this story is also quite significant for its message, for it tells us where we may find the well, and how and what we may drink of it. Here's that story:

So He came to a city of Samaria, called Sychar, near the parcel of ground that Jacob gave to his son Joseph; and Jacob's well was there. Jesus therefore, being wearied from His journey, was sitting thus by the well. It was about the sixth hour. There came a woman of Samaria to draw water. Jesus said to her, "Give Me a drink." For his disciples had gone away to the city to buy food. The Samaritan woman therefore said to Him, "How is it that You, being a Jew, ask me for a drink since I am a Samaritan woman?" (For Jews have no dealing with Samaritans.) Jesus answered and said to her, "If you knew the gift of God and who it is who says to you, 'Give Me a drink,' you would have asked Him, and He would have given you living water." She said to Him, "Sir, You have nothing to draw with and the well is deep; where then do You get that living water? "You are not greater than our father Jacob, are You, who gave us the well, and drank of it himself, and his sons, and his cattle?" Jesus answered and said to her, "Everyone who drinks of this water shall thirst again; but whoever drinks of the water that I shall give him, shall never thirst; but the water that I shall give him shall become in him a well of water springing up to eternal life" (John 4:5-14).

Now, there's more to this story, but let's start here, for this story is chock full of deep spiritual information. Though it tells us nothing whatsoever about religion—except that the rituals and dogma of religion really don't matter at all—it does tell us about both drink and food that have to do with a deeper well within us, a well that has to do with spirit and truth. It wouldn't matter who it was who said this. It could have been Buddha, Mohammad or Gandhi. It is the message that matters most here. And why it is important right here and right now is because we need to know what to do and how to live if the duality trance state turns out to be total mythology.

We've just run through several chapters that, while demonstrating the complete heresy of the duality trance state, have informed us that there is a way of being that has nothing to do with good or evil, but rather with the completion of consciousness in *only Christ truly*. This way of being is one in which we receive ourselves as having the Christ nature, or the Buddha nature—the nature that is our truest I AM nature. And it is this nature to which Jesus refers when he meets this Samaritan woman at the well.

If the Bible is woven through with wisdom, as I suspect that it is—though I in no way believe that it is inerrant—then this idea of men meeting women at the well is significant. It is significant first because putting the masculine archetype together with the feminine archetype in the psyche is what brings us to wholeness. As we said in Chapter 3, the healthy feminine is that which carries us to the internal so that we can gather all that is found there, and the healthy masculine carries what was found there out into the external world as manifestation.

So, at many other wells significant protagonists in the story of God and man, as presented in the Old Testament, the masculine met the feminine. And at this well in Samaria, again, the masculine meets the feminine. And this feminine was the quester—the one who asked just the right questions to facilitate the inner journey. And for every question she asked the Master-Teacher takes her deeper into her own psyche.

So, from a metaphorical perspective, here's what happened. Jesus asks her to give him a drink. He does not necessarily define what kind of drink, nor does he use the word *water* in his request. He simply asks her, the feminine, to give him drink. He is asking his own inner feminine to take him to that inner world where he will find that living water of which he speaks later. And she asks, how can you ask me for a drink, aren't you a Jew? She is saying, the feminine cannot go within here, for there is a split—a chasm between God and humanity, between the conscious and the unconscious, between the internal and the external—where the external tells her that she and Jesus cannot associate. His response is this: Actually there is no split, you just don't know it.

Wait, that's not at all what he said. What he said was "If you knew who it is who says to you, 'give me a drink' you would have asked Him and He would have given you living water." And according to traditionalists, this means that Jesus and Jesus alone has this living water, and only he can give it to us. But from a metaphorical and metaphysical perspective, every time Jesus referred to himself, he was referring to the I AM within each of us, for he came to show us that we are all gods. So, from this perspective when he made the above statement, he was really saying, something like this: "If you only knew the I AM you are, you would be guided to this living water."

But she wants to know how this can be, as we all do. How can you do this, she said, you don't even have anything to draw the water out. Where do you get this living water? And, you are not greater than Jacob are you? That last question is where we all get stuck. We assume that locating this water has something to do with greatness—greatness that is greater than other humans who are not so great. This is why we have selected Jesus to be the only human ever to be both God and man. Do you have the kind of greatness, she asks, that can make me believe in you?

Wasn't it Jesus who said, "Truly, truly, I say to you, he who believes in Me, the works that I do shall he do also; and *greater works than these* shall he do" (John 14:12-emphasis added)? Just prior to this verse in 14:6, he had said, "I am the way, the truth and the life." The word *I* there is *ego* (εγω), which means *me, I am he, me, it is I*. And *am* is *eimi* (ει), which means *is, are, was, am, will be, I am*. So, the word *I am* has the same meaning as *I AM that I AM*, spoken to Moses from that burning bush. In Chapter 3 we discovered Charles Fillmore's interpretation of these words: "I-am—I-was—I-will-be because I-am—I-was—I-will-be the power to be eternally I" (332). So, what Jesus was really saying here is I AM is the way, the truth and the life.

And that same meaning is used again as he says: He who believes in I AM, the works that I AM does shall he do also; and greater works than these shall he do. In other words, Jesus recognized and lived from his own I AM nature, and because he did, he did great works. But, he tells us, anyone who recognizes his own I AM nature can not only do the same things that he did, but even greater things than he did. So, here he is clearly telling us that we don't need to think of him as the one and only God/man.

So, when the Samaritan woman asks this question, she is trying to find out if Jesus is great enough for her to believe. And he answers her in the same way: *Everyone* who drinks of this water will thirst again, but *whoever* drinks of the water that I AM gives will never thirst again. It isn't about greatness, he says, it's about the drink that I AM gives. And he goes on to say that the drink that I AM gives will become within that person who drinks it, a well of water springing up to eternal life.

Here is the real well. It is the one found within us. And we must be able to dialogue with the feminine—the one who leads us inward to find it—for she asked, "Sir, give me this water, so I will not be thirsty, nor come all the way here to draw." And that was the beginning of her inward trek. And his answer is very curious:

> He said to her, "Go call your husband, and come here." The woman answered and said, "I have no husband." Jesus said to her, "You have well said, 'I have no husband'; for you have had five husbands, and the one whom you now have is not your husband; this you have said truly" (vs. 16-18).

Now, why, if the woman asked for water, did Jesus tell her to go get her husband? That's not an answer to her request. But the journey inward begins with telling the truth. The woman had to begin the process of finding this living water by telling the truth. My guess, just based on the moral codes of the time, is that this was a truth with which she was not so very comfortable. But as we can see, Jesus didn't judge her, he just noticed out loud that she told the truth.

And her response was that she recognized him as a prophet and then she went directly to the conundrum of separation—you worship this way, and we worship that way. She wanted to know from this prophet, which was the correct way. But, of course, he answered that neither were correct, for:

>...an hour is coming, and now is, when the true worshippers shall worship the Father in spirit and in truth; for such people the Father seeks to be His worshippers. God is spirit and those who worship Him must worship in spirit and in truth (vs 23-24).

These verses have been seen as a mystery to traditionalists who have a hard time figuring out how to worship in spirit and in truth. They've basically decided that this means that one's worship has to be heartfelt and sincere. And that's where they left it. But this woman, this separated Samaritan woman represents our supposed separation from the divine, and her question, as to which is the correct method of worship, has everything to do with that separation. The duality trance state has us all believing that there's some kind of special person and special formula by which we will find the straight and narrow pathway to connection with the divine. And since none of us is special enough to find that formula, we are left believing that only Jesus had it, and we must now, not only worship God, but also Jesus, in order to be connected—or at least that's the Westernized version of it.

But here we see that simply seeing and acknowledging what she was doing in her life was the key that turned the lock on the door to this amazing information. Such truth telling lacks judgment. Not only did Jesus not judge her for her life as it was, but she did not judge herself either. We see nothing here of confessions or recognition of sin, or asking for forgiveness. We only see that she acknowledges the truth of her choices.

How many of us are living in denial of what we are doing in our lives? How many of us further deny any responsibility for what we are doing in our lives? We do this because we live in the duality trance state. We think that things that we are doing are wrong, bad or sinful and we should be ashamed of ourselves. So, rather than owning those things and taking responsibility for our choices, we deny that we are doing them. We deny it to ourselves and if challenged we deny it to others—all because we fear our own judgment and that of others. But here, the woman simply says, "I have no husband." And Jesus says, "Yep, that's true, you are living with this guy, and you've been married five times."

When Jesus told her to go get her husband, she could have just turned on her heel and gone to get the guy she was living with. There was no reason for her to acknowledge the fact that she was not married to him, other than her own need to clarify the truth. "Here's how I've lived," she could be saying. When we get to the point in our lives where we say, "here's how I've lived" and we are gut-level honest about not only what we've done, but, without judgment, why we have done it, we often find that at base, we have been bargaining with the duality trance state.

Bargains, as you've probably surmised, always carry and *IF* and a *THEN*. *IF* I do this, *THEN* that will happen. *IF* I can pretend to myself that it will be okay if I settle for this life, when I really want a passionate, full, potent life, *THEN* I won't notice that I'm only half alive. THAT is the bottom-line bargain of all of our other bargains. Because some part of us knows. It knows that we are essentially divine beings. It knows that we can live into *greater things than these shall you do*. It knows our power, our love and our peace. And it tells us about these things at least often enough for us to either talk ourselves out of it, or experiment with it. We learn of our power in our nightly dreams—as we choose different scenarios in which to participate. That choosing done in dreams tells us that we have the power. We learn of our love for self, others and life itself through our deep connections, but also through our angers, our hatred and our fears. Why would we be angry at all if some part of us didn't want to take care of us? Why would we hate, if we didn't first love. Why are we afraid if life really means nothing to us?

But our judgments keep us from looking, from listening, from seeing this essence of who we really are. In fact, they keep us stuck in the duality trance state. Our judgments tell us not to look to see what we are up to, because if we ever really see it, we might find out we are bad people. Or, in the case of someone who is living out the bad-guy role, our judgments might help us see and feel how much we really do care about others, and about ourselves. It is our judgments that put us in denial, and make us lie to ourselves and others about who we are. And our judgments come from our belief that we are separate from the divine.

Yet this woman, this separated woman, this woman who was considered by the Jews to be impure, told the simple truth—this is how I am living. And Jesus filled in the blanks—not only is this how you live today, but here's how you have lived up to this point. And she did not argue. She did not deny. She further acknowledged the truth he had spoken by saying something like, "Whoa, you must be a prophet!" And later when she ran to her home, she was shouting on the streets, "Come see the man who told me all the things that I have done; this is not the Christ is it" (v 29)? And just so, telling ourselves all the things we have done *is* the Christ. Yet, more is to be revealed.

First, the word *Father* as Jesus uses it in the above passage (vs 23-24) and in other places in the Gospels is not *abba*, as is commonly thought. In fact, abba is only used once by Jesus in Mark 14:36, when he was praying to have "this cup removed from me." Rather the word for *Father* is *Pater*, which we delineated in Chapter 6 and discovered its bottom-line meaning to be something like *source*. But there is another very interesting meaning to this word: *animated by the same spirit as himself*. Jesus refers to his Father in other passages as the originator of his own activities, even going so far as to say: "I can do nothing of my own initiative" (John 5:30). What he is saying here to this woman, and again just a few verses later, in this statement about his own initiative, is that he is animated by the divine within him—*who is the same as he*. And when he tells us that we will all one day worship in spirit and in truth, he is telling us that our worship will be *to live animated by the divine nature within us*.

The words *spirit* and *truth* tell us much about how this happens. The word used here for spirit is *pneuma* (πνευμα)— which, at its root, means *breath, breathe* or *wind*. There are many other more traditional meanings attributed to this word, including Holy Spirit, but it also means *the nature of Christ*, and *the disposition or influence that fills and governs the soul of anyone*. The Christ nature, like the Buddha nature, is a disposition and influence that fills and governs the soul of anyone. Jesus recognized his oneness with the divine; he saw himself as moving, thinking, talking, acting, breathing as one with the divine. And he now says that anyone who so desires, may also do the same— and further that doing the same is the only true worship.

The word used for *truth* in this text adds yet more to this meaning, for it is *alētheia* (αφλησθεια), which means both *objectivity* and *subjectivity* with regard to the truth, both *candor of mind* and *truth as personal experience*. It is rooted in *alethes* (αφλησθησζ), *true, loving the truth, speaking the truth, truthful*. And that is rooted in both *A* for *alpha, the beginning*, often used as another word for Christ, and in *lanthano* (λανθασνω), *to be hidden, to be hidden from one, secretly, unawares, without knowing*. This truth of which Jesus speaks is both objective and subjective, both candor of thought and personal experience. But it is also our beginning, our origin in our own Christ nature (or Buddha nature, or divine Self), which is hidden from us in the unconscious.

So, at the base of humanity is this unveiled reality of who we are, which is our origin as soul, which though it can be experienced, hasn't been because it has been hidden in the unconscious. This word *truth* then reveals the secret divine nature of humanity, which is the Alpha, the originator, the generator of all. Jesus said, *I AM the truth,* using that same word, *alētheia,* for *truth.* So here's what he was really saying: I surrender to my truest essence — though that essence of humanity may be hidden from everyone else, I surrender to it, so that I AM that essence. Further, that essence is the I AM — which truly allowed Jesus to say I AM that I AM. This is what made him capable of living out what's come to be called the Christ nature. The Buddha nature — the self that is no self — and the Christ nature are the same thing: divine Self. In other words, the Christ or Buddha nature is not made up of the sum total of our past influences found in our identities, our masks, costumes and roles. It is found in our essential beingness that is the originator itself.

So, what Jesus is really saying to this woman is that if she wants to drink of this living water, she has to see what is hidden — the veritable essence of her own being. The word *worship* adds even more to this, for it is *proskuneo* (προσκυνεϖω), which means *to kiss the hand of, as a dog licks the hand of his master.* The dog knows from whence comes all that he needs or wants, and just so, true worship is knowledge. It is simple knowing from whence comes all that we have and are. Jesus had this kind of knowing, so much so in fact that he knew that everything he did, said and thought came from this inner source, this truth that was hidden from everyone else.

And in spite of Jesus' efforts to show us this truth, it has remained hidden behind a dogma that says that no, the divine is not within us, it was only within Jesus, for we are impure and unable, therefore, to contain the divine. But it is this place hidden in the depths of the collective and individual unconscious where we know who we really are. We know that we, like Jesus — and like many of the other great spiritual leaders, as well as all of humanity—are constituent parts of the wholeness, the oneness that is *I-am—I-was—I-will-be because I-am—I-was—I-will-be the power to be eternally I*. It is impossible to separate from this essence—for it is the truest part of our being and our lives. So, Jesus tells this woman—the metaphor for the journey inward, which allows us to become aware of who we are—that the only truth of her life is this essence and this essence is living water, that springs up to eternal life.

Eternal is *aionios* (αιφωᾶνιοζ), *without beginning or end, that which always has been and always will be*. It is rooted in *aion* (αιφωᾶν), the word used often by the Gnostics as a noun, which meant *ageless ages*. We delineated the meaning of this word in Chapter 6 and concluded that it and its root words meant incessantly, invariably, and perpetually. And as we saw then these meanings do not tell us of a heaven that happens only after death but of an evolutionary process that is happening right now, all the time. Here the word refers back to the word *life, zoe* (ζοε), *possessed of vitality, life, every living soul,* which is rooted in the primary verb *zao* (ζαο), *to live, breathe, be among the living, to enjoy real life, to have true life and worthy of the name, active, blessed and endless in the kingdom of God, living water, having vital power in itself and exerting the same upon the soul, to be in full vigor, fresh, strong, efficient, powerful*. This life to which Jesus refers, then is not life after death, but a continual evolution that is incessant and which offers such amazing potent vitality that it can be considered nothing less than absolute abundance.

Do we want in our everydays for anything more than this? We are rarely conscious of it, however, because instead, we are living in the duality trance state. But here Jesus is saying that we don't have to live in that state, we can come alive, we can come to awareness that we are, have been and always will be alive, because we are, were, will be, because we are I AM, I was, I will be the power to be eternally I.

This is the well within us. And just as Jesus had no instrument with which he could draw from it, there are no techniques we can use to draw from this well. Rather we fall into it. We drink it and it drinks us. We are consumed by it, and we consume it—because it is who we are, and we are who it is. The well from which we drink is the eternal, vigorous, pulsating, fresh, soul, united with and inseparable from the divine. When we drink of this well we breathe life itself, for we are soul enmattered and matter ensouled.

We tend to think that if we are matter, we cannot also be spirit or soul, but we are both. Matter is spirit at base and spirit inhabits all matter. Spirit and soul are both synonymous with divine Self. Quantum physics is coming closer and closer to proving this as a reality—with its studies of quarks, what is below them, and the Unified Field Theory. But whether that ever happens or not, we all know it. Deep within our deepest essence we all know the truth—but we fear living into it, because to do so would be taking on our whole power, and owning responsibility for it. But the truth is we already have that power and that power is responsible for itself.

10

The Ocean

Have you ever wondered what it might be like to have the capacity to breathe under water? I mean, we can breathe everywhere else on planet earth. Why can't we breathe under water? True, when we arrive at the highest heights on the planet, the air is thinner, and so we must train ourselves to breathe at these heights, but we can still breathe there. So, why are we forbidden this sojourn under water? Well, I'm sure that many who don't think the kinds of "weird" thoughts that I think might find my question to be a bit on the ridiculous side. I mean, it's apparent that we can't breathe under water because we don't have gills. But these same people—usually more or less scientific types— would assert that we evolved from some kind of primeval slime or something like it—an argument I can't legitimately dispute. Yet, I do wonder, if that is true, why we didn't develop gills *and* lungs, as did some amphibians. Why is it that when we want to explore the ocean's depths, we have to strap on some special equipment that allows us only a certain range and depth?

Of course, I may never know, but what I do know is that from a psychological and spiritual perspective, if we are going to ever learn how to drink of that living water we referred to in the previous chapter we are going to have to develop psychological and spiritual gills. We are going to have to learn to breathe under water. And we are going to have to learn how to do this without getting the bends.

First, and most importantly, we are all already doing this. Lifetime after lifetime, incarnation after incarnation, we are slowly getting acquainted with the deep ranges of our being. That *is* after all why we are here. We are here to walk through the duality trance state to the other side of duality—oneness. We are here to ultimately and finally finish the question about duality—putting it to rest once and for all, not only for ourselves but for all posterity and for the entire universe. So, as we evolve into more and more truth about who we really are, we are slowly and more and more consciously stepping into the ocean.

As a symbol for the unconscious the ocean is an excellent metaphor, for it tells us of the vast regions of unknown material within the individual and collective mind, wherein we will find both the ferociousness of our fears, and the wonders of organic life itself. So, what we don't know is that while on a conscious level, we are slowly stepping into the ocean, on an unconscious level we've been swimming there all along. By bridging the gap between the conscious and unconscious world we begin to realize that flow that carries us from one truth to another to another until we know who we are.

In the previous chapter we saw that Jesus promised living water to a woman who had no clue what he was talking about. Nevertheless, she told the truth of her life and then ran to tell others how powerful her experience with this Master-Teacher was. That is how the journey into the unconscious begins—by simply telling ourselves the truth. Sometimes it begins with something as simple as the recognition that we have lied to ourselves and/or others about something. That recognition allows us to step into the sea. And then a wave's undercurrents swallow the sand right out from under our feet—for the next thing that happens after that recognition is a judgment—and we step back closer to land in order to get a grip. We can stay right here at the edge of consciousness for many lifetimes if we so choose—stepping in, stepping out, stepping in, stepping out. And we'll tell ourselves that well, at least we are trying to be honest, and that's a good thing, right?

We are trying so hard to do the *right* thing that we are getting it all *wrong*. Self-judgment only keeps us from learning to breathe underwater. That is why, when we meditate, we are taught to suspend all judgment and just sit with whatever comes up. And each time we delve into the deeper regions of ourselves, where we find some peace, which had previously been unconscious to us — we are learning to breathe underwater.

The ocean is primordial, in that from the unconscious emerges everything else that we have since become. The ocean of the unconscious holds all of the information we need about our origins, about our essence, and about all that keeps us from recognizing and living into that essence. So, when we get a little thread of information, a little piece of the hem of the garment of truth, we are both delighted to find it, and terribly frightened of it. We want to know more and we don't want to know more. Mostly, we don't because we fear our own judgment, which will ultimately mean we don't like ourselves, even hate ourselves; we fear the judgment of others, who will not like or love us if they learn the games we play, the bargains we make and the nature of our so-called sins; and we fear the ultimacy of judgment, as in the myths we've heard about hell, and bad karma, etc. For these reasons it is very difficult to relax into the mystery of our own souls.

But all of those reasons are created by the duality trance state. So, the closer we come to suspending our belief in its persuasions, the more willing we become to step into the ocean and keep stepping till we lose ground and must learn to swim the depths. Just now, and for the remainder of this Chapter, then, let us suspend our belief in duality in much the same way that we might suspend our belief in the life outside the theatre when we go to a movie and get completely involved in its story as if it were our own.

Meet Selena, daughter of Joe and Bonita Webster. Selena grew up in a middle-income neighborhood, attended a middle-income school, befriended middle-income peers, and ultimately married a middle-income man and took a middle-income job. Selena is the average American, Brit, European, Japanese, Australian woman. There's really nothing all that outstanding about Selena. She's got her issues and her talents; she's got her faults and her good points—as we say.

But Selena, like all of us, has lived mostly from the cultural and familial mores of her world, and she's basically out of touch with the other world under the sea of her unconscious. Yet like many middle-income folks, she's developed this vague sense of discontent—a slight awareness that this is not enough—not really something missing, just not really enough. Selena begins to take yoga classes, and from there she gets involved in some meditation groups and begins a daily practice. And one day, during her morning meditation, she slips beyond the duality trance state, beyond morality, beyond land, and turns up right smack dab in the middle of the ocean.

Without a splash she arrives under the surface where the quiet overtakes her and she begins to hum and throb with gentle sway of the truth. She's not even watching herself in this place—there is no observer—just the experiencer. Here she stays listening to the nothing that is everything until slowly she begins to wonder how this is happening and how it could possibly be happening to her—after all does she deserve this experience? Then just as suddenly as she arrived, she finds herself on land again. As she sits momentarily on the beach of this experience and tries to figure out what just happened, she looks around her at the others in her meditation group to see if they might have experienced anything like it. When everyone is finished with their meditation, she asks if anyone else has ever had an experience like hers. They tell her that they envy her and only wish they could. But Alice speaks up and says, "maybe not exactly like yours, but something similar."

Alice and Selena meet for coffee after work that day to talk about their experiences. But though Alice says that she's spoken with others who have had similar experiences, Selena thinks that this must mean that she, Alice and the others are somehow special, because "not everyone gets to have an experience like this, yes?" And Selena wants more. So, she begins to practice meditation two times a day. But though she is able to touch the fringes of that depth through an emotional experience with joy or a feeling of deep peace, she can't quite "get there" again.

She was already bored with her life when she started, now she is very frustrated. She wants to live in that state of total experience for the rest of her life, but she can't figure out how to do it. She reads every book on the planet on meditation, and New Thought, and she continues her meditation practice—but practice it is, for she just keeps waiting to arrive again at the Carnegie Hall of meditative experiences.

But as Selena continues her practice she begins to become aware of things in her life and the thoughts, feelings and behaviors that are not really true for her anymore. First thing was her job. She hated her job. Didn't used to, before all this meditation stuff happened, but now, she hates getting up in the morning and going to this stale place and working with these milquetoast people to accomplish exactly nothing. But, this is what she'd trained to do and changing it now, was a bit like trying to get on another boat mid-river—it's a bit rocky. So, she just didn't do anything, and she kept hoping for that experience to happen to her again as it had before in her meditation.

The next thing that she noticed was that she carried with her a great deal of tension in her relationships, starting with her parents and moving through that with her husband and children all the way to her friends and acquaintances. She began to wish they'd all just go away and leave her alone—and in fact, she began to spend more and more time alone in meditation. But the tension would not go away. At first she thought that the reason she felt this tension was because she really only wanted that peace she felt that special day. But slowly she began to realize that she'd felt that same tension all of her life.

It seemed to her now that she'd always been trying to get *them* to approve of her, like her, even love her. She was always trying to figure out what *they* needed and expected of her before they ever even hinted at it, so that she could give it to them—and then they would like her, approve of her and even love her. And now, since she'd experienced the deep vibration of truth, she just knew to the core of her being, that she was going to have to stop doing this.

At first she thought that this meant that she'd have to somehow stop caring what they thought. But as she just watched and listened to what was going on inside of her with each encounter with another person, she began to realize that it wasn't really about stopping anything. It was about starting something else. And what she wanted to start had to do with paying attention to her own internal urgings, passions and compassions, and then acting according to their impetus.

Of course, she stumbled around quite a bit with this at first. It was entirely new to her. And she had two voices to contend with—the one that told her that *if* they didn't approve of her, *then* she would be totally abandoned by them. They would reject her outright—and then she would have to face herself in the mirror and see that she was utterly worthy of such rejection. That voice was loud, and provided her with a compulsive, knee-jerk reaction to every encounter, which meant that she very often caught herself trying desperately to please them, rescue them or otherwise win their approval.

And that internal critic came up too. That voice that said, "You are so stupid, why can't you get it right! Look they just got you going again! How long is it going to take you to get it?!" At first, when this happened, she would find herself in the slough of despond. She wanted fiercely to only participate in that beautiful peace she felt that day when she landed in the sea, but she kept screwing up! But then she began to realize that every time she caught herself giving in to that knee-jerk reaction to please them, she was also a) getting it sooner each time, and b) realizing some new element of her reaction that she'd not seen before. In other words, each time she took a step back toward land, she remembered something she left back there, that she was going to need for the rest of her journey. And, she was getting closer and closer to being able, in the moment, to thinking, feeling, acting and telling the truth.

And then she began to be aware of a third voice—a much more subtle voice, but one she could feel kind of humming down deep inside of her. That voice was the voice of peace. The more she lived her own truth, the more apparent this voice became to her. And every now and then, she was able to really do that with someone. Really do it—where she seemed to hear the same old siren call to crash her boat on the same old rocks; but instead she stood up straight, took a deep breath and told her truth. She also began to behave more out of that truth making itself more and more profoundly evident to her. She began to make decisions based on that truth rather than on pleasing others. And the feeling of elation, personal freedom and empowerment that she got from this became its own reward. But then, there was the guilt. It came in like a rogue wave and knocked her off her feet, so that she floundered and sputtered in the early waves just off the beach of her consciousness.

That guilt told her that she was selfish, small-minded and inconsiderate of those whose needs she has just betrayed. These people needed her to continue to please, rescue and otherwise take care of them. What were they going to do now? How could she be so self-centered and insensitive? And everything, it seems *every*thing within her, urged her to go back and undo what only moments ago she felt so good about doing.

She finds herself lying on the beach now coughing, and sucking the air for all she is worth. But instead of rushing back into the waves she bows to this position, just surrendering to lying there winded and wet. As she does, she decides to stay right here for a minute. She needs to allow this to be, this war within her own psyche. She does not need to win right now; she just needs to hear the clink of the swords. And as she listens she begins to hear within the syncopated rhythm of each clink, the sound of truth coming through.

She sits up and holds that position in the brine of small waves lapping now around her, and she looks out to sea and here is what she sees. Guilt has been her way of swallowing herself, keeping herself secret from herself. Guilt has been the rationale for staying stuck in smallness, for not allowing her Self its true size, shape and form. Guilt seduces her into thinking that if she gives into it, she is right, and good, and that is good enough—she doesn't have to seek anything more and she can stay right here on the beach and never have to brave the waves again.

She sees now that guilt is holding her hostage to a compulsive way of interacting with others, a way that means doing the same old thing in a repetitive fashion, almost like a ritual prayer, that asks and asks for this one thing: please let them like me. She isn't good. She is manipulative. She isn't bad either, she's just believed that manipulation was how she might survive. But now she sees that surviving this way has kept her from living. She has survived on dishonesty and manipulation, all the while telling herself that she was a good person for doing so.

This knowledge does not come with judgment, but with certainty. Of course, that is short-lived because here comes another wave of guilt. And it goes that way for a while, with Selena developing clear vision, only to have it go away again momentarily as she falls on her knees again and again as the waves roll in. But on her knees, she is able to hold on to the ever moving sand and grab hold of some fresh new insight about herself and her life.

Eventually, she stands, ready again to walk through the waves and dive into the next rogue wave knowing that she can swim beneath its turmoil through to the other side. And once past it, she will begin the process of figuring out what to do about that career she no longer enjoys; and then what to do about that challenge she's taken on to raise children; and then what to do about that next challenge, and then what to do with this joy, and this peace, and this opportunity, and that new challenge. And each time she *looks* into the depth of one of these surface issues, she is like a snorkeler peering into the depths from above; and each time she *sees*, she is swimming those depths.

It's really all about vision. As Selena has evolved, she has begun to look, not only at surface issues that present, but at the hidden meanings and issues beneath them. And she's stopped looking to others for the answers to her life. She doesn't need them to like her. She doesn't need to fix them. She doesn't need to live her life based on fear that she's not going to get it right. She needs to see. She needs to see what is beneath, where the whale sings and the coral grows in strange and meaningful patterns. She needs to see, and see more. The problem has never been her guilt, her attempts to manipulate, or her "sin." The problem has been her blindness. She hasn't seen who she really is.

And when all the guilt, manipulation, traps and judgment are gone—who is she now? That is the question. And it is the only question ever worth asking—or going through the trouble to answer. The sea is wild at the surface, but calm at its center. We have to walk through the wild and learn to swim to the center.

Now let's look at Adam. Adam was once a little boy who lived with two drug-addicted parents who only ever bothered to notice him at all when he got into trouble. So trouble is what Adam did. And when he got into trouble, his father would punch and kick him, yelling at him for how stupid he was, and how he was going to grow up to be a nothing, "a big fat nothing!" So, Adam began to get in fights at school, as both a way of releasing the anger he felt at his own helplessness, and as a way of bullying others as his father had bullied him. At least if he was a bully he was alive and could mostly get what he wanted. In fact,

Adam got to be so good at it, that when he joined the neighborhood gang, he moved up quickly in the ranks, and eventually became the gang lord. He was smart and slick and he didn't care about anyone or anything—except his sister, who still lived in that hell-hole with his parents.

He'd always protected her, but now that he had all this power, he knew that the only one who could be blamed if something happened to her, was him. And something threatened to happen to her every day, sometimes several times a day. It's a busy job being a gang lord—you know you have to have eyes in the back of your head. So, Adam got some of his loyal devotees to watch out for his sister. One of them, Ricky, took a liking to her—and began to get really angry at anyone else who also liked her. But she didn't like him and snubbed him every chance she got. One day, Ricky just had enough, and he snapped. He ended up raping her and beating her up so badly that she was hospitalized and finally died.

Of course, the first thing that Adam did was tell his gang what had happened—and Ricky was taken down in a matter of hours. But then, Adam began to slowly unravel. How could he have been so stupid to leave Ricky in charge of her? At first, Adam just hit the bottle and the rock harder. He tried to stay in a stupor for a week or so, but he knew that he and his gang were all vulnerable if he kept that up. And then he just became enraged. He began going around starting fights and winning with everyone he could think of until he literally started a gang war.

Adam had been trying for so many years now not to feel anything, that when this pain rocked his world, he was completely lost in it. It was as if his ship had turned over at sea and left him floundering out there in the ocean with no rescue in sight. And he didn't deserve to be rescued anyway—after all he'd escaped his parents' abuse and left his little sister there to endure it alone and then he'd sent her a rapist and an abuser to be her guardian. That and all the other bad things he'd done began to weigh on him so hard that he couldn't do anything at all. Either he was going to die, he thought, or he was going to have to do something different—even his gang was in danger because of him.

Adam ran away, took an alias and ducked into a drug rehab center and halfway house, asking them to help him stop using and help him get out of the gang. His gang thought he was dead and got themselves a new lord, and went after the gang they thought killed him. But Adam was tucked away in the treatment facility and halfway house hating himself and thinking of ways to take his own life.

Instead, what began to occur to him, through the counseling and group therapy that he received, was that this whole thing, the whole entire thing started because he was trying to put on an identity that would enable him to survive his parents, and then the world. *If* he was a "bad dude" *then* a) he'd be noticed enough to feel he existed and b) he might be strong enough to *be* noticed and survive it. He'd bargained with the reality in which he found himself by giving up on who he really was and becoming someone else entirely in order to make it through.

When his sister was killed, however, he began to get in touch again with who he really was—a sensitive kid who loved deeply and had a great deal of compassion for others. But this was really hard to put together with the things he'd done. He'd hated his parents, never did a single solitary thing to help them; beat up whoever he had to beat up and he'd even killed someone in a knife fight in which it was kill or be killed; he'd used and sold drugs, had had sex with whomever, whenever, and he was just plain mean and abusive most of the time. So, how could he dare to call himself sensitive and compassionate?

He stayed right there in that mental, emotional and spiritual conflict for a while—not moving forward, not moving backward, just sitting in the waves and contemplating. Eventually, the counselors at the rehab center told him that he should work a

Fourth Step on his life, providing himself with a "fierce moral inventory" of his actions. He did that, writing for weeks about all the "bad" things he'd done, and finally confessing them to one of the counselors there. But this just stirred up another battle within him. Somehow during the writing and the confession, he felt two polar opposite things. On the one hand he felt really bad about what he'd done, but on the other he felt this cold pride come up like the sharpened and just polished shiny blade of a knife. That cold pride had defined him for most of his life. He knew it and had worked hard to earn it. That cold pride said, "Yes, I'm bad—watch this!" But the other side had a voice too, and it felt like a little shameful shrimp of a human being, the "big fat nothing" his father always predicted, who was utterly ashamed of being so small and helpless. That little shrimp had been cowering behind that bully identity like it was some kind of savior.

What was he to do with that cold pride, and what was he to do with that little shrimp? And what was he to do with the rage that still festered inside of him waiting for the slightest opportunity to come out. And come out it did, several times while he was there in treatment and then the halfway house—at the slightest provocation. But each time it did, because he was looking at it now, Adam was able to see further and further into the depths of that old identity. He was able to see that the provocation was not to anything real or sacred in his life, but to that cold pride. That cold pride said, "I'm not only somebody, but I'm everything and you are going to give me what I want when I want it or I will hurt you—because if you don't, you remind me of the sniveling little 'big fat nothing' hiding behind my pride." He wasn't afraid that someone might hurt him or steal his clothing, cigarettes or billfold; he was afraid that they would steal his identity. He was afraid that they might see that sniveling little nothing and come in and wound his heart again just as his father had.

And now he could see that that cold pride was a response to his father's abuse coupled with his mother's indifference and absence, and though he had lived entirely out of it, he knew that it was false. Yet, did that make the sniveling little nothing true? Was the sniveling little nothing who he really was? Previously those two had seemed to be the only options. But as he sat in the waves, close to the edge of the unconscious and letting the unconscious present its material to him, he also began to consider that part of him that wanted so badly to protect his sister. Who was *that* guy?

That guy was a guy who cared deeply about significant people in his life. That guy was tender and thoughtful and wanted only the best for her. That guy read her stories at night when the parents were passed out in the living room or gone. That guy even protected her from her father's abuse, and tenderly potty trained her when her mother fell out on that job. That guy was someone Adam could like. But that guy was also lonely and sometimes felt overwhelmed and hopeless. And wasn't that just a bit too close to the sniveling little shit he didn't like? Wasn't loneliness the same as self-pity? Wasn't feeling hopeless a sign of weakness? And after all was said and done, wasn't he still bad for doing the things he'd done?

Adam continued to sit in the waves, throughout the days and nights of his treatment and subsequent move to the halfway house. After a while, it began to occur to him that just sitting with himself—and all the different aspects of himself—was making him like himself a lot more. He was able to see the strength that can only be found in the observer—who watches and listens to what is going on within. He began to see the sitting, watching and listening as a position of great self-love and empowerment. He began to like the sitting, listening and watching in and of itself, regardless of what he saw, heard or wanted to get up and run from.

And because he liked this sitter/watcher he began to stay there for longer and longer periods of time, and because he was able to do that, he was able to not only sit and watch himself but sit and watch others as well, tapping into that intuitive part that had always been quite active in his life, but used for other purposes. He was able to point out to others in the group things that he saw and felt from them, and they began to be impressed with his insight. That feedback made him trust this aspect of himself even more.

Thus, Adam began to stretch himself beyond the beach, to walk deeper and deeper into the waves, asking the hard questions and finding that just being willing to ask was sometimes enough. As time went by, Adam began to live more and more from the position of the sensitive, the compassionate and the sitter/watcher, and the more he lived from that, the more he trusted it, and the more he trusted it, the more he was willing to risk stepping further into the waves. By the time he left the halfway house and went into the working world, he knew that what he wanted, had always wanted, really, was to work as an EMT.

So, he started back to school and became an EMT, and if he'd stopped right there, the story would be good enough for most, but Adam didn't stop there. He continued to work on deeper and deeper aspects of himself until he found the spiritual component of his psychology. And though he attended no church, temple or mosque, as he worked his 12-Step program, Adam began to explore his own authentic spiritual beliefs. He began to meditate and as he did, he found deeper and deeper regions within his innermost being where peace flooded in over him like an easy breeze. Slowly he began to define this part of himself as his truest essence. He received all manner of insight as if it came as a download from his uppermost chakras. His compassion for others increased and his ability to love and take exceptional care of himself likewise increased. Adam was learning to inhabit heaven—his divine Self in the now. Today, Adam walks the planet as both a teacher and an EMT rescuer, with keen vision of who he is and the power to recognize Self in every encounter with other.

These fictionalized stories were developed as a composite picture, piecing together tiny little scraps from the stories I've heard and participated in over the years as a therapist, author, and speaker. But they tell the story of how we begin to tell the truth. They tell the story of how we may begin the process of learning how to drink that living water that springs up to the life that always was and always will be within us, and finally learn to swim in the ocean depths beneath the well. As we can see, that process works exactly the same, whether we've lived identified with so-called *goodness* or so-called *badness*.

It isn't that Adam gave up his evil ways and became good; it's that he began to get more closely aligned with who he really was. And it isn't that Selena started out as a good person who became a better person; it's that she became more closely aligned with who she really was. Ultimately who both Selena and Adam are is divine Self. And the closer aligned they become with that, the more they inhabit heaven in the present moment—right here on planet earth.

11

For All We Know

I believe it was Blaise Pascal who said, "...it is not certain that everything is uncertain" (Pascal 185). He spent a lot of time and energy trying to single-handedly dismantle the notion that we could know things by reason alone. Unfortunately, he couldn't prove that either. But he did push us to consider what we think we know or what we think we must know. And for all we know, he was right.

Now, we could go on a long tangent here about certainty and whether or not it can ever be trusted. We could spend many words discussing the fact that there is really very little that we can actually know—but even that is an unknown, so why bother. But we've talked in this book about two different kinds of knowledge—and both have to do with how and what we see. The first kind of knowledge came from the tree of knowledge of good and evil. Most traditionalists view this knowledge as reality: There definitely is a good and a bad, and if you don't believe it, just look around. The problem with this view is that when we look around we see what we've been trained to see. And the question is, does that perceptual agreement actually equate to knowledge?

Whether it's judging a thing to be *bad* or judging a thing to be *good*, or whether it's trying to make excuses or rationales for why a thing that looks *bad* is really *good*—judgment of all kind comes from this trance state in which we see only that which we've been trained to see. So, where is the knowledge in that?

The word used for *knowledge* in the phrase *the tree of knowledge of good and evil*, is da'ath (דעת). It means *knowledge, perception, skill, discernment, understanding,* or *wisdom*. It originates in the word yâda' (ידע), a word we've seen before and which means many things, including, *to know, to learn to know, to learn by experience, to perceive, to see, to find out, to make oneself known, reveal oneself* and *to be known.* So, traditionalists would have us to believe that the tree of knowledge of good and evil was meant to introduce us to evil. Like naughty children who had eaten from the cookie jar from which they'd been told not to eat, they were to learn their lesson—but in what seemed a rather harsh way—by being cast out of the Garden of Eden. But I have to ask: How are people who are supposedly born into original sin ever supposed to learn that lesson? If knowledge is what we are looking for, how will we who are evil learn to be good?

Some Eastern traditionalists would answer that our journey is the journey from ignorance to bliss. That we evolve from a state of ignorance in which we do many immoral and even evil things, until we finally move off the wheel of reincarnation into nirvana—or a state of bliss in which we do not suffer and there is no more need for reincarnation. If we go with that, we'd have to recognize that there are very few people who have reached this state of bliss. So, what about the rest of us?

Western traditionalists would answer that the only solution to the dilemma of sin is forgiveness. If we go with that, we have to ask: Did Jesus fail? If Jesus really came here, knowing that he was working with people who were, at their core, basically bad people, to forgive them of their sins and teach them how to be good now that they'd been forgiven—*what happened?* Why are so many people still living in what even they would call sin? Why are there still so many who, even though they have been forgiven and "born again," are basically living in sin, though they may strive mightily against it? But traditionalists have an answer for that too. They would shake their heads in despair blaming the *ruler of this world,* i.e., Satan. He tricks the minds and hearts of even well-intended Christians. So, then what do we do with verses like this:

For as the rain and the snow come down from heaven, and do not return there without watering the earth, and making it bear and sprout, and furnishing seed to the sower and bread to the eater; so shall my word be which goes forth from my mouth; it shall not return to me empty, without accomplishing what I desire and without succeeding in the matter for which I sent it (Isaiah 55:10-11).

Wasn't it the word of God, or *'elohiym*, which spoke the beginning of our history here on planet earth into being, back when the earth was formless and void? Wasn't that word something like, "Let there be light" and "let there be an expanse in the midst of the waters, and let it separate the waters from the waters" and "let the waters below the heavens be gathered into one place and let the dry land appear" and "let the earth sprout vegetation... plants...fruit trees..." and "let there be lights in the expanse of the heavens to separate day from night..." and "let the waters teem with swarms of living creatures, and let birds fly above the earth" and "let the earth bring forth living creatures after their kind..." and finally "let us make man in our image, according to our likeness, and let them rule over the fish of the sea and over the birds of the sky, and over the cattle and over all the earth and over every creeping thing that creeps on the earth" (Genesis 1)? And when they had made humans, wasn't it *'elohiym* who blessed them saying, "Be fruitful and multiply, and fill the earth, and subdue it, and rule over the fish of the sea and over the birds of the sky, and over every living thing that moves on the earth" (1:28)?

Wasn't this an example, even to traditionalists, of the divine sending out the word? Well, if that is true, why has it returned to him so empty—so devoid of success—even to the point that it isn't man who rules the earth but Satan? What is going on here? Did *'elohiym* lie? No, of course not, we sputter, but just look around—I mean obviously the world is ruled by Satan. There is so much evil, so much greed, and personal aggrandizement, political manipulation, drugs, alcohol, murder, depravity, and abuse. How could it possibly be true that Satan doesn't rule this world? So, we conclude that man has screwed it all up—sinful creature that he is—he has developed an alliance with Satan in the same way that if he'd chosen to do so, he could have allied with the divine instead.

And this belief has been so perpetuated throughout the world, that most people believe it—even if they do not come from traditional Western religion. Somehow we've just screwed it all up—I mean look at us—we really can't say that at our core we are good people, can we? Just look around! God didn't fail—we did. So, where does this leave the word of God that cannot return to him empty?

The New Age/New Thought movement responds by saying that everything on the earth plane is illusion. It isn't real. We've just made it all up. In other words, God's word has not returned to him empty, we've just made up a world of suffering in which to live. The real world, they say, is the world of bliss in which we can live if only we will refuse to think or feel anything "negative" and avoid TV, radio and media that is "negative." I've spoken to those who espouse this belief and asked questions like "Isn't this a bit Pollyanna-ish?" Their answer is, "Maybe it is, but I'm happy, so what difference does it make." And their idea is that if everyone thought like they thought, they'd be happy too.

These viewpoints run the gamut of explanations as to the conundrum of the suffering world and what we can do about it. All three viewpoints, Eastern, Western and New Age/New Thought each answer the basic question as to why the world is what it is—i.e., why we suffer. We suffer because we are ignorant, we suffer because we are sinful, we suffer because we've made up a world of suffering. But what if the question isn't why do we suffer? What if that question only covers the surface of the question as to why it is that God's word appears to have returned to him empty? What if the real question is, Who am I?

Both the Bible (and many other sacred texts) as well as the *Course In Miracles*—most often used by New Agers as a kind of Bible—tell us that we are divine Self—but most of us either don't notice this being said or we don't put any emphasis on it whatsoever. In fact, if we study the texts of most of the world's major religions—really study them, rather than just take them at literal or surface value—we will find that they all say this same thing: We are divine beings. My recent book *The Law of Attraction: The Soul's Answer To Why It Isn't Working and How It Can*, devotes an entire Chapter to some of the sacred world texts, such as the *Surangama Sutra*, the *Mahayana Mahaparinirvana Sutra*, the *Bhagavad Gita*, some Sufi poetry, as well as the Bible to find out what these texts have to say about who we really are. So, I won't go into all of that again here, though you are certainly welcome to explore this independently. But suffice to say, that this notion of ourselves as divine beings leads us to that second kind of knowledge.

And if we go back to the meaning of the word *knowledge*, as it is referred to by the tree of knowledge of good and evil, we can't walk away from those definitions without recognizing that they are leading us to find out who we really are. And this knowledge is based in experience, rather than just an acceptance of what we've been told. But Western traditionalists would tell us that acceptance of what we've been told is faith, and rejection of what we've been told is lack of faith. And it was that same kind of thinking that led the church to condemn people to death for questioning the reality to which the church had attached itself. In fact, it is why Galileo was sentenced to prison when he stood up for the Copernican theory that the earth revolved around the sun. The church had attached itself to the theory that the sun revolved around the earth because the earth just had to be the center of the universe. Most people cite this history as evidence of the clash between science and religion. But I think it says far more about how we define faith.

I do find it very interesting that this notion of faith, as described in Hebrews 11:1 in the New Testament of the Christian Bible, as, "assurance of things hoped for, the conviction of things not seen" is assumed as a kind of knowledge. We just know what we know—even if all that we know is what we've been taught to know. Yet, while on one side of the mouth traditionalists seem to be telling us that we should believe in "things not seen," on the other side, their knowledge is based entirely in what is seen. Look around, they say, for evidence of evil. And where would they like us to look for evidence that God's word will not return empty? But it is equally interesting that New Agers will say that what is not seen is the only assurance we have of things hoped for. And many of us, including traditionalists, scientists, politicians, historians, and followers of all faiths, assume that what they espouse to be truth is fact.

The word *faith,* as it is used in that verse in Hebrews is *pistis,* (πιῶστιζ), which is all about *belief,* or *the conviction of the truth of anything.* But it is rooted in the primary verb *peitho* (πειῶθω), which means *to persuade, to induce one by words to believe, to make friends of, to win one's favor, gain one's good will, or to seek to win one, strive to please one, to tranquilize, to listen to, obey, yield to, comply with, to trust, have confidence,* or *to be confident.* Now, I don't know about you, but for me, this changes the connotation of the word *faith* entirely. Taken in this context alone, we see that faith, unlike the knowledge that is the journey of experience, is but a form of brainwashing. We must learn to believe, we must be persuaded, befriended, won over, pleased and—the most informative of all—we must be tranquilized.

In 1 Corinthians 13:13, we read this: "But now abide faith, hope, and love, these three, but the greatest of these is love." The same word, *pistis,* is used for *faith* here. Hebrews tells us that faith *is* the assurance of things hoped for—so this pretty much puts *faith* and *hope* in the same category. But love is greater than either. And love is a growing, reaching, experience—something we can come to know with that same kind of knowledge referred to above (*yâda'*). We will be speaking much more about love in an upcoming Chapter.

But the word *assurance,* as it is used in the verse in Hebrews is also interesting. It is *hupotassō* (υϑποταϖσσω), which means *to arrange under, to subordinate, to subject, to obey, to submit to one's control.* It was a Greek military term meaning *to arrange under the command of a leader.* It is rooted in both *hupo* (υϑποϖ), *by* or *under,* and *tasso* (ταϖσσω), which means *to put in order, to station, to place in a certain order, to arrange a place, to appoint, to assign, to appoint to one's own responsibility or authority, to appoint mutually.* When we put this together with the word *pistis,* what we might conclude is that faith is defined as *persuasion by our own appointment.* We obey the persuasion we receive from others, or—a much more hopeful definition—we obey the persuasion of our own authority. Either way it is our own appointment. But if our own authority is that which allows us the experience *to know, to learn to know, to learn by experience, to see, find out and make oneself known or reveal oneself and be known,* then it is the same as *knowledge.* But if our own authority gives over to external locus of control, then we are being persuaded to agree to something that may or may not be true. So, essentially then, the verse in Hebrews is telling us that **our persuasions are all about the authority we give over to hope.** Now there's a thought. The question then becomes: Who has authority over our hope?

But if knowledge really means *to know, to learn to know, to learn by experience, to perceive, to see, to find out,* and *to make oneself known, reveal oneself* and *to be known,* then we might have to consider the journey itself as knowledge. If it is true, as we've said in previous chapters, that the journey here to planet earth is really all about uniting form with formlessness, then what we are doing here is learning what we need to learn to make that happen. If we really are co-creators—a part of the original *'elohiym* —who took on form in order to unite it in knowledge with formlessness, then what we are learning about separation is just as important as the ultimacy of seeing again that we've never been separated. Knowledge is learning to know. Knowledge is learning by experience. Knowledge is finding out. Knowledge is making oneself known. Knowledge is revealing one's Self. Knowledge is coming to be known.

Those definitions are very different from our modern and Westernized version of the word *knowledge*. Our modern Western version is found in the definition of the word *fact*. If it is fact, you can know it. Plain and simple. If it isn't fact, then it cannot be known. Plain and simple, black and white—totally Western. But that is not the definition of the word as it is given to us in the phrase *the tree of knowledge of good and evil*. There the *process* of discovery *is* knowledge. There, the *process* of revealing the true essence of one's Self *is* knowledge. This is a much more fluid definition, for it speaks of evolutionary process in the same way that the definition of *heaven* speaks of evolutionary process. This gives us all plenty of room to play with the creative process itself.

That is what we came here to do: to play with the creative process. We, as a part of *'elohiym*, are dabbling in what it is like to paint the house green—no, blue—no, yellow. We are writing the play and deciding on different roles in the play from one incarnation to the next, living out the dramas, as if they were the truth, in much the same way that a method actor will become his or her role. We are finding out what it is like to live an *as-if* life, in which we live *as if* we were separate from the divine. In the process, over many incarnations, we are slowly learning who we are. THAT is what the tree of knowledge of good and evil is really all about. And when we chose to eat of that tree, it is just possible that we were *not* disobeying a directive.

Genesis 2:17 has been translated to mean: "but from the tree of the knowledge of good and evil you shall not eat, for in the day that you eat from it you shall surely die." In Hebrew that looks like this:

סֹת: התא'אד בות 'אר 'ל לאכא: נמ יכ מוי לאכא: נמ התֹם התֹם התֹם

The literal translation of the Hebrew sentence is:

tree knowledge good evil no (or *–not, without,* or *before time*) to eat or be eaten from (or *–out, since, so that, both* or *either*) that (or *–for, because, surely* or *nevertheless*) day to eat or to be eaten from (or *–out, since, so that, both* or *either)* to die, to die

Now, I double-dog dare you to translate that sentence into a meaning that is without a doubt meant to be translated as we've translated it. I'm not an expert in languages, but seriously, can we really be certain what is meant by this ancient sentence? And yet, we have based our entire world view, on which we have based everything else in the world, on that single sentence. Everything we believe to be true about duality comes from the *metaphor* presented by this tree—whether we are Jewish, Christian, Muslim, Hindu or of another faith—somehow we screwed up. For if Adam and Eve were told not to eat of the tree, then they disobeyed—and everything in our world is based on their disobedience—or as Western traditionalists put it—on our original sin.

But what if, instead this sentence is really saying something more like: death will come as a result of eating and being eaten by the journey on which you are about to embark—the journey of knowledge of duality? This changes things entirely, in fact, what it means on a metaphysical level is that because humanity had incorporated the duality trance state into its way of living, Life— that Life that is of the living water that Jesus offered the Samaritan woman—was going to be harder to access, for not only did humanity consume the duality trance state so that it became a biological component of the body/mind, but we were also consumed by it. And all the changes we discussed in Chapter 4 were a result of this choice.

Traditionalists insist that eating of the tree of knowledge of good and evil was wrong. We should not have done it. But from this new perspective of both the interpretation of the word *knowledge,* and the potentialities inherent in this possibly very misunderstood sentence, it was not wrong at all, it was simply the choice we made as part of our co-creative effort to unite matter with spirit, form with formlessness. The other option was to stay in the subtle body without any awareness of physicality — and never ask the questions that are essential to creating something new and different from anything that had ever been created before. But if we had taken that option, all would still be formless and void and form would not be able to unite with formlessness.

As we've said, in order for form to so unite, it has to first experience itself fully as form. In much the same way that we often have to go to the fringes of death before we really can appreciate life, so it is that form has to go to the fringes of form — just form with no attachment to formlessness — before it can see that form and formlessness are one. Form has to answer every creative question relevant to the experience of life as form, and run through the gamut of potential answers to those questions before it can finally experience the answer, the creative answer that unites form and formlessness. And once form sees itself as one with formlessness, and formlessness sees itself as one with form, the entire universe will shift into a completely new phase of development. We might say, well it sure is taking us a long time to get this thing figured out. But time is relative. What feels long to us as form, is really only always the eternal now in formlessness. And once we know ourselves as both form and formlessness, then time will no longer be necessary anyway.

And if what we are doing here is *knowledge as journey* then we also have the option of knowing what it is like to live here, right here, as both form and formlessness. Many of the world's Yogis have experienced this. The ability to heat up the body with the mind. The ability to become invisible. The ability to levitate, to move matter around with formless energy. Quantum physics is also demonstrating the union of form with formlessness through many of its experiments, so that, for example, one commonly known experiment demonstrated that two connected electrons broken apart and spun off into entirely different directions would act simultaneously exactly the same from a great distance apart. These are some of the things we understand now as the union of form with formlessness. But there is another way of knowing this union—there is the knowledge of home. There is the ability to inhabit heaven now.

So, what is it like to inhabit heaven now? It is like those all-too-rare moments that all of us have experienced at one time or another in which we see clearly, if even for a flash of a nanosecond, that life is full and rich and powerfully potent right now. Every one of us has had at least one, but most probably several of those moments. Very often they happen around a serious or potential loss or an exceptional view of nature. Both nature and loss tend to put us in touch with the deeper aspects of ourselves so that we are more attuned and therefore can hear the gentle whisperings of insight and understanding that are always circling around the psyche looking to build a home in its branches. But those moments are very often later dismissed as a rarity all-too-easily lost in the chaos of living in the "real" world. Actually, they are little windows to the soul—the divine Self—heaven.

Inhabiting heaven means inhabiting your deepest essence, coming to live from there. But like Jacob, most of us wrestle with our angels instead of taking up residence with them. We've learned from Adam and Selena's stories how we might go about the process of inhabiting heaven now. Coming to inhabit heaven is the same as the coming to know the Self. We experience our way into that knowledge. We experience first the hem of the garment. But once we've made contact, once we've had an affective or subjective experience with the Self, we are now opened. Through that tiny opening we can begin to allow the light to pour in, or we can simply close the door again.

What keeps us from inhabiting heaven now is not sin or immorality. What keeps us from inhabiting heaven now is the fact that we are closed to experiencing heaven now. We've been trained to believe that life is just the way it is and there's not much we can do about it. We've been trained to believe that it is blasphemous to realize our deepest divine nature. But our training often runs counter to these glimpses of heaven we get and dismiss in the name of that training. All that is left to us then is the journey of experience that reveals the divine Self.

People who inhabit heaven now are no better, no more moral than anyone else. They may appear to be, but they are not. They are simply more open. Being open is all about reception. It's not about doing, acting, giving—it's about receiving. And in order to inhabit heaven now, we simply must be open to all that there is to receive of truth, of love, of the potency of raw LIFE energy.

Thus it is that meditation as an experience is so important to the process of inhabiting heaven, because from the position of stillness, we come to know. The statement "Cease striving and know that I am God" from Psalms 42:6 doesn't mean sit still so that you can learn that you are not in charge. It means when we stop trying to find the divine, we learn that we *are* divine. It means that as we are still we can hear the soul talking to us, that we can feel the stirrings of divine energy within us, that we are able to step into ourselves and just be with that deep internal essence. And the more we do that, the more we come to know. And what we come to know is not some external God who wishes for us to be better people. What we come to know is that we are already the salt of the earth and the light of the world. We are the essential divine energy. We are the way, the truth and the life.

And the more we know that, the more we choose to live that truth. So, inhabiting heaven is first inhabiting the truth of who we are. That means we tell the truth to all facets of ourselves, leaving no stone unturned. It means that we allow the divine Self to sit in its wonderful stillness and witness everything we do, say and think. It means that we can be in that truth, without judging ourselves, but in full awareness of divine Self as one with all of it. Second, it is living from that truth, instead of from the lies of duality. So, when duality comes knocking on heaven's door to tell us that we should be afraid, that we should worry about whether or not we will have enough, or whether or not someone does or doesn't like us, or whether or not we are doing the right thing, or whether or not we should get *them* back for how badly they've treated us; we receive that energy and take it with us again to the stillness that is divine Self and remain open to receiving more. Just as Selena and Adam did we receive each thing that arises in the stillness and we allow it its say and we allow it to show us every aspect of itself so that it gives us its fullest message.

You see we've got it all backwards. We think that we should be about the business of living right, about the business of doing, about the business of serving God, or others. But that's not at all what inhabiting heaven is about. It is about *receiving* the love that is ours, it is about *receiving* each aspect of ourselves as if it had value, it is about *receiving* the grace of life energy that radiates in and *as* us, it's about *receiving*. The Buddha knew this, Arjuna was taught this in the Bhagavad Gita, the Gnostics knew this, Brahman of the Hindu faith is this knowledge, and Jesus knew this—and that knowledge is the only difference between us and them. All that we are and all that we ever will be is about reception. Receiving the divine within us from the divine within us. Receiving all that is from the source of all that is. And when we live in that kind of reception, we are inhabiting heaven now.

Notice, however, that I did *not* say that heaven is a state of constant bliss. That, I'm afraid is what we are looking for. A state. We are hoping to live in a mood. But heaven is not a mood. Heaven is the very essence of Life energy itself. Heaven is the tree of Life. It is a deep abiding sense of Self as stillness that is the source of all movement. And like that tree of Life, it grows— eternally. And the birds of the air nest in its branches. Heaven is the discernment that recognizes falseness immediately, so that when we appear at its door looking for bliss, it tells us to go look elsewhere. But when we open, when we simply open to the essence of who we are, we begin to experience Life. Will there be joy there? Yes. Will there be peace there? Yes. But is this a mood? No. Heaven is your Life, not your mood.

And what about suffering? Once we begin to inhabit heaven, will there be suffering? We've all been taught that in heaven there is no suffering, so does this inhabitation provide us with that long-sought world in which suffering does not exist? What the essence of a soul knows is far beyond suffering. Suffering is the surface energy that forces us to look deeper. It serves no other purpose. Suffering is a derivative of the duality trance state in which we live as if we are separate from our own deepest essence. But suffering is *not* an external event.

Events, circumstances and relationships don't cause us to suffer. Suffering occurs as a result of our blindness to who we are. Suffering is always an inside job. Suffering is what we choose as an internal response to an external event. For example, we respond to loss with suffering. But when we chose to see it, deep within us there is some part of us living in reception of this so-called loss. The reception is the process of acceptance of the shift in consciousness that is the natural next step in our evolution. We actually think that we can lose people, places, things, and circumstances. But we never lose anything. And if we were living fully absorbed by the soul, we would walk through the process of acceptance receiving every change in our lives as a gift.

But can a person learn to suspend the suffering version of life in favor of the one in which we see the truth of our lives? Once we see the truth there is no other version of life. The truth of loss to death is that there is no death—our relationship to that person continues as they exist in formlessness, and we in form and formlessness. But with regard to our emotional responses to loss, first they are influenced by our interpretation of that loss. And second, emotion is also divine energy. When we stay present with our emotions for long enough we see that they are giving us a divine gift. As we cry we may also find the richness of life in those very tears. As we let go we realize ourselves and our connections at a deeper level.

The reason we think of our emotions as difficult or easy (or as they are too often labeled, *positive* or *negative*), is because we want to have that mood of constant bliss. In fact, those of us on the spiritual path often judge ourselves for not having constant bliss, as we saw Selena do. We tell ourselves that we must be doing something wrong, that if we were doing it right, we'd be living in bliss. But if we were to be able to suspend that fallacy for a few moments and look into how we actually feel—without the notion that we *should be* feeling something different nagging at us—we would no longer see the "difficult" or "negative" emotions as difficult or negative. They would simply be feelings we would feel. We would seek to be present with those emotions as if they were special and beautiful aspects of living a poignant and rich experience—which is what they actually are. Each one of them comes into our awareness to give us a gift.

On the surface and from the perspective of the duality trance state, we see our emotions as painful, heavy and laborious—so that we have to *work on* them to make them transform into something else less painful, heavy and laborious. But from the perspective of the soul, the divine Self, there is no division, no separation, and all things are divine. What does this mean in a practical sense? Well, it means that we can let go of our judgments and just have an experience with our emotions and find out where that takes us.

When we think of heaven, we generally think of it as a final place. The quality of the word carries connotations of finality and structure. It is the *place* at which we will finally arrive, a place that is perfectly place and perfectly final, and perfectly perfect. But as we said earlier, we are not looking for perfection, we are looking at a kind of eternally ongoing evolution that is constantly completing itself. This means that when we have an emotion, we can lean into its experience and let it carry us to a new mystery of Self. We can't know heaven as fact. Heaven can only be known as an ever-evolving experience. We do not leave the world and its events, people, and circumstances to live in a rarefied atmosphere of sated bliss when we choose to inhabit heaven now. We enter the world through the openness of divine Self. We encounter the world *as* divine Self. We impact and are impacted by the world *in* divine Self.

And the only way to know this is to have that experience for yourself. Step into the stillness within you. Open yourself to its influence over you; allow yourself to fall into that stillness and let it wash over all of your feelings, sensations, thoughts and beliefs. Be still and just be with that stillness. It speaks of and for itself in small whisperings, like the little clicking sounds your computer makes when it is downloading something. Being with beingness is heaven. Being still is knowing I AM divine Self. Being still is an experience of that knowledge of who we actually are. And as we are still we receive. We receive the abundant rich love of the divine Self, we receive sacred information as awareness as it downloads. We receive because we are not in the way of receiving. We receive because being still *is* the knowledge I AM.

I encourage deep daily meditation because the minute we step into the stillness we cease striving, which means that all that is available to the divine is available to us. I encourage deep daily mediation that grows into deep walking mediation that evolves into deep talking meditation, that becomes deep Self-awareness in everything we do, say and think. I encourage it because it ultimately becomes one of the channels of initiation. Remember that Jesus said that he did nothing of his own initiation. The divine Self was initiating everything. When we step into the stillness often enough, it begins to initiate our lives. And as it initiates it reveals more and more about the Self as initiator until one day we wake up and realize we are not just touching heaven now and then, we are inhabiting it, right here, right now on planet earth. This is the word that does not return to the divine empty. Form and formless have been united. But whether we get this now, or get it in the next or the next incarnation, the word which is divine creativity in action *will* eventually have us all living in the knowledge of who we actually are as divine Self.

But how do we know this is true? Fact is, we don't—not in any kind of factual way anyway. We don't know for a fact that there was ever any such thing, either metaphorical or real, as a tree of knowledge of good and evil or a tree of Life. We don't know for a fact that heaven exists at all. In fact, we don't know much at all for a fact.

But if knowing is the discovery process of experience itself, then yes, we can know all of this as experience. We can know this as we discover it within ourselves. We can begin to touch the hem of the garment of the I AM that we are, and as we experience the healing of that awakening, we can begin to receive more and more of it as we become still in order to receive. We can receive our eternal home in heaven right now, right here on planet earth. We can inhabit heaven now. And in so doing, we can begin to un-know duality as the only fact of our lives. And for all we know the apparent uncertainty of receiving will become the only certainty of our lives.

12

The Wide Expanse of Love

We've found ourselves a narrow, confined little space in which to live and breathe. And we've molded ourselves to its form, all the while wearing blinders lest we begin to see beyond its tiny absolutes. It told us what to do and we conformed. It told us how to think and so we thought. It even told us how we should feel, and so we forbade any other feelings to come into awareness. We can define ourselves by this confined little space—whether we are *good* people or *bad* people—according to the definitions given to us by the duality trance state.

According to Western traditionalists, Jesus instructed us to stay in this narrow space, for he said:

Enter by the narrow gate; for the gate is wide, and the way is broad that leads to destruction, and many are those who enter by it. For the gate is small, and the way is narrow that leads to life, and few are those who find it.

This verse has been used over and over by fundamentalists whose safe passage into an externalized version of heaven is meant only for the few who have their particular religion. But when we look at the root meanings of the words here, we find something entirely different from what we've been taught. The word *narrow* here is *stenos* (στενοωζ), which means *narrow* and *strait*. But it is rooted in *histemi* (ι&στημι), which means something very different. That word means, *to cause to make stand, to bid, to stand by—as in the presence of others, in the midst, before judges;* and *to place, to make firm, to fix, to establish, to uphold, to sustain the authority or force of anything, to be of steadfast mind.* So, basically, Jesus is using the word *stenos* as a metaphor which will help us attain to its deeper meaning. Enter, he says, by the way that causes you to stand in the midst, established, upheld and sustained by your own authority and force, for in so doing you will be lead to life—to living water.

But that's not all, for the word *broad* is *platus* (πλατυῶζ) and originates in the root word *plasso* (πλαϖσσω), which means *to mold* or *form* and *is used of a potter*. And the word destruction is *apoleia* (αφπωϖλεια), which means *to destroy as one destroys vessels*—i.e., those made by a potter—and *to perish—as money perishes*. *Apoleia* is rooted in *apollumi* (αφποϖλλυμι), which also means *to destroy or perish*. But *apollumi* is rooted in *apo* (αφποϖ), which means *of separation, the state of separation* or *of origin*. So, here Jesus is basically saying the same thing that was said to Adam and Eve by *'elohiym*, informing them of what they were looking toward when they incorporated the duality trance state into their bodies and minds. He is saying that the way of the duality trance state molds us to fit its origins in separation. But, and here's the amazing part of this statement: the mold will be broken. We cannot forever stay in this place in which we believe that we are separate from the divine. We will eventually break open to become who we really are.

So, while traditionalists and fundamentalists everywhere insist that to leave the narrow little place in which we live wrapped in our shrouds and perpetually wearing our blinders lest we see something else beyond that which we've been taught, what we can now know is that both paths are ultimately going to lead us to our Selves. The one allows us to stand in our own power and find our own living water; the other provides us a mold which must ultimately be broken so that we emerge from separation into oneness.

The thought that there is more than one path and that all paths ultimately lead to the same place is profoundly disturbing to many traditionalists and fundamentalists. And actually to most of us it is disturbing, because we all want for the *bad* guys to get their due—and if we've been *good* we want our due too. That's how much we are still connecting the dots between our place on the continuum between the polarities of *good* and *evil* and reward or consequence—as if there were some kind of magic thread that binds them together.

But remember the statement we read earlier in Chapter 6 in which Jesus said: "for He causes the sun to rise on the evil and the good and sends rain on the righteous and the unrighteous" (v 45)? This statement clearly tells us that there is no connection whatsoever between our fortunes and our position on the duality polarity. But many say that the following statement, made in Galatians by that letter's author, was actually made by Jesus: "Do not be deceived, God is not mocked; for whatever a man sows, this he will also reap" (6:7). It's a little, no, a lot like bad karma— and it's in direct conflict with this other statement made by Jesus in the Sermon on the Mount. So much for the inerrancy of the Bible.

Yet the Bible doesn't have to be inerrant to tell the gentle truth of our innate and profound I AM nature, any more than knowledge has to be seen as fact. And if I were to decide on my own—which is what we all do—which of those two statements were correct in their essential wisdom and love, I'd have to go with the one made by Jesus. Jesus alludes to this same message when he reminds his disciples of a "saying" commonly used during the historical point of reference in which he lived: "For in this case the saying is true, 'One sows, and another reaps'" (John 4:37).

If the duality trance state is true, then yes, we are likely to reap what we sow. But if it is false, then there is no connection between our goodness or badness and the fortunes or misfortunes of our lives. This doesn't mean that if I run a red light in front of a cop I'm not likely to get caught, but it does mean that my moral character does not produce its own consequence. So, if we are going to drop out of the duality trance state, we are going to have to come to terms with the idea that it rains and shines on both the so-called *good* and the so-called *bad*—for there simply are no such terms.

When Jesus spoke to the Samaritan woman at the well, he said nothing about worshipping in goodness or badness. But he did say something about worshipping in spirit and in truth. If you can't get behind a single other word said in this book, try to get behind this: When we spend all of our energy deciding what is good and what is bad, we don't have much left for what is spirit and what is truth. In fact, we don't even really know how to define those words.

But here is what is spirit and here is what is truth: Love.

Beloved, let us love one another, for love is from God; and everyone who loves is born of God and knows God. The one who does not love does not know God, for God is love (1 John 4:7-8).

Teacher, which is the great commandment of the law? And he said to him, "You shall love the Lord your God with all your heart, and with all your soul, and with all your mind. This is the great and foremost commandment. The second is like it, You shall love your neighbor as yourself. On these two commandments depend the whole Law and the Prophets (Matthew 22:36-40).

Those two laws were written into some of the most difficult of all books of the Bible to read, Deuteronomy (6:5) and Leviticus (19:18). And they were surrounded so thickly with other rigid and much less meaningful laws that we hardly even knew they were there. But they were.

What is even more interesting is what follows these two statements in those books of the law. The command to love the Lord your God with all your heart, mind and soul, was followed by this: "And these words I am commanding you today shall be written on your hearts" (Deut. 6:6). Yes, and where else could such a command be written—for how else will we make our hearts obey?

And the command to love your neighbor as yourself, goes like this:

You shall not take vengeance nor bear any grudge against the sons of your people, but you shall love your neighbor as yourself; I am the Lord.

Now that last commandment could be read like this:

You shall not take vengeance nor bear any grudge against the sons of your people, but you shall love your neighbor as yourself—I AM that I AM.

The difference in the second interpretation is that the command is telling us why we should love our neighbor as ourselves, for like us, our neighbor is I AM that I AM. Remember that in Chapter 3 we learned that Charles Fillmore, author of *The Metaphysical Bible Dictionary,* told us that the word *Lord* should be translated as *I AM.* So, when the writer of Leviticus wrote that command, he may or may not have really known the power behind his statement—but our translators took the potency right out of it. Why? Because they lived and interpreted from the duality trance state.

But how does a person love the I AM with all the heart, mind, and soul? Well, from the perspective of the duality trance state, it is impossible, for we are at bottom, sinful people. And from that perspective, this is why we needed to develop so many other laws: because we couldn't trust the human heart, mind and soul to love in this way. In other words, we had to constrain ourselves, circumscribe our sins, and then with the little that was left, we were to love God and neighbor.

Truth is, we spend very little time in our churches, mosques and synagogues talking about these commands without the "should" attached. We tend believe that unless we are fairly consistently told to love, we just won't. The human heart just doesn't have the capacity for the kind of love that is being spoken of in these verses. But it should, shouldn't it? So, let us just work harder at loving. Try to be kind, and giving. Try to stifle anger. Try to avoid selfishness. Try to stop judging. Try to turn the other cheek. Just keep trying and even though we all know we will never really succeed—because we were born in original sin—just keep trying. And just ignore the fact that no good deed goes unpunished.

Whew! I don't know about you, but I'm tired just reading that paragraph—and I'm feeling pretty hopeless too. We are fighting against a strong headwind there, don't you think? And the headwind is made up entirely of the duality trance state. In fact, it tells us that we will fail, but that we should do our best anyway.

Here is what is spirit and what is truth: "not by might, nor by power, but by my Spirit says the Lord of hosts" (Zechariah 6:2). Jesus knew this truth completely, for it is he who said, "I can do nothing of my own initiative" (John 5:30). From the duality trance state, in which we are split off into consciousness and unconsciousness, split between wrong and right, good and bad, humanity and divinity, we will not ever be able to love. This is what John meant when he wrote that those who do not know God cannot love. We do not know ourselves to be divine, therefore, we cannot really love. That statement, "not by might, nor by power, but by my Spirit says the Lord of hosts," could be interpreted thusly: Not by might, nor by power, but by my Spirit, says I AM. In other words, the belief that we are separate from the divine has absolutely no power. But I AM within us has all the power and can do whatever it wants. And what it wants is to love.

But from the duality trance state, we operate out of the several things we call love. We call possessiveness and jealousy love. We call power over another person love. We call obsession love. We call trying to change another person love. We call security love. We call worry love. But none of these things are love. Love is absolute unconditionality. We do not earn it. It cannot be created or contrived. It is a gift that comes to our awareness already whole.

Remember that we said that the healthy feminine aspect of our psychology had to do with the internal journey in which we go inside and receive what we've found there. The healthy masculine energy then takes what was found there and gives it to the world through manifestation. It works the same with love. We must first go within to receive love, before we can take it out into the world.

The reception of love comes about as a natural part of the inner journey. As we go within, as did Selena and Adam in the previous chapter, we begin to relate to ourselves differently. We tend, over time and the effortless effort of sitting with the Self, to develop more and more compassion for ourselves, until finally we begin to really enjoy our own company, to actually relish in the deliciousness of our own thoughts and feelings, to seriously desire to take care of and protect our newfound precious Self. It's very much the act of falling in love with ourselves. This is self in a process of receiving love from Self, until finally there is a union between self and Self, so that all is Self. This is loving the Lord your God—the I AM that I AM we are—with all of our hearts, our minds and our souls. This is heaven.

It is at that point that we can, like Jesus, say that we do nothing of our own initiative. This means all that we do is coming from the soul—or the Spirit—as Jesus put it. This is worshipping in spirit and in truth. This is the prayer in "my name" of which Jesus spoke so often. Prayer is worship for it honors truth and spirit. And prayer in my name is prayer that comes from the I AM that I AM. "My name" is I AM. And if I become the Self, then I have become I AM. If I AM that I AM, then I am praying *in* that name. If I am living life as I AM then I AM praying in the name. If I am living Life as I AM then I AM not taking the Lord's name, I AM, in vain. This is all there is of love. Love that loves because its very essence is love.

What will that look like when it becomes action? Well it will look a lot like Jesus looked as he behaved. It will look a lot like Buddha looked as he behaved. It will look a lot like Paramahansa Yogananda, Ajahn Chah, Teresa of Avila, Ghandi, Thomas Merton, Táhirih, Maharishi Mahesh Yogi, Mother Meera, D.T. Suzuki, William Blake, Hildegard of Bingen, Ram Dass, Thich Nhat Hanh and many more. But love is not some sickeningly sweet emotion. Nor is it that which makes us sacrifice ourselves for others. Love is not a should or an ought. Love is not a duty or an obligation. Love is not all nice and sweet—sometimes it calls the Pharisees vipers. Love does not just tell the truth, however. Love *is* truth. It is the only truth, for there is always only love, as there is always only divine energy. Love is who we are. Love is compassion and grace in a combination that removes initiative from the duality trance state and gives it to the divine Self or soul.

Love is not our definition of unselfishness, or worse, selflessness—love is Self in reception *as* action. Let us say that again: *Love is Self in reception as action.* In other words, love is something we receive from divine Self, which radiates into us and out of us as divine action. Love cannot be given. Did you hear what I said? *Love cannot be given by us to others.* All of our assumptions about love tell us that we should be loving and kind to others, that we should put others first, that we should be patient and loving and kind and bear all things, believe all things and hope all things. But the problem with this thinking is that we assume a *should* in front of that love. We assume that 1st Corinthians 13 is telling us what we should do. But actually it is telling us *how we are loved*. It is telling us that this is the only definition of love there is, and from the duality trance state, we simply have not a clue about what love really is. Everyone, living identified with duality, who tries to love in this way fails— because it simply cannot be done in separation consciousness. Rather this love is divine love that comes to us and becomes us. The minute we put a should in front of it, it ceases to be love.

So, love is not worrying about others, witnessing to others, or striving to serve others. Nope. Love is not taking care of others, protecting others, or even the current jargon, "being there for" others, or "having each other's backs." Love is not anything we can ever do from the duality trance state.

Love is the realization, the reception of who we are. When we fully know that we are so richly and potently loved by the divine Self, which is not far away in some rarefied world while we suffer down here in the real world, but is rather the essence of who we are; we become aware that love *is* the natural essence of our flesh, blood, bone, thought, emotion and sensation. Then when we look at others, we know that they are likewise divinely loved and that *love that we are* effortlessly radiates to them through the oneness we are. We do not see them as needing us to heal them, for they are divine beings on a journey of their own to full consciousness of that reality. They do not need us to protect, take care of, be there for or take their backs. They, like us, are fully empowered to experience divine Self as they choose on their journey. If they do not see that, that's because their journey belongs to them and they will take it in the way the soul has orchestrated for them. And each little thing in which they engage or which they encounter along the way is getting them there, in much the same way that regardless of what the molecule of water is doing, the river is still carrying it to the sea. Like we have now ceased to judge ourselves for our journey, we will cease to judge them for theirs. And it is only then that intimacy can be richly enjoyed by both parties. And it is this intimacy that is the definition of true compassion.

Compassion is not feeling sorry for another human being, or trying to fix, help, heal or otherwise make their lives different. Rather, those things define attachment, which according to Buddha, is the antithesis of truth. Compassion is not wishing another's life would be different. Compassion is not hoping and praying that others will see how they are screwing up their lives. Compassion is not trying to *help* them—a term so often used as a euphemism for trying to control or change them. Compassion is intimacy. Compassion is knowing someone in the Biblical sense, according to the word *ginosko* (γινωσκω), *to know, to understand—an idiom for sexual intercourse.* That's not to say that we will have sex with everyone, but it is to say that we realize our oneness with everyone. We come to know them deeply, expansively, intimately, and they us, because we are one with them and they with us. That is the definition of compassion—even though the dictionary would disagree—because when we know who we are, when we become intimate with divine Self, we see clearly that pity is a totally unrealistic stance. In fact, it tells us a lie. It tells us that we are separate from the divine and that life is impossibly hard and people are often helpless before its challenges.

Love is expansive. It moves us beyond the narrow confines of the duality trance state, and allows us to see the reality of ours and others' lives. Love is creative. It allows us to effortlessly create from its fertile ground more and more love and more and more ways to create. Love is not faith or fact. Love is knowledge—the kind of knowledge described in Chapter 9 as experience that brings us to full understanding of who we really are. Love knows itself as the discovery process of an ever expanding universe. Love is that discovery process itself—for there is absolutely nothing more loving than the freedom to explore all of the options of the creative impulse of which we are each and all a constituent. Love lets go; duality holds on. Love receives all things; duality judges all things. Love expands all things; duality diminishes all things. Love is willing to plunge the depths of the psyche to find the soul; duality fears the psyche and believes the soul to be unknowable until after death. Ultimately, love is everything and duality is a whole lot of nothing.

Morality springs whole from the duality trance state in which all is not one, nor is all to be received. Morality separates, while love unites. Morality tells us what we should do; love tells us who we are. Morality tells us who we should be; love is willing to find out who we really are. Morality creates a narrow path; love expands the universe and includes all.

From the duality trance state and from the codes put forth by morality, we have defined love as far, far less than what it really is. We have said that if we love others we should enable them in their addictions, in their compulsions and in their spiral into further emptiness, by petting, pitying and taking responsibility for them. We should not confront them with the truth of their behaviors because that would be unloving. And because we have this *should* about love, we try to deny any feeling that doesn't feel sweet and giving toward the victims of our enabling. We repress the resentments that would inform us of the truth which sets us free. We repress the anger that comes up to tell us that we need to stop deluding ourselves about how we can take care of those who will not take care of themselves. And we pay no attention to that little man on our shoulders informing us that we are only doing these things out of our own control needs, rather than out of our immense and gracious love.

We have said that love means that we should always feel kindly towards others even when they are abusive to us. But how is this loving? In fact, it is lying. First, it is telling ourselves that we will recognize no other feeling besides sweetness. It is telling ourselves to repress every other feeling, such as fear, resentment or anger, which might inform us of the truth of our relationship. It is telling ourselves to pretend, to repress, to deny, to lie. Further, it is informing those who abuse us that doing so is okay and that they don't really have to stop. It is informing those who abuse us that we are powerless and incapable victims—when in fact we have all of the power of I AM at our disposal. It is informing them that all of the blame and aspersions they cast upon us are true—when in fact these are just rationales (lies) they use to continue to do what they do. What they do doesn't help them; it only furthers their alienation from the Self. So, how can we call our sweet support of their abusive behavior love? And yet we do. But love is the truth, for the truth and only the truth—so help me God—sets us free.

We have said that love means that we should tolerate the intolerable and accept the unacceptable by "turning the other cheek." The passage from which that idea is lifted is taken out of context from Matthew 5:39, "…whoever slaps you on your right cheek, turn to him the other also." But that text is part of the sermon we mentioned in Chapter 6, in which it is clear that Jesus was not laying down yet more laws for us to obey, but turning us from the external to the internal for the answers to our questions. So, this part of that speech actually goes like this:

> You have heard that it was said, "An eye for an eye and a tooth for a tooth." But I say to you, do not resist him who is evil; but whoever slaps you on your right cheek, turn to him the other also. And if anyone wants to sue you, and take your shirt, let him have your coat also. And whoever shall force you to go one mile, go with him two. Give to him who asks of you and do not turn away from him who wants to borrow from you.

And then he went on to say:

> You have heard that it was said, "You shall love your neighbor, and hate your enemy." But I say to you, love your enemies, and pray for those who persecute you in order that you may be sons of your Father who is in heaven; for He

causes His sun to rise on the evil and the good, and sends rain on the righteous and the unrighteous. For if you love those who love you, what reward have you? Do not even the tax-gatherers do the same? And if you greet your brothers only, what do you do more than others? Do not even the Gentiles do the same? Therefore, you are to be perfect, as your heavenly Father is perfect (vs. 43-48).

As we said in Chapter 6, the final outcome of this sermon is that we are to become complete in our evolution toward full awareness of who we are as divine beings. So, when Jesus says that we are to turn the other cheek, he does not intend to lay down another law that says we *should* turn the other cheek, literally allowing someone to hit us again. He is telling us that laws alone will never get us there; and yet, all the law will be fulfilled when we become who we really are. So when we take literally the statement "turn the other cheek," we are missing the point entirely.

That said, one of the most interesting parts of that statement is this: "But I say to you, do not resist him who is evil." The phrase *him who is evil* does not refer to a person, but is actually the one word, *evil, poneros* (πονηροΰζ), which means, *full of labors, annoyances, hardships, pressed and harassed by labors, bringing toils, diseased or blind, bad, evil, wicked.* It is rooted in *ponos* (πoΰνoζ), *great trouble, intense desire,* or *pain.* And *ponos* is rooted in *penes* (πεΰνηζ), which means *poor,* and comes from the primary word *penos* (πενoσ), *to toil for daily subsistence.*

Because all that was said after *do not resist evil* is metaphorical and illustrative of how one would avoid resisting evil, the statement is extremely important. Further, because that statement leads head on into the statement about how we are to love and how we are to be complete—it is even more important. The word for *evil* in this passage is that same understanding we now have of what was said by *'elohiym* when they prophesied to

Adam and Eve about what it was going to be like for them after they'd incorporated the duality trance state into the body/mind: they were to live lives full of labor and hardships, and they were going to have to toil for daily subsistence.

If we do not resist lives full of labor, hardships, annoyances, disease, blindness in which we toil for daily subsistence, then we receive those things as part of the oneness—thereby stepping outside the narrow confines of the duality trance state, ceasing all judgment about how it should be and receiving the gifts those things have to offer. Our labors, hardships, annoyances, diseases, blindness and toiling are but aspects of the duality trance state. We think of these things as enemies and we believe that no one in his right mind would love them. But it is our hatred of them that keeps us separate from the divine gifts these things bring with them.

This means, not that we should allow someone to hit us again, neither in the metaphorical nor the real, as it has been translated to mean, but that we learn to *be with* those things that present as evil, from the dualistic mindset. This means that if we have a so-called *negative* thought, we are to walk a mile, no, two miles with it. We are to become intimate with it—for that is the nature of divine love. We are to allow it its say, to listen to it as we would a frightened little child. When poverty looks like it's about the take the shirt off of our backs, we are to lean into that vision of life so that we allow it to speak its fears, and listen to it as we would a frightened little child. When duality slaps us on the right cheek we are to receive that slap as the love it actually is, for, regardless of how we are interpreting the events of our lives, all things are useful to the soul for our awakening. Everything is a gift of love from the divine Self to the false identity we call self. When we receive it that way, we are operating from the love that is the very essence of divine Self.

Now, I know this seems to be asking a lot, and it is radical, but our judgment of these things as enemies keeps us from seeing the truth of the love that is in them. It keeps us confined in a narrow place where we can only see ourselves as worthy if we can somehow avoid the suffering to which other less hardy, less righteous, less intelligent people are restricted. But if we see ourselves as I AM that I AM then we can be still and know that we are I AM, receiving whatever is there to receive as the love that it is. This is the reception of the love of the Self for the self, which ultimately unites the two into one, in the completion to which Jesus is directing us. This is why Jesus said that when we stop separating good from evil, we will be "sons of your Father who is in heaven." We will be the children of our origins in divine Self when we remain open to receiving all the gifts found in everything that comes our way. This doesn't mean that we sit around and do nothing, it means that *everything we do is reception*.

This requires far more than merely following a behavioral rule that says that we *should* turn the other cheek, give away our coat, walk that other mile and give to those who wish to borrow. It requires that the soul be the initiator of our hearts, minds and bodies. It requires that we completely understand "not by might, not by power, but by my Spirit, says I AM." It requires that we come to know that the soul (another word for spirit) is the one who orchestrates every movement, every thought, every emotion, every belief—so that we can do nothing of our own initiative—we can do nothing from the duality trance state, but do all through the power of the I AM.

This is the flow from internal to external that is required for us to become whole. This is what Jesus meant in the very next chapter of Matthew, when he prays "Thy will be done on earth as it is in heaven" (6:10). He meant that we are already in the flow that, like a river that runs to the sea, carries us from I am to I AM. And if I AM is love, then this river, this flow is love. And we can get there right here, right now on planet earth. In fact, we already are there, we just don't know it. We don't have to wait to die to be fully initiated by soul or divine Self. Jesus prayed that divine will would pervade planet earth—that all-consuming love would consume planet earth completely. He certainly prayed in the I AM nature, and so we know that his prayer is answered.

Divine will is currently being done on earth as it is in heaven. Though we may not be aware of it, divine will is currently being done all the time. This does not mean, as is typically thought, that all the *bad* things that happen are really God's will—or worse, God's punishment. It means that divine will utilizes everything we do, say, think and feel, whether dualistic or not, to bring us closer and closer each second of every day to full awareness of who we are as divine beings. This is the flow of divine energy that when we become conscious of it fully defines everything we do, say, think and feel. This is all-consuming love that unites all the varying aspects of us into oneness, so that we expand as it continues to expand. And this flow defines who we actually are. Our essential nature is all-consuming love. We can choose, anytime we wish, to fall backwards into that flow through surrender to consciousness, or keep doing what we do from the duality trance state. When we choose surrender, when we choose falling backwards we open the door to our mansion in heaven right here, right now on planet earth.

13

Precious Clarity

It's all in the eyes, as they say. And, indeed, perception is every-thing. What we see is how we live. And what we see is based entirely on what we believe. That great amorphous *they* says, "seeing is believing." But I say, believing is seeing—what we believe is what we see. So, if perception is such a dominant force in our lives, how do we begin to perceive clearly? How can we develop perception that is based on the soul's vision, rather than on the vision created for us out of the duality trance state?

I have a friend who once told me that when we want to pray for people, instead of asking God to heal them or help them, we should "see them as healed," and "see them as helped." Of course, like anything else we can contrive such vision, so that we work hard to create a mental image, rather than simply believing them healed or helped, but his point was well made. Believing is seeing. So, if it is true that our vision is created from our beliefs, and we believe in the duality trance state, how will we change our beliefs?

We contend with this quite frequently in my practice as clients reach the stage in their experiential process in which they've begun to dialogue with different aspects of themselves. They encounter some part that just will not allow any shift in the belief that says that they are worthless, or that they really should feel guilty about not taking care of their manipulators. They want to change that belief but meditating *at* it, Reiki-ing *at* it, talking *at* it, fussing *at* it, even yelling *at* it makes no difference. So, they come into therapy the next time with this question: "How do you change a belief that doesn't want to change?"

Well, remember that we said that knowledge, as it is defined by the tree of knowledge of good and evil, is a process of discovery; it is finding out; it is making one's Self known; it is revealing the Self. Many of our beliefs are based on something we call fact, not really knowledge. We've been taught to believe that we are separate from the divine, we look around and see that there is good and evil in the world, and we say, well it's a fact, we *are* separate from the divine. Or, we've been taught to believe that we are unworthy and unlovable, and we look around and see that, yep, indeed, no one loves us and we have not done anything worth a hill of beans in our lives and so, it's a fact. We have been betrayed by family and come to believe that all people would eventually betray us, and yes, some really have betrayed us—so it is a fact—we will always be betrayed.

Of course, good scientists everywhere would assert that this is nowhere near the scientific process of research, but rather is some form of deduction that connects dots that may or may not be connected. But we do it. We do it every day—and for entire lifetimes. And these beliefs can be very stubborn, even in the face of evidence to the contrary. Let's take Steve, for instance. Steve is the head of the Human Resources Department at a large corporation. He went after that job and got it, over three other people with more experience than he, mostly because of his people skills. He likes his job and he's good at it. Steve is also married and has two children, and he adores his wife and children, spending every possible minute he can with them. He doesn't ask for much more, because he's pretty content now with what he has. But Steve has never been content with who he is.

He comes from a "crazy" family, members of which he's had to rescue again and again from jail, bar fights, drug overdoses, and from bouts of domestic violence. He feels really sorry for these people because he knows that they came from the same place he did. And he feels very guilty that he somehow managed to get out of all of that and get into another life. So, whenever they call him, he's there, guilt and all. He's spent loads of money on them, and has had many weekends with his family disrupted entirely by their antics. But he's always there when they need him, saying to himself, "there but for the grace…"

Steve's belief is that he's just lucky and the other members of his family are not. And so of course, he should keep rescuing them, and maybe one day, they'll get lucky too. Even when other people recognize the hard choices he made to put himself through college and get his master's degree and work his way up to the position he has today, he still sees himself as a "crazy guy who got lucky." It's also luck to him that his wife loves him and that she was able to "give me" two beautiful children. So, when she tells him what a wonderful man he is, and what a wonderful father he is, that just doesn't really cross his radar screen.

Problem is that because Steve believes this, he carries around with him a low-grade depression, called dysthymia. He doesn't ever really get suicidal, but he doesn't ever really let himself completely love life either. So, when Steve arrives in therapy, trying to understand why he can't ever really just be happy, his therapist tries to help him get in touch with this belief system that colors everything in his life a muted shade of gray. She tries several different experiential techniques to help Steve see that he believes things about himself that are not true. And slowly Steve begins to see that yes, he does have these beliefs, and maybe they are not true. So, he begins a dialogue between these beliefs and the other countering self that does not believe these things anymore. But he just keeps running back into that stubborn sense of himself that he's just less than other people, because he comes from a bunch of "crazy people."

And one day he asks that fateful question: Well, how do you change a belief that doesn't think it should change? This is where we can really begin to see identity as the issue. Steve has identified with his family-of-origin, and in order to change his belief about himself, he has to change his beliefs about his family-of-origin. They are not crazy, helpless victims of the fates. They choose their lives, as does he, and for whatever reason, they continue to choose to live as they do. Indeed, they believe that what they are doing works for them in some kind of way or they wouldn't keep doing the same old thing. Further, Steve is helping them stay stuck in their patterns by rescuing them, so that they never have to stop and think about the fact that they have choices.

Steve has come from a family system in which disavowing the power of choice is part of their connection to each other. They all talk about luck, good luck and bad luck. Steve has had the good luck, and the rest of his family has had the bad luck. And they remind him of this anytime they need his help. He stays connected to them by disavowing their power to choose and they stay connected to him by disavowing their own. And if Steve stops to think about it, they rarely connect any other way. They call Steve when they need rescue, and he rescues them when they call—other than that, there's not much going on between them. A Christmas card once a year would probably be a whole lot less stressful on everyone, but they've been taught to believe that they are all just lucky or unlucky and this is what's left to them after that.

The answer, then, to the question how do you change a belief that doesn't think it should change is this: Ask it why it doesn't want to change. Steve believes that if he doesn't rescue his family members, he will not have any family at all. That idea is completely unacceptable to him, so he maintains the family belief system that people are just lucky or unlucky in order to maintain his relationship to family. Steve's resistance to changing that belief is based on his fear that he will not have a family if he does. And the truth is, it is possible that family will reject him if he stops rescuing. But it's also possible that they won't. And until he risks it, he'll never know. This risk-taking is the discovery process defined earlier as knowledge. Through such risk-taking he will reveal himself to himself.

So, if he goes to his family and just says, "I'm done, you're on

your own from now on. Don't call me for rescue ever again,"
then yes, they probably are going to feel pretty ashamed and
angry. And they are likely to suspend their relationship with
him—at least until they feel that they need rescuing again. But if
he goes to them and opens his heart, something else entirely is
possible. So, suppose he says something like this:

> You know I love you, and I really want to be close to you, but
> this thing we are doing is not really connecting; and it is not
> really loving. I'm lying to both you and myself when I
> convince us both that you need me to rescue you and can't
> make it without me. Of course, you can. But I haven't helped
> you do that, I've just helped you lean on me, because I
> thought that would keep us close. But I'd like to change that
> now and I'd like to spend time with you that isn't about me
> rescuing you, but just about being together.

There's no guarantee that such a statement will jar something
loose in family members—but it is the truth, and the truth sets
everyone who hears it free on some level. It's possible that they
will still get angry and still suspend their relationship with him
until the next time they need rescue, but if he says the same thing
every time they call for rescue and he makes the effort, in
between pleas for rescue, to spend time with them really
connecting without rescuing, they may just begin to get it. And if
they realize that he is literally changing the dynamic between
them, they might just find the courage to become their own hero,
in the same way that Steve has. Or, that truth might just sit down
there inside of them, until another incarnation, or another, until
they are ready to pull it out and use it. But even if they never get
it, still the most significant result of such a statement is what
happens inside of Steve. The courage it takes to make that
statement means that Steve has committed to himself in a whole
new way. And that commitment shifts things around inside, so

that Steve now believes more in the truth than he believes in the lie he's been telling himself for years.

So, Steve has to be willing to go within and ask the hard questions. He has to begin to walk the inner terrain, and to, without judgment, see what is in there. He has to be willing to open his eyes, and pull the shingles off the roofs of the blocked-in ceilings of his sky. And because, at his bottom-line essence, Steve is I AM, such vision is love. Such a vision of his complex interactive thought patterns and beliefs does not make Steve judge himself, and split himself off further from the I AM. It makes the Self love the self—until eventually, perhaps even in some distant incarnation—he will unite consciousness of self with consciousness of Self and begin to live from the initiative of his soul. This risk-taking to gain knowledge is the beginning of that initiative.

The only way looking inside ourselves creates judgment is when we peek quickly and then just as quickly throw what we've seen into one of the two categories, *good* or *evil*. I won't even bother to call that seeing—because it isn't seeing. It is simply furthering the blindness. One of the ways we can know when we are furthering the blindness is by how it makes us feel. If, for example, I glance inside and see that I've been passive-aggressive by being crudely sarcastic to a friend, and I quickly say to myself that I was stupid and shouldn't have done that, I might feel embarrassed and ashamed of myself. That shame furthers the split between conscious awareness of Self and unconsciousness the more I believe in it. Why? Because it keeps me from seeking further awareness. Why would I look any further when what I've just seen is enough to make me cringe? I'm not likely to grow from a position of shame. Though most traditionalists believe that we grow by shaming ourselves into it, what we really do is just pass around the same circle again and again. We run into shame, we do something to alleviate it and then we run into it again and again and we do something to alleviate it. Nothing has really changed and no conscious awareness has occurred. And since nothing has changed, traditionalists can use that information as evidence that humans are sinful.

But most of us can see our way clear to look further down the path if the light we are using is compassion for the self. So, if you are feeling shame in response to some vision of yourself, you might want to begin to question the shame itself, with questions like:

- What do you need, Shame?
- Tell me about the day of your birth, Shame.
- What are you hoping will happen when you shame me?
- What will happen if you don't shame me?
- What frightens you the most, Shame?

These questions allow us to begin to peer beyond shame, and even beyond the morality codes that hold us to the shame, and see something else within—something more akin to truth. These questions are brave, not because they are hard to ask, but because the answers ultimately lead us to freedom. Freedom is terribly frightening, because it seems to set us in some kind of free-fall as we let go of all of the rules and codes we've used as excuses for not surrendering to authenticity—to divine Self. Freedom means we get to decide whether or not we agree with that code, and if not, why not. Freedom means we can consciously decide on the next step and the next and the next without any shoulds, codes, oughts, ought nots, thou shalt nots or any other external locus of control. Rather freedom allows us to recognize that the locus of control is actually internal and always has been. So, when we make our choices to step in a particular direction, we get to decide if these steps become a running leap into flight, or if they turn us back to that little black box we've been living in.

Freedom allows us complete, absolute, 100% responsibility

for our lives. Freedom does not allow us to blame our circumstances, our parents, our financial situations, our childhoods, our traumas, our disabilities, our churches, temples or mosques, our religion, politics or our enemies for whatever goes on in our lives. Freedom does not know the words *fault* or *blame*. And the truth is we already *are* absolutely free; we've just strapped ourselves to our little boxes, with low ceilings and tight walls, *so that* we won't have to know we are free.

But when we ask these questions of shame, we are pecking at the walls and ceilings of our narrow little boxes, and as we do, we might just break through to see the sky, the primeval forests, the vast oceans and deep caverns of the inner terrain calling us to come explore. And once we consciously commit ourselves to that journey, even if we crawl back into our boxes for a moment, it will only be a moment, for we will forever after know the difference between how it feels to be free, and how it feels to be enslaved.

Another way to know when we have held to a pattern of furthering the blindness is when the only way we ever see anything about ourselves is when someone else tells us. If we find that others nag us, or point out the same thing again and again—it could mean that they are trying to point out a blind spot. A blind spot is usually placed strategically over a complex in the psyche. A complex is a pattern of thought, feeling and behavior that takes over without our conscious permission. This complex means that anything that offers us conscious awareness is quickly denied so that the complex can continue to control us. So, if you hear someone who loves you say anything like, "I've been trying to say this to you for years," or "can't you see that you just keep doing this same thing?" or "why can't you see what you are doing?"—it might be time to turn inward and see if they are trying to tell you something very significant to your own happiness. Often walking through the irrational and dualistic turns and twists of these complexes is the central challenge of our lives and can offer us greater awareness than any other objective goal.

It is equally important to begin to observe, to begin to see how we see. Such observation means standing back to notice how we are looking at life. Part of learning to see how we see is knowing the different kinds of vision available to us. As free persons, we could choose to see life at the moment or in the long-term through any of the following lenses:

1 Tunnel vision: The inability to see beyond one small, tight, rigid perspective.

2 Blinders: When we wear blinders we are like the mule pulling the rig—we must go only where our master tells us to go—like it or not, true or false. We are enslaved to the vision provided by the master—who or whatever that is.

3 Glass half-empty: The ability to see only a limited portion of hope, creativity or expansiveness in any given scenario.

4 Glass half-full: The ability to see lemonade when presented a lemon.

5 Head-in-the-sand: The choice to postpone looking at anything difficult.

6 Pollyanna: A naïve view of the world and life in which fear, anger and distaste are repressed in favor of a vision of pleasantness and pleasure.

7 Magical: Illusions connect dots that do not belong together, creating images of self, life and reality that are unfounded.

8 Bitterness: The view that all of life is hard, there is trickery and betrayal everywhere and nothing good will or could ever happen—at least not without a trap within it.

9 Cup overflowing: The realization that all things, people, places, events, and circumstances present us with a gift.

10 Divine light: The realization of who we are. With this vision we can see ourselves, everyone and everything else as divine.

No one of these visions is better than the others. But whatever vision we are using informs us of our current place in the evolution out of the duality trance state and into full awareness of who we are by cluing us in to our particular complex. In other words, if I fairly consistently use Pollyanna vision, I'm not likely to allow myself to feel the very anger I might need to feel in order to change the unpleasant circumstances I'm trying to avoid through the Pollyanna perspective. It's easier for me to just change the subject and pretend. It's harder for me to allow myself to consider the possibility that all of that energy I'm putting into pretending could be used to change my circumstances. If I can see that I'm using Pollyanna vision, however, I can at the very least provide myself with an objective assessment of some of my fears and complexes—which can enable me to see my way through them if I so choose.

If I fairly consistently have a bitter view of life, then I'm not likely to listen to anyone or anything that offers me hope, or presents me with an idea that I am the creator of my life. In fact, if anyone does try to do so, they are likely to be greeted with a good portion of my rage. They just don't understand how hard it is for me, and even if they did understand, they wouldn't be able to change it. Maybe other people get lucky, but not me. The door to new perspectives is then shut, and I can sit down on my toadstool the rest of the day croaking. This perspective does not offer me much of an opening to see how I'm using this perspective, but if by chance I were to have an epiphany so that I now see how I'm seeing, it could be life-altering, but if not that, then at least I could assess where I am.

Seeing how we see tells us where we are. It does not tell us we are bad, or not good enough, or too attached to ego—the current euphemism for doing it wrong. It simply tells us that for whatever reason, we've chosen this way to stay blind to who we really are—for to see might be terribly frightening. But notice that I said "might be" there, for once we take responsibility for our freedom, freedom isn't scary anymore, but exhilarating. The truth is we fear being afraid more than anything. We fear all of those notions in our heads about how we might *feel* if we stepped out of the black box for a moment and allowed ourselves to exhale. We don't know how we'll feel. We just tell ourselves that we are going to feel terribly afraid, and so we *are* terribly afraid of being terribly afraid. And this is how we talk ourselves out of even looking out the window, or through the crack under the door.

Yet if we choose to just look, really look, we will not only see a new vision of what is possible, but one of who we are as well. At that point we will be conscious participants in the mission of the I AM energy, from which it becomes possible that "greater things than these shall you do" (John 14:12)—for believing is seeing. The following is a metaphysical translation/ interpretation of John 14:12:

Truly I say to you, he who sees his I AM, the works that I do shall he also do; and greater works than these shall he do; because I AM has Source as its only point of reference. And whatever you ask empowered in your own I AM, that will I AM do, that the Source I AM may be glorified in you, its creation. If you ask I AM anything in that empowerment, I AM will do it. And as you receive the love I AM, you will be kept like a promise.

These words are extremely powerful. They tell us that we have all the power—for it has already been given to us. Human beings don't really know how to use power. The options for what to do with our power range a gamut between the two polarities, the first of which is to bow our heads and fake humility denying the power we hold in our hands, and the second is to use power as if it is control over others. We see power used in the world for bullying of all manner, and we eschew it so that we won't allow ourselves to sit in the same room as our power. Therefore, many of us hang around in the middle ground between these two polarities, so that we won't have too much power, and we won't ever have enough either. But we have *all* of the power.

When we beg God to meet our needs, we are denying our own power. When we plead with the universe to provide us with our desires, we are denying our own power. When we assume that others can block us and prevent us from having what is ours to have, we deny our own power. When we blame our parents, our teachers, our religions, our governments, our bosses, our financial situations, or anything else for our lives, we are denying our own power. We saw in Chapter 7, what can happen when we project all of our power onto a single political leader. The same thing happens anytime we give away any or all of our power to anyone or anything else. We suffer.

We have *all* the power. And if we not only believe but invest in that, then we will do greater works than Jesus did. If the stories of Jesus healing the sick and raising the dead are true, then what he was saying to us is that we will do even greater than that once we take hold of our own power. We so distort the story of Jesus when we say that the reason he was here was to die for our sins. Not only is that totally dualistic, but it belies most of what he did before he died. He came here, just as we all come here, but he did far more than most of us do. Why? Because he knew who he was.

But if we ask ourselves what could we do that is greater than he did, we have to ask, what is greater than raising someone from the dead. The answer? Not dying. What can we ultimately do when we own the full range of our power? We can stop living as if we are dead. We can live LIFE forever. Perhaps we can even live forever in form—perhaps even consciously choosing different forms as we go.

As we've said, once we complete the creative experience with duality, form and formlessness will be merged into one. We will be able to consciously participate in form and formlessness simultaneously. What that will mean exactly, I can't say. But I imagine that it will look like form that recognizes itself as spirit, and spirit that recognizes itself as form. The journey to the realization of that is where we are now. And what we see now, determines what we will do and say and think and feel now.

So, if we desire an upgrade to a new level of awareness, we are going to have to download the information that is already inside of us, waiting for us to click the "Download Now" button. But downloading doesn't mean that we become different or better or improved. It only means that we see who we really are. And what an amazing, phenomenal, fantastic voyage it is to know that where we stand right now is just as much a part of the process as is the final full consciousness of who we are—that consciousness referred to by many as *enlightenment*. I dare you now to stand, just gently stand in that awareness for just a moment—stand in that consciousness that everything, everyone, every situation, event and circumstance, every feeling, thought, behavior and subtle nuance of being is part of the process taking place right now to bring us to full disclosure, full revelation of who we are.

We can't avoid the journey. We are always on it. We are on it constantly and consistently. We have never *not* been on it. We may choose to upgrade our consciousness to a deeper awareness of what it is like to be on that journey, but we are always on it. We may choose to stay blind to what is actually happening— nevertheless we are still on that evolutionary journey. The process of coming awake is the process that carries us from blindness to seeing clearly. Again, it isn't a process in which we *become* higher or better or different; it's a process in which we slowly, incarnation after incarnation, wake up to see who we already are.

Everything we do, say, think and feel is a part of the alchemical shift and evolutionary change that is constantly taking place. Form is constantly becoming more and more aware of itself as soul. And soul is constantly becoming more and more aware of itself as form. Mind is constantly alchemically receiving body, and body is alchemically receiving more and more of soul. If I do something that most consider to be good, it isn't really good—that's just the name we gave it. Actually it is just a part of the process bringing me to more awareness of who I am and that of those whom my behavior impacts. If I do something that most consider to be bad or even evil, it isn't really—those are just the names we have given it. Actually it is just something I'm doing to further my awakening process and that of those whom my behavior impacts. This last one is the hardest for us to receive, for we cannot imagine that doing something we call *evil* will bring us ultimately to wholeness.

We can easily imagine that doing something we call *good* brings us closer to wholeness, but we cannot conceive of the possibility that doing something we call *bad* has the exact same result. But imagine for just a moment that—let's make it bad, but not serial-killer bad—you are embezzler. You take other people's money, because you see it cross your desk every day; because you hate the fact that you were put down and rejected by family as a "nobody," and felt shamed and betrayed by them throughout your life; because if you could just get enough money, then you could wash their shame out of your system; and finally, because you can. You take a little and then a little more and a little more, until one day you find that you are taking fairly large sums of money once a month. And from that money you build for yourself a beautiful home, purchase nice clothes and you even get to associate with the wealthier set, so that now you feel that no one can ever shame you again.

Now suppose that you get caught. And now everyone knows that you are a fraud. They look at you as that "nobody" you always were. Having experienced that wonderful high of being accepted by the wealthy makes this all the more devastating because everyone who believed you to be somebody now knows you are nobody. Not only that, but you are going to go to jail with a bunch of other nobodies. How do you cope with the enormity of this reality? You either die of it, or you find a way to live through it. Of course, the ways are various: You could figure out a way to steal money in a sneakier fashion so that you won't be caught again, should you get out of jail anytime soon; you could buddy up with some inmates who show you another way to live on the underbelly without having to get rid of shame; you could look in the mirror and see, really see with compassion, what you've been up to. And those are just a few of the options.

Whether you see it now or see it later, the soul is always really in charge. The soul may not choose the choices that you—in the duality trance state—are making, but it uses the energy and every aspect of the impact of those choices to create your evolutionary process. It uses the energy and potency of the psychological, physical, emotional, sensational and other experiences you are having as an embezzler to alchemically facilitate your ongoing evolution. So, in this or another life, the soul intends for you to eventually come to see yourself with compassion and to allow the Self—the soul—to genuinely love and take care of the self, until ultimately your consciousness of self and consciousness of Self are united. So this story we've just told is part of the alchemistry of life evolving into soul.

Alchemistry works like this: two chemicals impact each other in some way, so that each chemical changes into a little more of the other chemical and/or to something else entirely as a result. This is exactly how the stories of our lives impact and are impacted by the soul, so that both change and evolve into something else. Both formed body and formless soul impact each other so that each becomes aware of the divine reality within each. Soul becomes aware of itself as more body and body becomes aware of itself as more soul. So this story of your life as an embezzler will impact consciousness of Self and the Self will impact consciousness of the self, so that both will evolve to receive the other. Such reception is a direct result of seeing, at least glimpsing, who we really are. So, if instead of staying on the same path, you see yourself as a soul, rather than as an embezzler—the body/mind consciousness configuration will be altered to the same degree that you have come to see clearly. But even if you don't see the divine Self as a result of this experience, still the energy you used to embezzle money and try to regain a sense of self without shame is used by the soul to further your awareness if only incrementally in this life. Everything you do is energetically used by the soul to further your ongoing evolution toward full awareness of who you are.

This is exactly what Paul was trying to say in 1 Corinthians 13:12: "For now we see in a mirror dimly, but then face to face; now I know in part, but then I shall know fully just as I also have been fully known." Now you may only see yourself as an embezzler who got caught. Now you may only see yourself as nobody, but that is seeing in the mirror dimly. Yet each vision of yourself—regardless of how dim—is used by the soul as energy to bring you to the place in which you see yourself clearly face-to-face. More and more as time and incarnations speed by, we are all coming to see ourselves in the mirror of the soul, clearer and clearer. And that is really all that is going on here. Everything else is just hypnosis, the duality trance state in action.

When we get this, really get it, beauty becomes full of its own essence, light becomes more filled with light, a moment more full of its potency, laughter more filled with joy, tears more poignant, life more real and more rich. We don't have to strive after fulfillment—we already have it, right here inside of us—and because we see that now, we get to live into what is already ours. We don't have to seek, for the seeker is what is being sought, as the Buddhists say. We don't have to have to, for there is nothing that should be done—all is Being. This is heaven. The only heaven there ever was or ever will be. And it is attained simply by looking in the mirror and seeing clearly.

This vision is a precious jewel to be uncovered at the bottom of the sea roiling in the unconscious mind. This vision is crystal clear and it clarifies everything else. This vision is not magical or miraculous in the sense there is some supernatural force that creates and invigorates it. Rather it is über-natural—the most natural of all natural events. This vision is seeing the naked soul unfettered by the downsizing of the duality trance state. This vision is Self-revealed. It is ordered and constructed by the Self and it certain to come to all of us—for the word of I AM will not return to I AM empty. There is no need to wait to inhabit the Self that is heaven within. We don't have to be good or worthy enough. We just need to see what is already there.

Living in heaven is not at all difficult when we see the simplicity of Self-realization. It is simply surrender to truth. A gentle falling backward into the soul. Being still, we come to know who we are. We come home to the surrounding presence of the Self. This is not done by effort, strategy, or technique. It is done by realization. Hopefully this book is a part of the global realization, and perhaps even your individual realization. As you have read its pages, perhaps chakras have begun to open and kundalini has begun to rise up your spine, so that you begin to see, feel, touch and know the Self you truly are. If not, that's okay. I trust that along your journey you are awakening a little more every single moment. As am I.

But if you would like to see if you can see—be still. I don't mean stop your thinking. I don't mean suspend your ego. I don't mean anything that requires effort on your part. Just be still. In the stillness an awareness begins to arise, a sense of the Self, the enormity of soul makes its presence known, and for just that moment, you know I AM (you are) God. For so it is.

Works Cited

Fillmore, Charles. *The Metaphysical Bible Dictionary*. Unity Village, MO: Unity Books. 1931, 2000. Used with permission of Unity, www.unity.org

Dan, Joseph, Ed., Kiener, Ronald C. Translator. *The Early Kabbalah*. Mahwah, New Jersey: Paulist Press. 1986.

Kierkegaard, Søren. *Either/Or: A Fragment of Life*. Translated by Alistair Hannay. London: Penguin. 1992.

New American Standard Bible. La Habra, CA: The Lockman Foundation. 1960, 1962, 1968, 1971, 1972, 1973, 1977

Pascal, Blaise. Pensées. Translated by A.J Krailsheimer. London: Penguin Group. 1966, 1995.

Ryerson, Nancy. "Outside In: Virtuous Reality: Why your moral compass is more pliable than you think." *Psychology Today Magazine*. July/August 2011, p 32. http://www.psychology-today.com/articles/201108/outside-in-virtuous-reality

BOOKS

O is a symbol of the world, of oneness and unity. In different cultures it also means the "eye," symbolizing knowledge and insight. We aim to publish books that are accessible, constructive and that challenge accepted opinion, both that of academia and the "moral majority."

Our books are available in all good English language bookstores worldwide. If you don't see the book on the shelves ask the bookstore to order it for you, quoting the ISBN number and title. Alternatively you can order online (all major online retail sites carry our titles) or contact the distributor in the relevant country, listed on the copyright page.

See our website www.o-books.net for a full list of over 500 titles, growing by 100 a year.

And tune in to myspiritradio.com for our book review radio show, hosted by June-Elleni Laine, where you can listen to the authors discussing their books.

mySpiritRadio